San Francisco Architecture

Artworks, and Parks in
the Bay Area of California

Sally B. Woodbridge

John M. Woodbridge, FAIA

Chuck Byrne

Ten Speed Press
Berkeley | Toronto

Distributed by Ten Speed Press

Ten Speed Press
P.O. Box 7123
Berkeley, California 94707
www.tenspeed.com

Distributed in Australia by Simon and Schuster Australia, in Canada by Ten Speed Press Canada, in New Zealand by Southern Publishers Group, in South Africa by Real Books, and in the United Kingdom and Europe by Airlift Book Company.

Library of Congress
Cataloging-in-Publication Data

Woodbridge, Sally Byrne.
San Francisco architecture : an illustrated guide to the outstanding buildings, public artworks, and parks in the bay area of California / Sally B. Woodbridge, John M. Woodbridge, Chuck Byrne.— Rev. ed.
p. cm.
Includes index.
ISBN-10: 1-58008-674-8
ISBN-13: 978-1-58008-674-5
1. Architecture—California—San Francisco Bay Area—Guidebooks. 2. Public art—California—San Francisco Bay Area—Guidebooks. 3. Parks—California—San Francisco Bay Area—Guidebooks. 4. San Francisco Bay Area (Calif.)—Guidebooks. I. Woodbridge, John Marshall. II. Byrne, Chuck, 1943- III. Title.
NA735.S35W64 2005
720'.9794'61—dc22

2005001455

First Printing, this edition, 2005
Printed in the United States of America
1 2 3 4 5 6 7 8 9 10 — 09 08 07 06 05

Contents

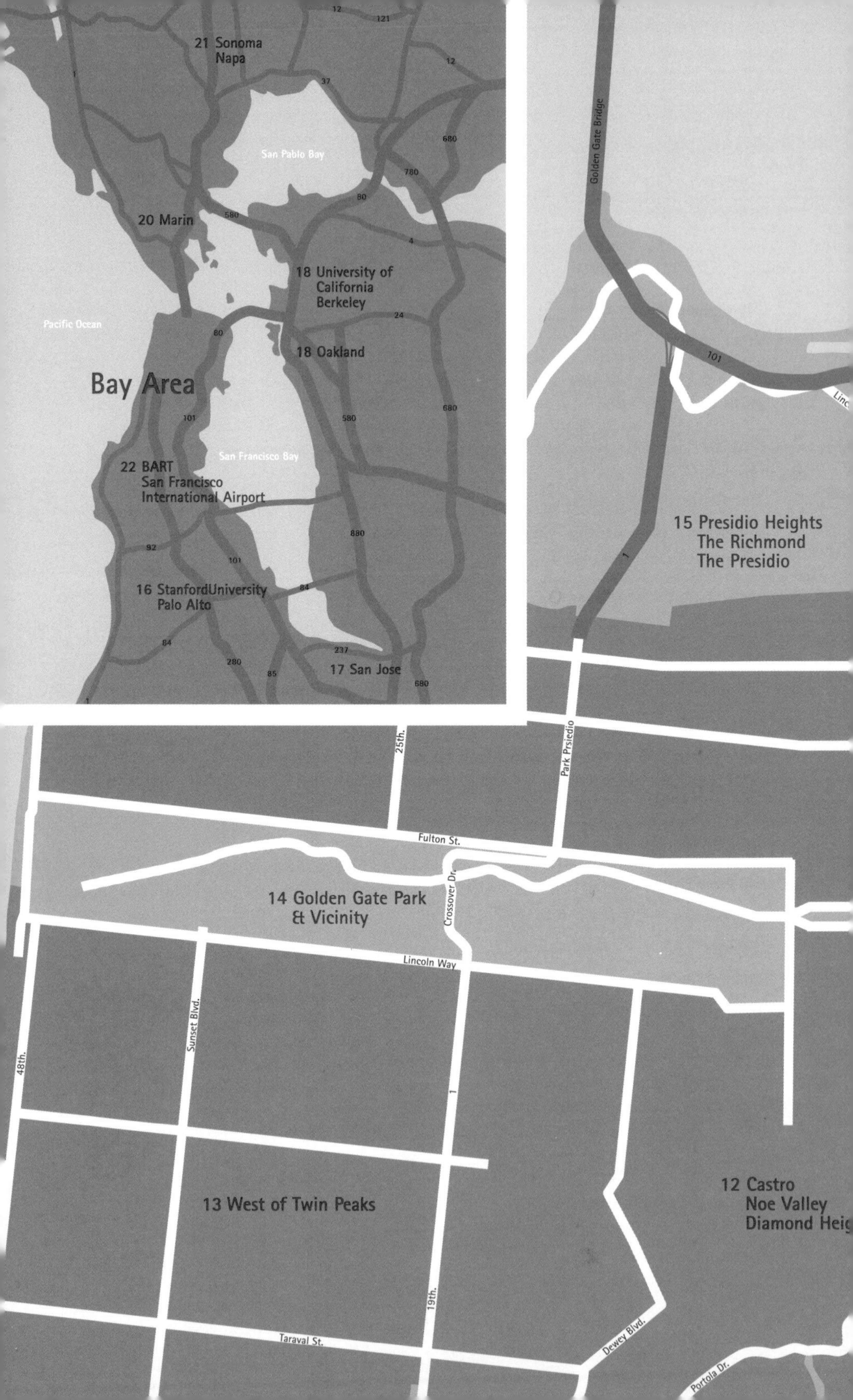

Bay Area
21 Sonoma
Napa
San Pablo Bay
20 Marin
18 University of
California
Berkeley
Pacific Ocean
18 Oakland
San Francisco Bay
22 BART
San Francisco
International Airport
16 StanfordUniversity
Palo Alto
17 San Jose
Golden Gate Bridge
15 Presidio Heights
The Richmond
The Presidio
25th.
Park Prsiedio
Fulton St.
Crossover Dr.
14 Golden Gate Park
& Vicinity
Lincoln Way
Sunset Blvd.
48th.
13 West of Twin Peaks
12 Castro
Noe Valley
19th.
Taraval St.
Dewey Blvd.
Portola Dr.

Area Maps

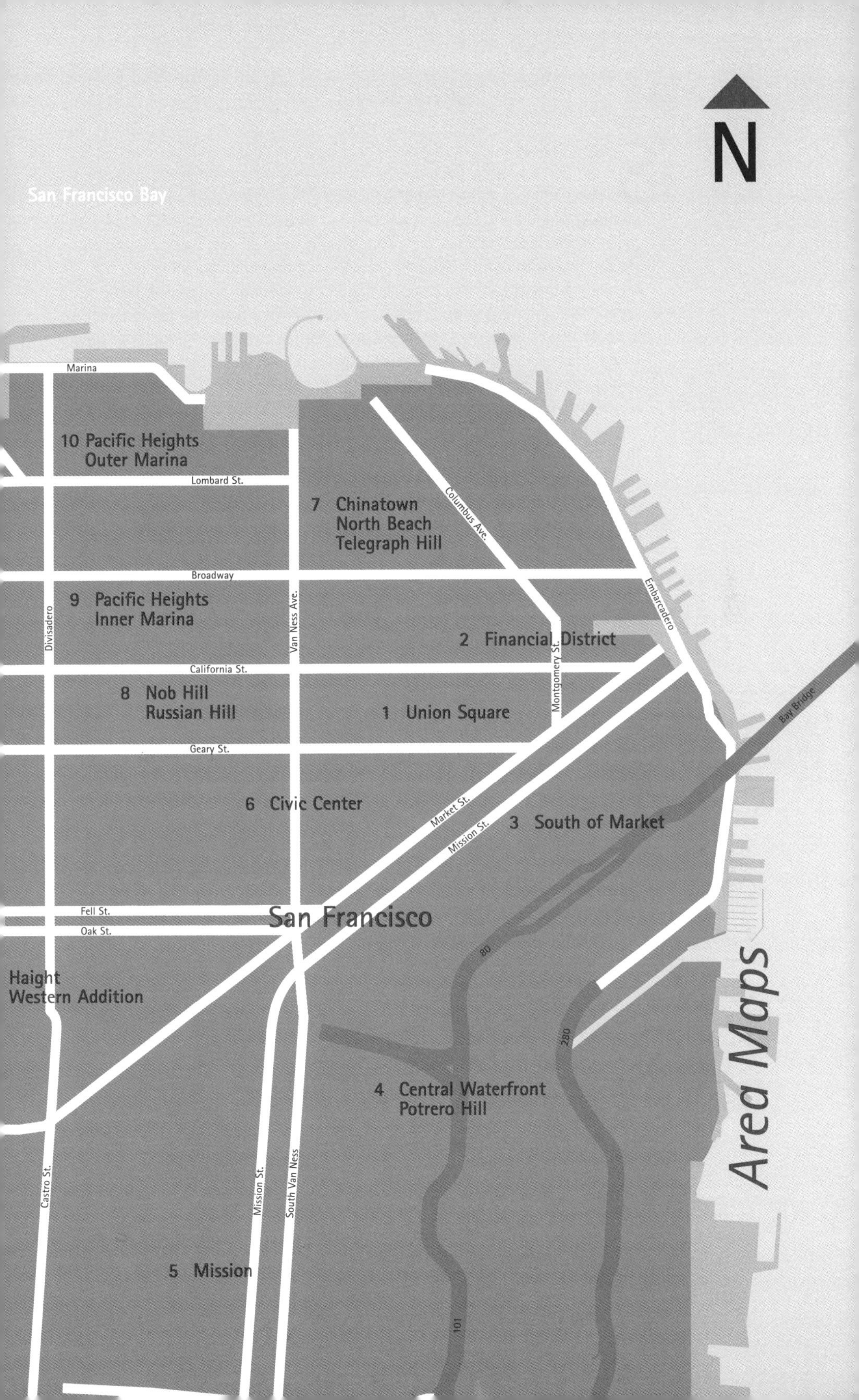

N

San Francisco Bay

Marina

10 Pacific Heights
Outer Marina

Lombard St.

7 Chinatown
North Beach
Telegraph Hill

Columbus Ave.

Broadway

9 Pacific Heights
Inner Marina

Divisadero

Van Ness Ave.

Embarcadero

2 Financial District

Montgomery St.

California St.

8 Nob Hill
Russian Hill

1 Union Square

Bay Bridge

Geary St.

6 Civic Center

Market St.

Mission St.

3 South of Market

Fell St.

San Francisco

Oak St.

80

Haight
Western Addition

280

4 Central Waterfront
Potrero Hill

Castro St.

Mission St.

South Van Ness

5 Mission

101

Guide to the Guide

Since 1960 we have co-authored four guides to the architecture of the San Francisco Bay Area. Each one has differed from its predecessor in scope and emphasis in response to changing tastes, new research in the area's architectural history, and our own evolving ideas of what constitutes a good guide. We believe that this, our fifth guide, is the best yet. Those of you who are familiar with our previous guides will note that we have increased the number of photographs to help users identify buildings and pursue their special interests, if any. Buildings have been omitted from this guide either because they have been demolished or appear to have failed the test of time. Often, in the case of houses, mature vegetation has made them invisible from public streets. Ever-increasing traffic has also made some places not worth the trouble of visiting by automobile. The good news is that a host of new entries reflecting the growth and change of the last twelve years more than balances the omissions.

The buildings and sites listed in this guide are visible from a public thoroughfare. In no way does the listing of any private building or site imply that anyone has the right to trespass on the property or visit the building. The hours that houses, museums, and monuments are open to the public should be checked by telephone or in appropriate publications. We strongly recommend consulting a good road map, particularly for the tours outside San Francisco, because the maps presented here are taken out of the larger context and meant for use within the subject area.

Acknowledgments

We are grateful for the generous help of the following people:

Robin Chiang, Jeremy Kotas, Stanley Saitowitz, Jay Turnbull, and Christopher Ver Planck, architects; Peter Albert, Manager, San Francisco/West Bay Planning Department, BART; Elizabeth Meyer, copy editor; Dea Bacchetti, Cary & Co; Chris Cary, public relations for LMS Architects; Elizabeth Quinn, public relations for Skidmore, Owings & Merrill; Elizabeth Byrne, UC College of Environmental Design Librarian, Judy Strebel, graduate student assistant, University Archives, San Jose State University Library; Dennis Letbetter, photographer; and Jack Stauffacher, typographer. Among the books we consulted, *San Francisco, Building the Dream City,* by James Beach Alexander and James Leigh Heig was particular helpful.

Introduction

Visitors to San Francisco often remark on its sparkling Mediterranean look, the result of sunlight reflecting off the patchwork of low, pastel-colored buildings marching over the hills, their bay windows looking out to sweeping views that seem to be at the end of every street. Compared to Mediterranean cities, even to many U.S. cities, San Francisco is quite young. Yet its 150-plus years of urban development are well represented in its architecture; an impressive number of interesting buildings live well together and repay repeated viewing. In spite of its terrain–even because of it–this is a great walking city, and we recommend seeing it on foot when convenient.

To look backward from present-day San Francisco to the barren fog-swept headlands that greeted Juan Bautista de Anza and his little band of Spanish settlers in the spring of 1776 requires an enormous leap of imagination. The scenic topography that seems so glamorous to us was problematic given the scarcity of water and the almost total absence of tree-cover to give shelter from the biting winds from the sea and the bay. We are told that the Indians shunned the San Francisco peninsula, and the Spaniards considered it a hardship post.

For nearly 60 years after the presidio and the mission were established hardly any other settlement existed. About 1835 when William A. Richardson, an Englishman, built his house near what is now Portsmouth Square, the village that became the city began. By 1846, when the Treaty of Guadalupe Hidalgo made California part of the United States, the village of Yerba Buena had attracted about 500 North Americans. In 1847 Jasper O'Farrell surveyed as far west as Hyde Street and, prophetically, out into the bay to the east. In the wake of the Gold Rush the grid was imposed over the hills with more enthusiasm for real-estate development than any logic based on the terrain. The panoramic views could hardly have been appreciated since the heights were inaccessible to horse and wagon.

Scarcely discouraged by devastating fires and a few warning earthquakes, development pushed more or less evenly westward through the remainder of the century. By 1906 the area bounded by Divisadero Street on the west, the bay on the north and east, and 30th Street to the south was well settled, mainly with closely packed two- and three-story wooden houses that are still a distinguishing feature of the city. Nob Hill and Pacific Heights and the grand boulevards of Van Ness and Dolores were the prime locations for mansions. The flatter lands–the Western Addition and most of the Mission district–were built up speculatively by builders using more or less standard plans with an endlessly inventive array of facades.

By 1906 the structure of downtown had evolved through a series of disastrous fires to something very similar to what it is today. Shopping was concentrated near Union Square, finance and business along Montgomery Street. Most business buildings had four to eight stories. The frames typically combined heavy timbers and cast-iron columns; the walls were brick sometimes clad with stone, but often with iron cast in elaborate patterns that imitated stone. Such structures had none of the resistance to earthquakes that either the residential wooden balloon-frame or the new steel frame offered. Nor were they fireproof, which proved an equal drawback since the worse disaster of 1906 was not the earthquake but the fire. Because the earthquake ruptured most of the water and gas lines, the fires that ignited everywhere defeated the firefighters. By the time the conflagration was finally contained by dynamiting Van Ness Avenue, the fire had destroyed all of the downtown business district and much of the nearby residential areas.

Even though the great Chicago architect, Daniel H. Burnham, had providentially completed a new plan for the city in 1904 that embodied the precepts of the City Beautiful Movement, the 1906 disaster was more of a trauma than a turning point in the city's development. The drive to rebuild was about as impetuous and greed-inspired as the gold-fever that had produced the early city. Things were put back pretty much as they were before, but since the value of the fire-proofed steel frame had been proven by the survival of the new skyscrapers, the post-fire business buildings used this structural system to increase their size and height.

The area adjacent to downtown became a zone of low- to mid-rise apartment buildings and residential hotels. Many were built in haste to rehouse the homeless; many more were buiit soon thereafter to accommodate the crowds expected for the Panama Pacific International Exposition of 1915 that was to celebrate the opening of the Panama Canal and the city's rebirth. Single-family houses dominated the streetcar suburbs and the older enclave of Russian and Telegraph Hills.

Assisted by improved transportation, the growing population pushed the limits of development south and west in the post-fire decades. After 1918 when streetcar service through the Twin Peaks tunnel became available to those residing in the Sunset Area, development pushed farther west over the sand dunes. Although the exclusive, planned developments of St. Francis Wood and Forest Hill were started, most of the housing in the Sunset and the Richmond districts was built for those of more modest means. Because of cheap land and low construction costs, builders could build and sell for less, thereby serving the growing demand for suburban living fed by the now-affordable automobile. The flat terrain was carpeted with boxy bungalows. Their stuccoed facades, as varied as their 19th-century counterparts, were derived from Hollywood images and based on both Mediterranean prototypes and contemporary styles such as the Moderne.

Little development took place during the Depression; in fact, the skyline remained virtually unchanged from 1930 to 1960. World War II brought all non-defense construction to a halt but produced major social upheavals that changed the social character of some of the city's older residential and commercial areas. One example was the Western Addition, where large numbers of defense workers occupied an area vacated by the infamous wartime relocation of the Japanese. Serious overcrowding was typical of the poorer parts of the city. Because of the flight to the rural suburbia of Marin County and the San Francisco Peninsula, fine Victorian houses were selling at bargain prices.

The 1950s brought urban renewal-or at least the planning for it. Redevelopment areas: the Golden Gateway, the Western Addition, Diamond Heights, and Yerba Buena were approved, cleared, and left like bombed-out wastelands, which have taken decades to refill. The 1960s saw the beginning of the boom in highrise office building, which continued more or less until the 1980s anti-growth initiatives. In 1985 the Downtown Plan, which limited north-of-Market development, was adopted. Downtown then began to spread across Market Street, the proverbial "slot" that seemed an unbridgeable barrier in the 19th and most of the 20th centuries. The high cost of land and construction together with the growth of neighborhood opposition to new development encouraged the trend toward preserving and rehabilitating older buildings. Today, many of the city's older residential and commercial areas have been rejuvenated.

The 1990s brought boom times to the high-tech industries, attracting new dwellers to the city from far and wide. Money flowed into new development, particularly in the SOMA (south-of-Market area) where multiple-unit buildings much larger than the flats and apartment houses of other boom times were constructed in former industrial areas adjacent to the south waterfront. The planning department codified a new building type, the Live/Work loft, originally intended for occupancy by artists and craftsmen, but soon allowed to accommodate others who worked at home, mainly in telecommunications. The building code for such lofts limited the number of floors to three with the main floor set at a height of 16 feet and a mezzanine limited to one third of the square footage of the lower floor. Accesssed by a stair from the main work area, the mezzanine was to be a sleeping area. Although a ban on Live/Work loft buildings in the late 1990s is in effect, purely residential buildings that observe the same code are still permissible, and the popularity of the loft plan has insured their continued development.

The coming of the ball park, the progress of major projects such as the University of California's San Francisco medical college campus in the China Basin area, and the start of a lightrail line out Third Street in the Central Waterfront area guaranteed the city's southward expansion even though the collapse of the so-called dot.com bubble in the late 1990s temporarily stemmed the development tide. Although the Bay Area did not recover speedily from the economic recession, new buildings of architectural merit, many of them in the pipeline before the tide turned, have been completed. In the past decade several city areas have been revitalized with new buildings and the restoration and rehabilitation of historic buildings. A prime example of this process is the civic center where the City Hall has been restored, a new main library has been built, and the old one rehabilitated as the new home of the Asian Art Museum. Perhaps the most dramatic change has occurred at the foot of Market Street where the restored and remodeled Ferry Building attracts happy crowds of commuters and others to its markets and restaurants.

New museum buildings–SF MOMA and the Yerba Buena Center for the Arts –have helped to shift the city's cultural focus downtown. The new de Young museum and the future Academy of Sciences museum complex will update Golden Gate Park's cultural offerings.

For the visitor with limited time to explore, downtown and the hills immediately around it show San Francisco's image and origins best. Here, the juxtaposition of hills and water, highrise and low buildings, mansions and shanties, along with the compactness of it all combine to make a kind of urbanity that exists in few other places in this country. The cityscape is so rich and varied that any guide to individual buildings should not be taken as the sum total of architectural interest. The city is full of happy accidents where minor buildings play major roles. So we urge you to walk, even at the pain of your leg muscles, to enjoy the surprises offered by this improbable conjunction of man and nature: the green of Angel Island seen at the end of a street, the cascade of little wooden houses tumbling down Telegraph Hill into the skyscraper canyon of lower Montgomery Street, or the fog making those often too solid towers ethereal and translucent.

macy's

1 Union Square

Union Square was the heart of San Francisco's shopping and hotel district even before the 1906 earthquake leveled its first commercial buildings. Laid out in 1850 during the mayoralty of John W. Geary, the informal grassy plot, then the heart of a residential district, acquired its name in the 1860s when pro-Union rallies were held there. Its civic status was further assured by the erection of the monument to Admiral Dewey's 1898 victory over the Spanish at Manila Bay. The 95-foot high column, designed in 1901 by Robert Aitken, sculptor, and Newton Tharp, architect, was dedicated by Theodore Roosevelt in 1903. The monument survived both the 1906 disaster and the 1942 transformation of the square into the first-ever under-a-park garage, designed by Timothy Pflueger in cooperation with the city park department. Built in wartime, the concrete structure was meant to double as a bomb shelter. In 1997, landscape architects April Philips and M. D. Fotheringham won a competition for the square's remodeling that was completed in 2002.

The Dewey monument is the only enduring element from the square's past. Surrounding the monument is a 245-foot-long granite plaza designed to accommodate large crowds and accessible from the streets that frame the square by a variety of steps and ramps. A performance stage is located on the higher, north side of the bi-laterally symmetrical square. Planted beds fill stepped terraces at the plaza's edge. A cafe occupies a small building on the square's east edge; the west side has a ticket sales booth. Overall the design provides opportunities for a range of social and cultural activities that connect the square to its surroundings.

One of the country's most compact and varied retail cores surrounds Union Square proper and extends to the adjacent blocks; it has been remarkably unaffected by the flight of shopping to suburban malls. The buildings on the square are a generally undistinguished but pleasing hodgepodge covering the period from 1906 to the 1990s. Bisecting the east side of the square is a narrow pedestrian street that was once a notorius alley lined with prostitutes' cribs, but is now a decorous shopping mall euphemistically called Maiden Lane. Union Square's development suggests that commercial vitality, not architecture, is its most significant aspect. Indeed, the economic advantage of location "on the Square" has furnished the impetus to change its character over the years, even in the face of considerable opposition.

1. Union Square
2. St. Francis Hotel *301-45 Powell St.*
3. Williams of Sonoma *370 Post St.*
4. Hyatt on Union Square *345 Stockton St.*
5. Commercial building *278-99 Post St.*
6. Former V. C. Morris Store *140 Maiden Lane*
7. Neiman-Marcus store *SE corner Stockton and Geary Sts.*
8. Former I. Magnin & Co. store now Macy's *101 Stockton St.*
9. Commercial building 200-16 Powell St.
10. Hallidie Plaza/Powell St. BART Station
    Bank of America *1 Powell St.*
    James Flood Building *870-98 Market St.*
11. Former Hale Bros. department store *901-19 Market St.*
12. Nordstrom/San Francisco Shopping Center *5th and Market Sts.*
    The Emporium *835-65 Market St.*
    Commercial building *825-33 Market St.*
13. Former Pacific Building Palomar Hotel and Old Navy Store *801-23 Market St.*
14. Fox Warfield Theatre *982-92 Market St.*
    Golden Gate Theatre *42 Golden Gate Ave.*
    Apartments *50 Golden Gate Ave.*
15. Eastern Outfitting Co. *1019 Market St.*
16. 9th District Court of Appeals building and the G.S.A. building *7th and Mission Sts.*
17. Former Hibernia Bank *1 Jones St.*
18. San Francisco Hilton Hotel *201 Mason St.*
    Downtown Center Garage *325 Mason St.*
19. Geary Theatre *415 Geary St.*
    Curran Theatre *445 Geary St.*
20. Clift Hotel *491-99 Geary St.*
    Bellevue Hotel *Geary and Taylor Sts.*
21. Alcazar Theatre *650 Geary St.*
22. Native Sons Building *414-30 Mason St.*
    San Francisco Water Department *425 Mason St.*
23. Bohemian Club *625 Taylor St.*
    Olympic Club *524 Post St.*
24. Former First Congregational Church *491 Post. St.*
    Medical-Dental building *490 Post St.*
    Elks Club *450-60 Post St.*
25. Metropolitan Club *640 Sutter St.*
    WCA *620 Sutter St.*
26. Apartments *980 Bush St. and 972 Bush St.*
27. Dennis T. Sullivan Memorial Home *870 Bush St.*
28. Former Family Club *545 Powell St.*
    Former town house *535 Powell St.*
    Academy of Art buildings *560 and 540 Powell St.*
29. Sir Francis Drake Hotel *432-462 Powell St.*
30. Medical-Dental office building *450 Sutter St.*
31. Notre Dame des Victoires *564 Bush St.*
32. S. F. Fire Station No. 2 *466 Bush St.*
33. Former Pacific Telephone & Telegraph Building *333 Grant Ave.*
34. W. & J. Sloane Building *220 Sutter St.*
    Former Goldberg Bowen Building/Bemiss Building *266-270 Sutter St.*
35. Former White House department store *255 Sutter St.*
    Hammersmith Building *301-03 Sutter St.*
36. Shreve Building *201 Grant Ave.*
    Hastings Building *201-09 Post St.*
    Phoenix Building *220-28 Grant Ave.*
    Head Building *201-09 Grant Ave.*
    Rochat Cordes Building *126-130 Post St.*
37. Bank buildings *744 Market St. and 1 Grant Ave.*
    Phelan Building *760-84 Market St.*
    Former bank building *783-85 Market St.*
38. Bank building *700 Market St.*
    Lotta's Fountain *Kearny and Geary Sts. at Market St.*
39. Former Hearst Building *691-99 Market St.*
40. Marriott Hotel *777 Market St. at 4th St.*
    Four Seasons Hotel *757 Market St.*

Previoous page: Union Square

Washington St.
Clay St.
Sacramento St.
California St.
Pine St.
Bush St.
Sutter St.
Post St.
Geary St.
O'Farrell St.
Ellis St.
Eddy St.
Turk St.
Golden Gate Ave.
McAllister St.
Hyde St.
Leavenworth St.
Jones St.
Taylor St.
Mason St.
Powell St.
Stockton St.
Grant St.
Kearny St.
Montgomery St.
Waverly St.
Commercial St.
Maiden Lane
New Montg
3rd St.
4th St.
5th St.
6th St.
7th St.
8th St.
Mission St.
Natoma St.
Howard St.
Folsom St.
Hallam St.
Harrison St.
Shiply St.
Bryant St
Bluxome St
80
N
1
2
3
4
5
6
7
8
9
10
11
12
13
14
15
16
17
18
19
20
21
22
23
24
25
26
27
28
29
30
31
32
33
34
35
36
37
38
39
40

1

1. Union Square

2. St. Francis Hotel

4. Hyatt on Union Square

5. Commercial building

1. **Union Square**
   1942, Timothy Pflueger; 2002, Philips + Fotheringham Partnership, Roysten Hanamoto Alley & Abey, Patri Merker Architects
   Geary to Post, Powell to Stockton Sts.
2. **St. Francis Hotel**
   1904-07, 1913, Bliss & Faville
   Tower, 1972, William Pereira
   301-45 Powell St.
   Gutted in the 1906 fire, the hotel was restored and enlarged by the first architects. In 1913 an addition on the Post Street end altered its symmetrical E shape. Typical of the Renaissance Revival style then in vogue, the building is treated like a stretched Italian palazzo with an ornate cornice and a ground floor arcade. Wide, rusticated bands running up the mid-section tie the top and bottom together. Light standards, presumably designed by Bliss & Faville, and boxed trees line the sidewalk in front of the hotel.
3. **Williams of Sonoma**
   1923, Reid Bros.; interior remodeling 2003
   370 Post St.
   An elegant small building originally designed for a men's clothing concern.
4. **Hyatt on Union Square**
   1972, Skidmore Owings & Merrill
   345 Stockton St.
   A well-mannered design with commercial space on the square and a mostly unshaded plaza. A special delight is the fountain set into the plaza steps. Designed by Ruth Asawa, the bronze reliefs on the drum were cast from "bakers' clay," a flour, salt, and water dough modeled by family members, neighbors, and scores of school children into scenes of San Francisco.
5. **Commercial building**
   1910, D. H. Burnham & Co., Willis Polk, designer
   278-99 Post St.
   A good example of a Neoclassical commercial building in which the "architecture" was designed to ride above the changing shop fronts.
6. **Former V. C. Morris Store**
   1949, Frank Lloyd Wright; rest., 1983, Michele Marx
   140 Maiden Lane
   Although this design anticipated the Guggenheim Museum's celebrated spiral, it was actually a remodeling of an old building into a retail space for the Morrises, purveyors of fine crystal and other interior

appointments. Greatly to their credit, subsequent owners restored the neglected interior and reinstalled Wright's furnishings.

6. Former V. C. Morris Store

7. **Neiman-Marcus**
   1982, Johnson/Burgee
   S.E. corner Stockton and Geary Sts.
   Replacing a revered landmark, the 1896-1908 City of Paris store by Clinton Day and Bakewell & Brown, this fancy box is clad in sandstone that mimics wrapping paper. The original store's great stained glass rotunda remains but not in its original central location.

7. Neiman-Marcus

7. Neiman-Marcus

8. **Former I. Magnin & Co.; now Macy's**
   1946, Timothy Pflueger
   233 Geary St.
   The elegant skin hung on this 1905 office building frame was made flush to keep off the pigeons, Union Square's most numerous residents. The design was so successful with shoppers and so discouraging to pigeons that it was used again in Seattle.

   Macy's
   1928, Lewis P. Hobart; 2002 remodeling, Patri Merker
   101 Stockton St.
   While the Macy's building that is visible on Stockton and Geary Streets reflects the styling of the time, the Union Square elevation has been updated more than once. The current glassy facade turned the store into a lantern to attract shoppers like moths.

8. Former I. Magnin & Co.; now Macy's

9. **Commercial building**
   1933
   200-16 Powell St.
   A Moderne jewel box that awaits restoration.

10. *Hallidie Plaza & Powell St. BART Station*

10. *Hallidie Plaza & Powell St. BART Station*

Market Street

Our first look at Market Street surveys the retail area, which, having risen with confidence after 1906, declined in the Depression and fell victim to the post-World War II suburbanization of living and shopping. Although generous injections of cash have periodically raised the tone of the street, the current wave of construction that will transform the block between Market, Mission, 4th, and 5th Streets is likely to have the most impact on the area as a whole.

Looking up Market St. from the Embarcadero

10. Hallidie Plaza

1973, Lawrence Halprin & Assoc.; 1997, elevator tower, Michael Willis & Assoc.

Powell St. BART Station

1973, Skidmore Owings & Merrill

One of the city's oldest transportation modes, the cable car, meets the newest one, the Bay Area Rapid Transit, at this historic transportation node of Powell, 5th, and Market Streets. From 1903-49 the San Francisco-San Mateo Interurban line ended near 5th and Market; the network of the Market Street Railway Company's lines served the area from all over, at one time requiring four tracks on the street. In the 1970s the city took advantage of the construction of BART to change the street pattern by extending 5th across Market to connect with the north grid and by closing the end of Eddy to vehicles. A sunken plaza named for cable car inventor Andrew S. Hallidie was created for access to the station. The idea was to woo a sophisticated public to Market Street by creating two pleasant, protected outdoor rooms clad in costly and durable materials, where civic entertainment would take place. For the most part fine and civil buildings strengthen the space; while the plaza's social use reveals center-city public life in all its colorful complexity. Tourists wait in line for the cable cars, evangelists harangue the bystanders, and street musicians play while street people sleep on the benches.

Bank of America
1920, Bliss & Faville
1 Powell St. at Hallidie Plaza
A handsome Renaissance Revival palace designed fittingly for the Bank of Italy, now the Bank of America. Bliss & Faville's competition-winning design reveals their admiration for McKim, Mead & White's University Club in New York. The architects economized by cladding the building's base in granite and the rest in less expensive terra cotta. The sculpture above the entrance is by John Portonavo; the interior is worth seeing.

10. Bank of America

James Flood Building
1904, Albert Pissis; 1992, restored to its original appearance.
870-98 Market St.
Virtually complete in 1906, the Flood Building was mostly rebuilt after the earthquake and fire. The rounded corner element is boldly articulated; the engaged colonnade is a leitmotif echoed in the Emporium and the former Hale Bros. store across the street. The architect intended to "give a touch of grandeur to Market Street." In front of 856 Market Street is the Albert S. Samuels Clock that Samuels and Joseph Mayer created in 1910 to stand across the street in front of the Samuels Jewelry shop.

10. James Flood Building

11. **Former Hale Bros. Department Store**
1912, Reid Bros.; rem. 1989, Whisler-Patri
901-19 Market St.
A commercial palace in the Renaissance-Baroque tradition, this building has a new version of the glass and metal canopy that was removed in a previous modernization.

11. Former Hale Bros. Department Store

12. **Nordstrom/San Francisco Shopping Center**
1989, Whisler-Patri
5th and Market Sts.
A successful contextual design that has raised the tone of this important intersection. The rotunda with its double escalators makes the movement of shoppers appear almost choreographic.

12. Nordstrom Francisco Shopping Center

The Emporium
1896, Joseph Moore; 1908, Albert Pissis; Bloomingdale's, KPF, 2006; mall by RTKL; Carey & Co., historic preservation architect
835-65 Market St.

12. The Emporium

Only the facade survives from Moore's original pre-fire building, which housed stores, offices, and the California Supreme Court. Using a strategy we now associate with historic preservation, Pissis kept the existing facade and designed the department store behind it with a skylit rotunda that was a standard component of late 19th-century department stores. The sandstone facade may have always been painted. The most recent renovation restores the rotunda to its original design. Additions are: a shopping mall, offices, a nine-screen cinema, and Bloomingdale's store, which will have its main facade on Mission St.

13. Former Pacific Building

Commercial building
1908, Lewis Hobart
825-33 Market St.
A respectable companion to its neighbors, Hobart's design observes their cornice line with a row of projecting balconies. As usual, ground floor remodelings have left the older architecture above with nothing to stand on.

13. Former Pacific Building
1907, C. F. Whittlesey; 1981, Whisler-Patri; 2002, Palomar Hotel/Old Navy Store, Gensler Architecture & Planning
801-23 Market St.
In form and decorative detail the building recalls Louis Sullivan's Carson Pirie Scott Store in Chicago. Restoration efforts improved the ground floor, but the cornice is sadly missing. Worth noticing is the color scheme of green tile and cream terra cotta over a red tile base. Whittlesey, who worked for Sullivan before coming west, said that he chose the colors "because the climate of our city is decidedly gray." The building's interior was completely remodeled in 2001-02 to house the Old Navy Store on the first four floors and the Palomar Hotel from the fifth to the eighth floor. The most dramatic part of the Old Navy Store is the third floor escalator landing where, to create more open retail space, several of the old building's concrete columns were cut off well above their bases and left hanging in midair, supported by massive steel trusses. The exposed structural system is awesome and worth pondering.

14. Golden Gate Theatre

14. Fox Warfield Theatre
1921, G. A. Lansburgh
982-98 Market St.

Golden Gate Theatre
1922, G. A. Lansburgh
42 Golden Gate Ave.

Apartments
50 Golden Gate Ave.
Two combination theater-office buildings designed by the prominent local theater architect, who also designed the hall of the Opera House. The Market Street theater district, formerly in the blocks from 5th to 8th Streets, started a comeback with the restoration of the Golden Gate Theatre in 1980. At No. 50 Golden Gate Ave., next to the theater, the facade is ornamented with grotesque heads.

14. 50 Golden Gate Ave.

15. **Eastern Outfitting Co. Building**
1909, George A. Applegarth
1019 Market St.
A remarkable bay window wall framed as though it were part of a monumental Classical colonnade.

15. Eastern Outfitting Co. Building

16. **U.S. 9th District Court of Appeals Building**
1902-05, John Knox Taylor; 1931-33, George Kelham; 1997 restoration and addition, SOM/Page & Turnbull, historic preservation architects
7th and Mission Sts.
A powerful expression of the Federal authority in Neo-Baroque with grand interiors. Restoration and rehabilitation of the building in the 1990s included a 45,000 square foot addition with offices, a law library and public reading room, and an inclosed, sky-lit courtyard. The addition is appropriately contemporary.

General Services Administration Building
2005, Thomas Mayne/Karen Hargarther Thomas
Mission and 7th Sts.
The site of this new federal complex is three acres across 7th Street from the U. S. Court of Appeals building; it features a 240-foot-high tower for the GSA set at a right angle? to the courthouse. The design of the tower emphasizes sustainability with the sun as the main source of light, operable windows, perforated steel panels on the south-facing elevation that will open or shut in response to sunlight, and translucent glass sunshades on the north side. The 7th street frontage has a cafe and plaza that will increase pedestrian activity in the area.

16. U.S. 9th District Court of Appeals Building

17. **Former Hibernia Bank**
1892, 1905, 1907, Albert Pissis
1 Jones St.
The city's oldest Classic Revival style bank had a colonnade splayed to fit the triangular site and articulated like a folded-out Roman temple. The domed rotunda recalls parts of the Paris Opera House, which Pissis surely saw during his student days at the Ecole des Beaux Arts in Paris. The interior is also notable.

17. Former Hibernia Bank

18. Downtown Center Garage

18. Geary Theatre and Curran Theatre

18. San Francisco Hilton Hotel

1964, William Tabler; 1971, 1989 tower, John Carl Warnecke

201 Mason St.

A succession of modish designs, the latest decidedly Postmodern. The 1971 aluminum-clad tower still holds its own, dominating the skyline in this part of town.

Downtown Center Garage

1954, George A. Applegarth

325 Mason St.

A straightforward, uncluttered structure with a double spiral ramp at the corner and a shopping arcade, one of the last–and the only Modern work–of a well known Beaux-Arts architect.

19. Geary Theatre

1909, Bliss & Faville

415 Geary St.

Damaged in the 1989 earthquake, the Geary was restored and reopened in 1995.

Curran Theatre

1922, Alfred H. Jacobs

445 Geary St.

The city's two major theaters reveal the versatility of the academic Classical Revival style. The facades have the same format, but the proportions and ornamental detail are sufficiently different to make each one a distinctive composition.

20. Clift Hotel

1913, MacDonald & Applegarth;1926, Schultze & Weaver

491-99 Geary St.

One of the most lavish of the area's many hotels, the Clift Hotel was built in anticipation of the incoming crowds for the 1915 Panama Pacific International Exposition. The client was a lawyer, Frederick Clift, for whom a "stone bungalow" suite was designed on an upper floor. (Photographs of the original interiors are in a case on the mezzanine.) In 1926 Schultze & Weaver, architects of the Waldorf Astoria and Sherry Netherlands hotels in New York, and the Biltmore in Los Angeles, designed a 240-room addition using the same exterior design. The original heavy cornice is now gone. G. A. Lansburgh designed the Parisian Room and the Redwood Room. Anthony Heinsbergen, another eminent theater designer, was his collaborator for the Redwood Room, one of downtown's most elegant public rooms in the Moderne style. The lobby was renovated in 2001 with furniture by Phillippe Starck.

Bellevue Hotel
1908, S.H. Woodruff; 1992, Roma Design Group
Geary and Taylor Sts.
A richly decorated Neo-Baroque exterior; the interior has had several renovations.

21. **Alcazar Theatre**
1917, T. Patterson Ross
650 Geary St.
Convincingly Islamic, and a great surprise on the street.

22. Native Sons Building

21. Alcazar Theatre

22. San Francisco Water Department

22. **Native Sons Building**
1911, Righetti & Headman / E.H. Hildebrand
414-30 Mason St.
Yet another Renaissance-Baroque commercial palace, this one is worth scrutinizing for its finely textured brick walls, graceful top floor loggia, and decorative detail, including panels by artist Jo Moro on the mezzanine.

San Francisco Water Department
1922, Willis Polk & Co.
425 Mason St.
A composition similar to the Native Sons Building, but with a more restrained use of materials and decorative detail. But observe that the ground floor drips with stony water which even runs over the keystone above the entrance arch. Inside on the north wall over the elevator is a mural by Maynard Dixon of the Sunol Water Temple built by the Spring Valley Water Company, the original clients for this building. The owner, William Bourn, was Willis Polk's patron. Polk also designed his house at 2550 Webster Street and Filoli, his estate in Woodside.

23. Former First Congregational Church

24. Bohemian Club

24. Olympic Club

23. **Former First Congregational Church**
1913, Reid Bros.
491 Post St.

Medico-Dental Building
1925, George Kelham/William G. Merchant
490 Post St.

Elks Club
1924, Meyer & Johnson
450-60 Post St.
This group of four buildings was designed by some of San Francisco's best known practitioners of the first quarter of the 20th century. Their range of size and type makes them interesting to compare with each other and with other examples of these architects' work.

24. **Bohemian Club**
1934, Lewis P. Hobart
625 Taylor St.

Olympic Club
1912, Paff & Baur
524 Post St.
Two distinguished club buildings. Although the latter is firmly in the Ecole des Beaux Arts academic Classical tradition, the former conveys the same exclusiveness with a touch of the Moderne. The bronze and terra-cotta plaques are by Carlo Taliabua, Haig Patigian, and Jo Moro, prominent local artist-members of this colorful institution.

25. **Metropolitan Club**
1916, 1922, Bliss & Faville
640 Sutter St.
Originally the Women's Athletic Club, the design previews Hobart's later Bohemian Club.

YWCA
1918, Lewis Hobart
620 Sutter St.

26. **Apartments**
1914, 1912
1086, 1060 Bush St.
Two examples of the great collection of post-fire apartment buildings that were built in a hurry on the south slopes of Nob Hill after the 1906 earthquake and fire.

Apartments
1909, Frederick H. Meyer
980 Bush St.

Apartments
1914, Grace Jewett
972 Bush St.

Two substantial Renaissance Revival apartment buildings, the latter by one of the few women architects in practice during this time.

27. Dennis T. Sullivan Memorial Home

1922

870 Bush St.

This building commemorates a tragedy of the 1906 earthquake that took the life of Fire Chief Dennis T. Sullivan, who was killed when the firehouse in which he lived shook apart. The memorial fund was used to build a new Fire Chief's home designed to resemble a firehouse.

26. & 27. left: 972 Bush St., right: 870 Bush St.

27. Dennis T. Sullivan Memorial Home

28. Town house

28. Former Family Club

1909, C.A. Meussdorffer

545 Powell St.

Town house

1911, C.A. Meussdorffer

535 Powell St.

Academy of Art College

1911

560 Powell St.

Former Elks Building, now Academy of Art

1909, A.A. Cantin

540 Powell St.

Built within two years of each other, these four buildings exhibit a wild variety of styles. The two by Meussdorffer illustrate his skill and confidence in rendering two period styles; the town house is a rare survivor in downtown. Both buildings have outstanding ornamental detail. Cantin's Elks Building improbably combines Classic and Mission Revival styles.

29. Sir Francis Drake Hotel

1928, Weeks & Day

432-62 Powell St.

31. Notre Dame des Victoires

32. S. F. Fire Station No. 2

Gothic motifs are freely used here to accentuate the hotel's stepped form, made fashionable by New York's 1918 zoning law for skyscrapers. The glazed void below the crown marks the Starlight Roof bar, a later addition that has a great city view.

30. Medical-Dental Office Building
1929, Miller & Pflueger
450 Sutter St.

30. Medical-Dental Office Building

One of the city's most admired office towers; its undulating wall inspired that of the former Bank of America Building at 555 California St. The skyscraper's low budget dictated the use of terra cotta instead of stone, and the minimal lobby. Although the smooth, continuous piers give the structure a vertical emphasis, the woven bevelled spandrels and corners create the appearance of a skin or wrapper that prophesied today's approach to cladding tall buildings.

31. Notre Dame des Victoires
1913, Louis Brouchoud
564 Bush St.
This church occupies the site of the city's first French church; is more significant as an historic center of San Francisco's influential French colony than as architecture.

32. S. F. Fire Station No. 2
1909, Newton J. Tharp
466 Bush St.
Appropriately, the city's first fireproof structure erected after the 1906 disaster, this work of civic monumentality expresses its dual function to house motorized equipment downstairs and people upstairs. A formal gateway to Chinatown was created at Grant Avenue in 1976.

33. Former Pacific Telephone & Telegraph Building
1908, Ernest Coxhead
333 Grant Ave.
A facade composed of boldly scaled Classical elements in projected and recessed forms. Coxhead's skill at manipulating the Classical vocabulary is nowhere better shown than in the entrance composition, where an elegant portal with a swan-necked pediment is fused with an arch tied at the top by an outsized keystone to the belt cornice above. Don't miss the giant columns' capitals.

33. Former Pacific Telephone & Telegraph Building

34. W. & J. Sloane Building
1908, Reid Bros.
220 Sutter St.

Goldberg Bowen Building
1909, Meyers & Ward
250-54 Sutter St.

Bemiss Building
1908
266-70 Sutter St.
Three handsome commercial buildings worthy of notice in an area that retains its post-1906 appearance. The W. & J. Sloane Building is the most conventional of the three; it now houses several art galleries. Bemiss's elegant, almost Miesian steel frame capped by a fringed metal valance accommodates what may have been the largest sheets of glass then available. The Goldberg Bowen Building's architects chose to decorate the frame with piers that erupt in floral bouquets at the cornice.

34. Goldberg Bowen building

35. Former White House department store
1908, Albert Pissis
255 Sutter St.
In 1968 an unusual preservation strategy converted what was once one of the city's major French department stores, the Raphael Weill Company, into a parking garage with shops on the ground floor.

35. Former White House department store

Hammersmith Building
1907, G. A. Lansburgh
301-03 Sutter St.
An improbable relic from the post-1906 earthquake downtown that makes much of its small scale, like a music box with a fancy lid.

35. Hammersmith Building

36. Shreve Building
1905, William Curlett
201 Grant Ave.

Hastings Building
1908, Meyer & O'Brien
180 Post St.

37. Wells Fargo Bank

37. Phelan Building

38. First Nationwide Bank

Phoenix Building
1908, George A. Applegarth
220-28 Grant Ave.

Head Building
1909, William Curlett & Sons
201-09 Post St.

Rochat Cordes Building
1909, Albert Pissis
126-30 Post St.

Five solidly respectable buildings, the first four of which compose a gateway to the heart of the shopping district to the west. The Shreve Building is both the most intact and the most luxurious in terms of materials.

37. Wells Fargo Bank
1910, Clinton Day
744 Market St.

Former bank building
1919, Bliss & Faville
1 Grant Ave.

Phelan Building
1908, William Curlett
760-84 Market St.

Humboldt Bank building
1906, Meyer & O'Brien
783-85 Market St.

A vintage Market Street intersection framed by buildings erected within four years of each other. The two smaller buildings illustrate the versatility of Beaux-Arts Classicism as well as the enduring power of the Pantheon as a prototype for religious and financial temples. Across the street the Phelan Building, built by a famous mayor and U.S. senator, is a fine traditional rendering of a steel-framed flatiron structure sheathed in terra cotta.

38. First Nationwide Bank
1902, 1906, William Curlett; Add. 1964, Clark & Beuttler
700 Market St.

Charles W. Moore was a principal designer of the corner addition, which echoes the form of the older building in a way that is clearly contemporary. The structure embraces the corner by making a major element of the stair tower.

Lotta's Fountain
1875, Wyneken & Townsend
Kearny and Geary Sts. at Market St.

Lotta Crabtree, the most highly paid American actress of her day, retired from touring in 1891 to

San Francisco. Her $4 million fortune went to charity; the best known gift is this fountain. The shaft was lengthened in 1915 by eight feet to better match the Market Street light standards. In 1916 the merchants paid for the bas-reliefs created by noted sculptor Arthur Putnam.

39. Hearst Building

39. Hearst Building
1909, Kirby, Petit & Green
691-99 Market St.
Of the three newspaper buildings that once stood on this intersection, this is the only one that still is identifiable. The entrance is a showpiece of terra-cotta ornament.

40. Marriott Hotel

40. Marriott Hotel
1989, Anthony Lumsden (DMJM)
777 Market St. at 4th St.
Often compared to an outsized juke box, the tower's form was shaped by the codes for setbacks to allow sunlight access to the street below. The mirror glass looks suspiciously like contact paper but glows dramatically at sunset.

Across the street at 54 4th St., the Victorian Hotel, c.1915 by William Curlett, recalls an earlier era of hotel building for the 1915 PPI Exposition in what is now the Marina district. Conveniently located near major interurban and city transportation lines, the hotel plan featured suites on the front for families and rooms on the back for servants. Many hotels like this one once occupied the south-of-Market blocks and served those who arrived at the now demolished Southern Pacific Railroad station, which stood at 3rd. and Townsend Streets.

40. Four Seasons Hotel

Four Seasons Hotel
2001, Gary Handel & Assocs./Del Campo & Maru
757 Market St.
A 40-story building that combines a 277-room hotel with 142 condominiums. The building was designed as an aggregate of forms clad with glass and metal panels; it respects the height of its older neighbors by stepping down to five stories on Market Street. The building provides a welcome contrast to the Marriott Hotel when seen from the gardens on Mission Street.

2 Financial District

Most of what is now the densest part of the city was once water. The shoreline was roughly at Montgomery Street; the east-west streets ended in wharves. To the south, the great diagonal of Market Street was laid out parallel to the road from the bay to Mission Dolores. To the north was the original settlement of Yerba Buena around Portsmouth Square, a collection of humble buildings that achieved city status overnight with the discovery of gold in the Sierra foothills. By 1850 a financial district fed by the Gold Rush had grown up around Montgomery and Washington Streets. The location was convenient to the Customs House, the gambling houses around Portsmouth Square, and the commercial wharves that extended out into the bay. These wharves soon became streets lined with buildings set on the hulks of abandoned ships. In 1850 two devasting fires drove the bankers out of crime-infested Sidneytown at the base of Telegraph Hill, whose denizens had set the fires, and precipitated the shift from wooden to more fireproof brick buildings. The more permanent structures were built to the south on choice sites cleared by the fire. The Customs House also moved to a brick building at Montgomery and California Streets. Other factors contributing to the move south were the improvement of the central wharves of Clay and Sacramento Streets and the cutting through of Commercial Street from the Long Wharf to Kearny Street. When the city's booming service economy surpassed that of gold in 1850, the ties to Portsmouth Square were loosened.

From 1850 to 1875 banks set the trend for the southward shift along Montgomery Street toward Market Street, influencing the relocation of legal services, real estate interests, and stock and insurance brokers. After 1888 the district began to grow vertically, encouraged by the advent of the earthquake-resistant steel frame. Buildings over ten stories rose on the fringes of the district and on California Street. Even the 1906 disaster did not dislodge the banks from Montgomery and California Streets; the intersection is still the district's heart.

Until recently the triangle these two streets make with Market Street defined one of the country's most compact clusters of skyscrapers. The forest of towers was dense but not overwhelming. A boom in office building that began in the late 1970s brought "Manhattanization" and public reaction in the form of anti-highrise initiatives of inspired futility. In 1985 the Downtown Plan revised height and bulk limits, created more restricted height zones, and instigated a yearly cap on development and a stringent project-by-project review. But by then the old scale was gone and the district's boundaries had pushed out, jostling Chinatown and Jackson Square and creating a larger and duller forest of towers on the much larger blocks south of Market. Still, the district is more dramatic than most of its kind, thanks mostly to the surrounding water which, since the removal in 1991 of the Embarcadero Freeway, damaged in the 1989 earthquake, is once more visually accessible. Unforgettable contrasts still exist at the district's edges, as when Montgomery Street bursts through its canyon into pre-fire Jackson Square and up Telegraph Hill, or when the cable cars climb California Street to Nob Hill.

2 Financial District

1. Former Pacific Telephone and Telegraph Building *134-140 New Montgomery St.*
2. Live/Work Lofts *85 Natoma St.*
3. 101 Second St. building
4. New Montgomery St. buildings
   Sharon Building
   Call Building
   Rialto Building
5. Sheraton Palace Hotel *633-65 Market St.*
   Monadnock Building *685 Market St.*
6. Hobart Building *582-92 Market St.*
7. Former Crocker Bank Headquarters *1 Montgomery St.*
   Mechanics Institute *57-65 Post St.*
8. Hunter-Dulin Building *111 Sutter St.*
   Hallidie Building *130 Sutter St.*
9. Russ Building *235 Montgomery St.*
   Mills Building *220 Montgomery St.*
10. California Commercial Union *315 Montgomery St.*
11. Former Bank of America World Headquarters *555 California St.*
    Mixed-use building *588 California St.*
12. Former Security Pacific Bank *300 Montgomery St.*
    Merchants Exchange Building *465 California St.*
    Insurance Exchange Building *433 California St.*
13. Kohl Building *400 Montgomery St.*
    Building *456 Montgomery St.*
14. Former Bank of Italy *552 Montgomery St.*
15. Transamerica Building *600 Montgomery St.*
16. 343 Sansome St.
17. Former Federal Reserve Bank *400 Sansome St.*
18. Former Bank of California *400 California St.*
19. Union Bank of California *350 California St.*
20. California Center *345 California St.*
21. Former Royal Globe Company *201 Sansome St.*
22. Pacific Coast Stock Exchange *301 Pine St.*
23. Adam Grant Building *114 Sansome St.*
    Former Standard Oil Buildings *200 and 225 Bush St.*
24. Crown Zellerbach Building *1 Bush St.*
25. Citicorp Center *1 Sansome St.*
26. Shell Building *100 Bush St.*
    Flatiron Building *540-48 Market St.*
    Heineman Building *130 Bush St.*
    Mechanic's Monument *Mechanic's Plaza*
27. Standard Oil of California Building *555-75 Market St.*
28. JP Morgan Chase Building *560 Mission St.*
29. Transbay Transit Terminal *425 Mission St.*
30. Foundry Square *First & Howard Sts.*
31. Poetry Plaza *199 Fremont St.*
32. Former Shaklee Terrace *444 Market St.*
33. Industrial Indemnity Building *255 California St.*
34. Tadich Grill *240-242 California St.*
35. 100 California St. building
36. 101 California St. building
37. 388 Market St. building
38. Former Pacific Gas & Electric Building *245 Market St.*
    Former Marson Bulding *215 Market St.*
39. San Francisco Federal Reserve Bank *100 Market St.*
40. Hyatt Regency Hotel *5 Embarcadero Center*
    Embarcadero Center *Battery Clay Drumm and Sacramento Sts.*
41. Former Alcoa Building *1 Maritime Plaza*
42. Pier I *The Embarcadero*
43. Ferry Building *Market St. and The Embarcadero*
44. M. Justin Herman Plaza *The Embarcadero*
45. Landmark Building *1 Market St.*
46. Audiffred Building *1-21 Mission St.*
47. Rincon Center *99 Mission St.*
48. 135 Main St. building
49. YMCA *166 The Embarcadero*
    Bayside Plaza *188 The Embarcadero*

Previous page: Transamerica Building

Green St.
Vallejo St.
Columbus Ave.
Broadway
Pacific Ave.
Jackson St.
Washington St.
Clay St.
Commercial St.
Sacramento St.
California St.
Pine St.
Bush St.
Post St.
Grant St.
Kearny St.
Montgomery St.
Sansome St.
Battery St.
Front St.
Davis St.
Drumm St.
Embarcadero
Steuart St.
Spear St.
Main St.
Beale St.
Fremont St.
Market St.
Mission St.
Natoma St.
2nd St.
New Montgomery St.
3rd St.
Delancy St.
Harrison St.
N
1
2
3
4
5
6
7
8
9
10
11
12
13
14
15
16
17
18
19
20
21
22
23
24
25
26
27
28
29
30
31
32
33
34
35
36
37
38
39
40
41
42
43
44
45
46
47
48
49

1. Pacific Telephone & Telegraph Co.

2. Liveork lofts

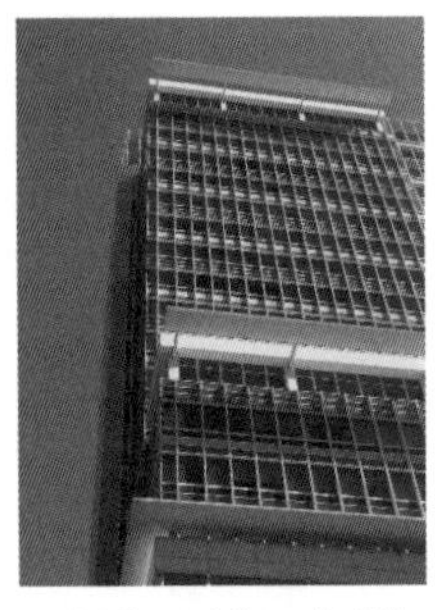

3. 101 Second Street building

1. **Pacific Telephone & Telegraph Co.**
   1925, Miller & Pfluege/A. A. Cantin; rest. 1990
   134-40 New Montgomery St.
   Eliel Saarinen's second-prize design for the Chicago Tribune Tower competition was the main inspiration for Timothy Pflueger's first skyscraper. Though the building appears as a stepped block from New Montgomery Street, it is a notched L from the southwest, contributing a welcome variety to the skyline. The eclectic ornament is well integrated into the building's form. The 1990 restoration included the recreation by sculptor Manuel Palos of the original 13-foot terra-cotta eagles that were removed from the top parapet in the 1950s. The black marble Moderne lobby is embellished with a stenciled ceiling a la Chinois and elaborate elevator doors.
2. **Live/Work lofts**
   1999, Jim Jennings Architect
   85 Natoma St.
   Known as the "Steel Arc", this loft building with steel walls that curve to form the roof is a pleasant surprise on this narrow street.
3. **101 Second Street building**
   1999, SOM; pavilion artworks by Charles Arnoldi and Larry Bell
   The central limestone tower is flanked by glassy slablike volumes that step down to the height of the building's more modest neighbors. The main entrance is a four-story glazed pavilion that also serves as a public exhibition area atop the roof. The glass wall of the mechanical equipment penthouse is designed to reflect the sun througout the day and thus contribute a glow to the city skyline.

New Montgomery Street

Now that the South-of-Market-Area has been developed with office and mixed-use buildings that the district north of Market could no longer accommodate, the story of this short street is worth recalling. In the late 19th century boom period capitalists William Ralston and Ashbury Harpending organized the New Montgomery Real Estate Company to develop the profitable south waterfront area. Rincon Hill, where the city's first millionaires had lived, was in the way; two stubborn residents, John Parrott and Milton Catham, stopped the street's progress at Howard by refusing to sell their property. Attempts to make New Montgomery Street the equal of its namesake faltered in bad times. The expensively improved lots did not sell when offered in 1869. Ralston then upped the ante by announcing the construction of the world's finest hotel, the Palace, at the head of the street–to no avail. Ralston's empire collapsed with the closing of the Bank of California on August 26, 1875; he drowned mysteriously that afternoon while taking his usual bay swim. The street lived on, never attaining the status its founders wanted, but boasting some substantial buildings that pre-dates those of adjoining streets.

4. **New Montgomery Street buildings**

Sharon Building
1912, George Kelham
39-63 New Montgomery St.
An L-shaped building that is not much more than a facade on the main street; the ground floor has a colorful old restaurant, the House of Shields.

Call Building
1914, Reid Bros.
74 New Montgomery St.
Originally built for the newspaper industry, the building is anchored at each end by a well-composed and richly detailed Classical pavilion.

Rialto Building
1902, Meyer & O'Brien; 1910, Bliss & Faville
116 New Montgomery St.

5. Sheraton Palace Hotel

5. **Sheraton Palace Hotel**
1909, Trowbridge & Livingston; rem., 1991, Skidmore Owings & Merrill/Page & Turnbull
633-65 Market St.
The airy opulence of the restored Garden Court in this block-size hotel captures the spirit of William Ralston's first Palace Hotel of 1873, long the west coast's finest. The warm brick exterior, stitched like a tapestry with terra-cotta ornament and crowned with a fancy

5. *Monadnock Building*

cornice, dignifies the whole block. The 1991 remodeling added a new section to the hotel and, best of all, restored the original ceiling heights and the grand public rooms.

Monadnock Building
685 Market St.
1906-07, Meyer & O'Brien
Interrupted by the 1906 earthquake and rebuilt afterward, the building was renovated in 1986-88. The entrance lobby has outstanding trompe l'oeil murals by the Evans & Brown Co. featuring famous people from the city's past who are identified on a handout available at the security desk. Do visit the sculpture garden in the interior court.

6. *Hobart Building*

6. **Hobart Building**
1914, Willis Polk
582-92 Market St.
An idiosyncratic design rumored to be a favorite of the designer. The bulding's eccentricity has become increasingly apparent with age, particularly when compared with its immediate neighbors. Shaped to address its polygonal site, the building had its bare flank exposed when a neighboring structure was torn down; the tower now seems to be peering over its shoulder in embarrassment. The ground floor remodeling is sad. Down the block at 562 and 567 Market Street. are two other buildings by Polk.

7. *Former Crocker Bank Headquarters*

7. **Former Crocker Bank Headquarters**
1983, Skidmore Owings & Merrill
1 Montgomery St.
A distinguished design, commendable for its sensitivity to both urban planning and preservation issues. The subtle play of light on the plaid pattern of polished and thermal-finished granite and the reflective, colored-glass windows change the tower's visual image during the course of the day. Next to the tower the pedestrian corridor through the barrel-vaulted Crocker Galleria is unfortunately interrupted by unsightly escalators. The roof garden created on the top of the old bank building's 1908 banking hall (designed by Willis Polk) is accessible from the upper level of the Galleria. It is a welcome, outdoor city room.

7. *Crocker Galleria*

Mechanics' Institute
1909, Albert Pissis
57-65 Post St.
One of the state's first educational institutions with a fine library on the arcaded floor. A mural by Arthur Mathews is in the marble elevator lobby.

8. **Hunter-Dulin Building**
1926, Schultze & Weaver
111 Sutter St.
A combination of the Romanesque and Chateauesque Revival styles with the building's shaft a clear expression of the structural frame and the chateau on top more staid than picturesque. The array of decorative motifs ranges from medallions with wistful young women shouldering garlands, to a belt cornice with squat eagles and ox heads, to a Neo-Norman arched entrance and the pseudo-Medieval lobby. This freewheeling approach to historicism typified this New York firm's work.

8. Hallidie Building

French Bank Building
1902, Hemenway & Miller; rem. 1907-13, E. A. Bozio
108-10 Sutter St.
An exposed-frame, Chicago School building that was embellished after the fire. The ground floor columns display a handsome scrolled shield with a caduceus, the symbol of Mercury, the god of commerce.

Hallidie Building
1917, Willis Polk
130-50 Sutter St.
Credited as the first use of the glass-curtain-wall, the facade of this building is more curtainlike than almost anything since. The elaborate cast-iron cornice, which resembles a Victorian window valance, contributes to the impression that the glass grid is a curtain. The fire escapes recall pull cords.

9. Russ Building

9. **Russ Building**
1927, George Kelham
235 Montgomery St.
For many years the city's largest and tallest office building, its Gothicized tower marked the center of the financial district until the 1970s, when it was dwarfed by a forest of new towers. The Gothic ornament is more perfunctory than inventive; the lobby is worth a visit.

9. Mills Building

Mills Building
1891, Burnham & Root; 1908, 1914, 1918, D. H. Burnham & Co./Willis Polk

Mills Tower
1931, Lewis P. Hobart
220 Montgomery St.
The only surviving pre-fire skyscraper that clearly reflects the great Chicago School tradition from which it sprang; the wall composition recalls Adler & Sullivan's Auditorium Building of 1888. Damaged but structurally intact after the 1906 earthquake and fire,

11. Former Bank of America World Headquarters

the building was restored and twice enlarged by Willis Polk, who headed the local D. H. Burnham & Co. office. Lewis Hobart's tower respects the original design. The arched entrance with its fine detail leads to a restrained lobby with a graceful branching stair and unusual foliated balusters.

10. **California Commercial Union**
1923, George Kelham/Kenneth MacDonald
315 Montgomery St.
Another Renaissance Revival design.

11. **Former Bank of America World Headquarters**
1969, Wurster, Bernardi & Emmons/ Skidmore Owings & Merrill/Pietro Belluschi, consultant
555 California St.
The city's most important office building but no longer owned by its largest bank. The tower's faceted form was partly inspired by Pflueger's 450 Sutter building. The height and dark red color insure its dominance of the skyline, but at sunset it becomes eerily transparent. The shaded, windswept north plaza has a polished black granite sculpture by Masayuki Nagare dubbed "the Banker's Heart" by an irate citizen. An opulent three-level banking hall fronts on Montgomery Street.

11. Former Bank of America World Headquarters

588 California St.
1987, Johnson/Burgee
The spooks on the roof are the talking points of this graceless try at reviving the 1920's skyscraper.

11. 588 California St.

12. **Bank building**
1922, George Kelham; rem. 1941, The Capitol Co.
300 Montgomery St.
A building remodeled to conform to the tasteful modern Classicism of the 1940s with great success. The ground floor remained intact, contributing an impressive colonnade to the street. The banking hall, refurbished by Baldwin-Clarke in 1978, is worth seeing as is the lobby inside the 300 Montgomery Street. entrance with its fine marble walls and Moderne lighting fixtures.

Merchants Exchange Building
1903, D. H. Burnham & Co./Willis Polk
465 California St.

Insurance Exchange Building
1913, Willis Polk
433 California St.
Two buildings with similar wall compositions and surface treatment. The Merchants Exchange (rebuilt after the fire) served as a local model for later build-

ings in the financial district: the Matson and PG&E buildings on Market Street. An interior skylit arcade leads to the old Merchants ex-change hall, attributed to Julia Morgan. Mimicking a Roman basilica, the hall is lavishly detailed and bathed in a natural light. The seascape paintings are by William Coulter. In the old days, merchants assembled in this hall where news about the ships coming into the harbor was transmitted to them from the lookout tower on the roof.

13. Kohl Building

13. Kohl Building

1904, Percy & Polk; 1907, Willis Polk
400 Montgomery St.

Restored by Polk after the fire, the ground floor has suffered the usual depredations. The entrance portico is still a fine composition; the marble lobby is mostly original. The best part of the building is its ornate top.

456 Montgomery Building

1983, Roger Owen Boyer Assoc./MLT Assoc.

13. 456 Montgomery Building

A highrise tower set back from the street to incorporate the temple-form facades of Albert Pissis's 1908 Anton Borel & Co. bank and Howard & Galloway's 1908 Sutro & Co. The latter is the more carefully detailed and costly design. In 1841 when the Hudson's Bay Company was located near here, this was the waterfront. Commercial Street, from Montgomery down to the bay, was the Central or Long Wharf, begun in 1848 and extended in 1850 when it was the city's major pier. The first U.S. branch mint in California was located at 608-10 Commercial; in 1875 the U.S. Subtreasury Building replaced it, was gutted by the 1906 fire and rebuilt as the one-story structure now tucked under the Bank of Canton, at 558 Montgomery, SOM, 1989. The old building now houses the Pacific Heritage Museum.

14. Former Bank of Italy/Bank of America

1908, Shea & Lofquist
552 Montgomery St.

A rich facade that, like some other buildings in the district, economizes by using expensive granite cladding on the ground floor and inexpensive terra cotta to mimic granite on the upper floors. The white marble interior is a real jewel box. Historic views of the city are on display.

15. Transamerica Building

1971, William Pereira & Assoc.
600 Montgomery St.

The butt of many jokes when it first appeared, this pyramid tower has settled into the affections of many people; its pointed top is now a valued anchor for the eye amidst all those unmemorable others.

16. 343 Sansome St.

17. Former Federal Reserve Bank

15. Transamerica Building

Still, the way the building rests spiderlike on the ground, ignoring its context, is hard for many to forgive. Next door is Redwood Park, completed in 1971 by Tom Galli.

16. **343 Sansome St.**
    c.1930, Hyman & Appleton; 1990, Johnson/Burgee
    A 1908 building restyled in Moderne and now joined by a restrained Postmodern design with Sullivanesque detail.

17. **Former Federal Reserve Bank**
    1924, George Kelham; 1991, Studios Architecture/ Kaplan, McLaughlin, Diaz
    400 Sansome St.
    A design in transition from the academic Beaux-Arts tradition on the ground level to the Moderne style on the upper part, as you can see by comparing the Ionic capitals of the free-standing columns with those of the giant pilasters above. The lobby, with murals by Jules Guerin, and the former banking hall are worth a visit. The Battery Street. entance was modified in 1991 to connect with the Embarcadero Center.

18. **Former Bank of California**
    1907, Bliss & Faville

Bank of California Tower
1967, Anshen & Allen
400 California St.
The banking temple at its best, with a beautifully detailed Corinthian order for the colonnade. Inside, the banking hall is a great cage with a coffered ceiling. Next door, the 1967 tower's fretted floor spandrels pick up the rhythm of the fluted columns. The ground floor cornice of copper stamped with a curvilinear pattern holds its own against the Classical riches of its neighbor.

18. Former Bank of California

19. Union Bank of California
1977, Skidmore Owings & Merrill
350 California St.
A sculptural, contemporary version of the Classical skyscraper with the corners visually strengthened by paired columns. Panels of precast bosses attempt to overcome the blankness of the typical office tower; expanses of glass permit a view into the banking hall. At the top of the wall at the back of the property walrus heads wreathed in rope peer over tiny icebergs. Forlorn relics, they solemnly represent the Alaska Commercial Building that once occupied the site.

20. California Center

20. California Center
1986, Skidmore Owings & Merrill
345 California St.

J. Harold Dollar Building
1920, George Kelham
341 California St.

Robert Dollar Building
1919, Charles McCall
301-33 California St.
To get the prestigious California Street address for this office building/hotel and preserve two landmark buildings that were headquarters for the Robert Dollar Steamship Lines, this highrise tower was planted in the middle of the block and provided with shopping arcades that permit circulation through it. The twin towers of the eleven-story hotel at the top of the building are linked by glazed skybridges.

21. Royal Globe Insurance Company

21. Royal Globe Insurance Company
1907, Howells & Stokes
201 Sansome St.
An exemplary Edwardian building. The entrance composition and ornamental detail of the base and attic sections provide a visual feast. The company had a similar building in the east with the same cladding.

22. 155 Sansome St.

22. Pacific Coast Stock Exchange

1915, J. Milton Dyer; 1930, Miller & Pflueger
301 Pine St.

This mausoleum-like block is a 1930 remodeling of a temple-front structure that had housed the U.S. Treasury. The monumental pylons in front have cast-stone sculptures representing agriculture and industry by Ralph Stackpole. The trading hall interior has a curvilinear grill made of thin metal strips laid endwise on a frame to form a lightweight ceiling beneath the air plenum, an ingenious way of creating an apparently changing depth of field that the same architects used in Oakland's famous Paramount Theater.

22. Pacific Coast Stock Exchange

Office tower

1930, Miller & Pflueger; 1988 renovation, Patrick McGrew Associates
155 Sansome St.

The tower next to the stock exchange originally served as the administrative wing of the stock exchange; it has a restrained Moderne entranceway and a glamorous lobby. The City Club occupies the tower's 10th and 11th floors, which originally housed the Stock Exchange Club, designed by Michael Goodman in Pflueger's office. The exceptionally fine interior has a mural by Diego Rivera in the stairwell and numerous artworks by local artists Harry Dixon, Robert Boardman Howard, Ralph Stackpole and Arthur Putnan. The club is open to visitors in the afternoon if no member events are scheduled. A detailed information sheet is available at the reception desk on the 10th floor.

23. Adam Grant Building

1908, Howard & Galloway; 1926, Lewis Hobart
114 Sansome St.

Only six floors of this office building were completed

when it opened in 1908; the rest were added by Hobart in 1926. The building was designed by John Galen Howard, who did his best-known work as the first supervising architect of the University Of California in Berkeley.

Former Standard Oil Building
1912, 1916, Benjamin C. McDougall
200 Bush St.

Former Standard Oil Building
1922, George Kelham
225 Bush St.
Two buildings with richly detailed exteriors. The last named has a Mediterranean crown a loggia capped with a red tile roof supported by a heavy, corbeled cornice.

24. Crown Zellerbach Building

24. Crown Zellerbach Building
1959, Hertzka & Knowles/Skidmore Owings & Merrill
1 Bush St.
The first of the city's glass-curtain-walled towers in the first and best of the tower-plaza settings. The air-conditioning console is set in to permit the glass to extend unbroken from the floor to above the ceiling, a design feature no longer affordable for most clients. The same goes for the elegant but extravagant placement of the elevators and stairs in their own mosaic-clad tower outside the office block. The playful round building, originally a bank, is an integral part of the gently sinking plaza with a fountain by David Tolerton.

25. Citicorp Center

25. Citicorp Center
1910, Albert Pissis; 1921, George Kelham
1984, Pereira & Assoc.
1 Sansome St.
Originally the London Paris National Bank. When the Citicorp tower was built the old banking room was converted to one of the most atmospheric atriums in town.

26. Shell Building

26. Shell Building
1929, George Kelham
100 Bush St.
A slender, stepped tower clad in rusticated beige terra cotta. Shell forms are well integrated into the design even when nearly out of sight. The projecting shells near the top conceal lighting that occasionally turns the crown to gold. The entrance lobby carries out the general theme.

Flatiron Building
1913, Havens & Toepke
540-48 Market St.

28. JP Morgan Chase Building

Heineman Building
1910, MacDonald & Applegarth
130 Bush St.

Mechanic's Monument
1894-95, Douglas Tilden, sculpt.; Willis Polk, arch.
Mechanic's Plaza
Polk designed the base of this heroic sculpture by Tilden, a deaf mute who was an internationally known artist. James Donahue gave the monument in memory of his father, Peter, who in 1850 started the state's first ironworks and machine shop, established the first gas company for street lighting in the city in 1852, and later initiated the first streetcar line. Bronze sidewalk plaques note the original shoreline of Yerba Buena Cove.

27. **Former Standard Oil of California Building**
1964, 1975, Hertzka & Knowles; plaza garden by Osmundson & Staley
555-75 Market St.
The plaza with its lush garden by Osmundson & Staley steals the show here. The intersection offers a chance to compare changing fashions in corporate plazas. Ecker and Jessie are two mid-block streets that reveal the possibilities for creating lively pedestrian passageways in the large South of Market blocks.

28. **JP Morgan Chase Building**
2002, Cesar Pelli & Assoc./Kendall-Heaton; Hart Howerton, landscape architect
560 Mission St.
A 433-foot-high rectangular tower with a notable dark green steel frame that is a departure from the light colored highrise buildings of the past. Pelli credits the Hallidie Building on Sutter Street as his inspiration. For that lowrise building Willis Polk designed the first-ever glazed wall hung like a curtain beyond the structural frame. Pelli's curtain walls have extra horizontal bands of steel framing the windows on the lower floors, a minimalist decorative touch that enlivens the grid. The plaza east of the building has a sculpture by George Rickey near the reflecting pool.

29. **Transbay Transit Terminal**
1939, Timothy Pflueger/Arthur Brown, Jr., and John J. Donovan, consulting architect
425 Mission St.
Designed to handle the Key System trains that ran across the Bay Bridge from 1939 until 1958, this is now a bus terminal. The functionalist Moderne box encloses a well-designed circulation system. The

construction of this terminal signaled the demise of the Ferry Building as the prime gateway to the city. Plans for a new terminal building and transportation hub are in progress.

30. Foundry Square

30. Foundry Square
2003, Studios Architecture;
Joel Shapiro bronze sculpture in plaza of Building 2
First and Howard Sts.
Four ten-story buildings were designed for the corners of this intersection, but in the wake of the dot.com bust only two were built. Thus a feeling of suspended animation afflicts the two unbuilt corners where a parking lot and a former factory building still stand. The glass walls of the new buildings face small plazas and are separated by four-foot air plenums, a thermal zone that reduces the need for heating and cooling. The outer walls of laminated glass vary in transparency with the amount of direct sunlight. Undulating metal roofs ride above the buildings, signaling them from far away.

32. Former Shaklee Terraces

31. Poetry Plaza
1997, KMD architects with Paul Kos, artist, and Robert Haas, poet
199 Fremont St. at Howard St.
A lyrical space in more ways than one. This small plaza wraps around an historic 19th century brick building that once housed the Marin Electric Company. Granite rocks, including one that weighs 82 tons, punctuate the plaza. Robart Haas composed his poem, "Daisylaps," to run along a stuccoed wall that faces the north wall of the brick building and leads to the street. The poem begins with: "an echo wandered through here what? an echo wandered through hear it?" Although birch trees along the wall shade some of the poem's words, they seem to add to its message. Two water faucets high on another wall drop water into a copper basin, replacing a waterfall that the budget ruled out.

33. Former Industrial Indemnity Building

32. Former Shaklee Terraces
1982, Skidmore Owings & Merrill
444 Market St.
The rolled-back Market Street facade and finely scaled flush aluminum skin make this one of the more ingratiating of this generation of towers. It is connected by a hyphen to the 1908 Postal Telegraph Building by Lewis Hobart at 22 Battery Street.

33. Former Industrial Indemnity Building
1959, Skidmore Owings & Merrill
255 California St.
Once a giant, now a moderate-sized tower, but still

36. 101 California Street Building

37. 388 Market Street Building

39. San Francisco Federal Reserve Bank Building

remarkable for its deference in scale and wall composition to its neighbors, particularly Lewis Hobart's 1910-17 Newhall Building at 260 California Street.

34. Tadich Grill
1909, Crim & Scott
240-42 California St.
The restaurant started up in 1865 on the site of the Transamerica pyramid and moved here later. The interior is a fine period piece, but the facade also deserves notice for the simple elegance of its terra-cotta frame

35. 100 California St.
1959, Welton Becket & Assoc.
One of the early postwar office towers. The metal bolts on the piers were added later for seismic safety.

36. 101 California Street Building
1982, Johnson/Burgee
An elegant silo that adds grace to the skyline; the less elegant glazed atrium at street level is an awkward interruption to the silo's descent to the ground, but the plaza is a welcome open space even if it does face north.

37. 388 Market Street Building
1987, Skidmore Owings & Merrill
The most successful design to date for a Market Street triangle, this teardrop-shaped tower is a mix of offices below and six residential floors at the top.

38. Pacific Gas & Electric Company
1925, Bakewell & Brown
245 Market St.
An engaged colonnade with a giant order topped by freestanding urns is the climax of this imposing facade. Clad in terra-cotta cast to mimic granite, the decorative detail is exceptional. The sculptural group by Edgar Walter over the entrance is particularly fine.

Matson Building
1921, Bliss & Faville
215 Market St.
The Matson was once the mainland headquarters for Hawaii's Big Five corporations. Like its neighbors, the building was designed to evoke the princely age of commerce embodied in the Renaissance palace. Nowadays these mercantile palaces recall the time when large office buildings lined the streets at uniform heights and spoke the same civilized language.

39. San Francisco Federal Reserve Bank Building
1982, Skidmore Owings & Merrill
100 block Market St.

A monumental loggia along Market and a reticent, granite-clad stepped facade distinguish this complicated building, which has everything from executive offices to money-warehousing operations.

40. Golden Gateway Phase One

40. Embarcadero Center

1967-81, John C. Portman, Jr.

Bounded by Clay, Battery, Sacramento, Drumm, California, and Market Sts. and M. Justin Herman Plaza

An 8 ½-acre portion of the 51-acre Golden Gateway Redevelopment Area fostered by M. Justin Herman, San Francisco's entrepreneurial Redevelopment Agency director from 1959 until his death in 1971. Called a city-within-a-city, the project was built incrementally over 14 years in tandem with the growth of the financial district. Often scorned in its early stages as a merely formal gesture at multilevel urbanity, its present daytime population now fills its many levels. The complex of four towers linked by footbridges plus the Hyatt Regency Hotel is exceptional for its successful integration of shopping–on the first three levels of each block-sized podium–and office towers, whose coverage is limited to one-third of the site. The towers, clad in rough-finished, precast concrete, are composed of slablike elements stepped to create 10 to 14 corner offices per floor instead of the usual four. Their slender profiles are a welcome departure from the heavier towers on the skyline. The city's requirement that one percent of development money be spent for art has endowed the Center with a number of works of art, including sculptures by Willi Gutman, Michael Biggers, Nicholas Schoffer, Anne Van Kleeck, Louise Nevelson, Barbara Showcroft, and Robert Russin; and tapestries by Francoise Grossen, Lia Cook, and Olga de Amaral. Circulation is baffling, but directories in each building give the locations of shops, restaurants, and works of art.

40. Embarcadero Center

Hyatt Regency Hotel

1989, John C. Portman, Jr.

333 Battery St.

The Center is introduced on Market Street by the Hyatt Regency Hotel, completed in 1973, and one of Portman's most successful atrium hotels. The great interior space has a monumental spherical sculpture of aluminum tubing by Charles Perry titled Eclipse. Seen from the Embarcadero, the staggered floors of the hotel recall an old-fashioned typewriter keyboard. A dreadfully dull main entrance addresses the automobile rather than acknowledging its importance as a gateway corner to pedestrians.

40. Hyatt Regency Hotel

41. Alcoa Building

41. Alcoa Building

42. Pier 1

41. Alcoa Building

1964, Skidmore Owings & Merrill; Sasaki Walker Assoc., landscape architect

1 Maritime Plaza

The major office tower in the Golden Gateway Redevelopment Project. Alcoa was the first design to use the seismic X-bracing as part of its structural aesthetic. The idea was used again in Chicago's Hancock Building, designed in the firm's Chicago office. The formal plan for the garden squares on top of the garages was intended to create the effect of an outdoor sculpture museum. Major pieces are by Marino Marini, Henry Moore, Charles Perry, Jan Peter Stern, and Beniamino Bufano; the fountain is by Robert Woodward. Although the rooftop plazas are convincing as pedestrian precincts, the street level is a grim reminder of what happens when an area is abandoned to auto traffic. A seismic retrofit of the Alcoa building in 2003, for which the architects were not consulted, appears to have compromised the design of the lower part of the structure. Golden Gateway Commons, the last phase of the redevelopment project, was designed by Fisher-Friedman and completed in 1987. Sidney Walton Park, bounded by Jackson, Front, Pacific, and Davis Streets was designed by Peter Walker and endowed with four sculptures by Marisol, Joan Brown, George Rickey, and Jim Dine; the fountain is by Francois Stahly. The small park has an inviting, restful atmosphere reminiscent of European city parks.

42. Pier 1

1932; 1999-2001, restoration and adaptive reuse, SMWM; Page & Turnbull, historic preservation architects

The Embarcadero

Built during a maritime industrial boom, this former warehouse building, like the other piers along the Embarcadero, had two sections, the two-story bulkhead with offices on the street end and a storage shed that extended 770 feet into the bay. A long period of minimum use took its toll of the structure, which was finally slated for renovation in the 1990s. The result is an office building that houses the Port Authority in the bulkhead space and new offices for the AMB Property Corp. in the back section. Since the pier was an historic property, the architects were constrained in their choices for structural additions and materials. Steel-framed mezzanines were used to create additional floors without altering the pier's exterior. A new glass curtain-wall inserted in the original arched entry permits a view of the gangplank-like ramps leading up to the mezzanine. The renovated building is notably "green" with operable windows and a radiant floor system that uses bay water to heat and cool the interior. To meet seismic codes without disturbing the historic building's integrity, steel piles were driven into the bay floor outside the structure along the building perimeter. A six-foot-thick concrete cap over the piles created more than an acre of new open space, a promenade around the building that offers views of the bay and of the bay side of the Ferry Building.

43. Ferry Building

43. Ferry Building

43. Ferry Building Plaza

43. Ferry Building

1895-1903, A. Page Brown/Edward R.A. Pyle, State Dept. of Engineering; 1999-2003, SMWM; Page & Turnbull, historic preservation architects

Before the bridges and the demolished freeway were built, this was the city's transportation hub. Some 170 ferries docked every day disgorging their passengers for an easy walk to downtown offices or to the trolley line up Market. The completion of the bay bridges, the Key System, and the Transbay Terminal diverted much of the traffic to rail, bus, and auto. When the ferries stopped in 1958, the building was converted into offices, which involved a mezzanine floor that intercepted the great skylit galleries that ran the length of the building. Several plans for the building's restoration were made in the next decades, but none was implemented. Near the end of the 20th century plans were made for resumption of ferry service that promised to activate the disused and abused structure. In 1999, SMWM's plan for restoring and refurbishing the building was adopted; its focus was the 660-foot-long second floor passenger gallery that originally provided access to the ferries. This so-called "nave" was also opened up to the first level to create a daylit public market hall with generous stalls leased

43. Ferry Building Plaza, trolly stop

43. Embarcadero trolly platform

43. *Embarcadero Promenade, sculpture*

to local food purveyors that extends the length of the building. An outdoor market takes place in front of the building on weekends.

The inappropriate remodeling over the years of the bay side of the Ferry Building led to rebuilding it with a design close to that of the original. The Agriculture Building that stands south of the Ferry Building is a richly ornamented relic of the 1915 Panama Pacific International Exposition. The plaza in front of the building, which divides the Embarcadero roadway, was designed by George Hargreaves, landscape architect. The plaza's trolley shelters were designed by Stanley Saitowitz.

43. *Information pylons*

Embarcadero Promenade
1982, MLTW/Turnbull Assoc./Donlyn Lyndon
Promenade Ribbon
1993-99, Vito Acconci, Stanley Saitowitz,
Barbara Stauffacher-Solomon
The promenade stretches along the waterfront and is accompanied for two and a half miles by a public art project: a concrete parthway with a center strip of glass brick illuminated by fiber optics.

Information pylons
1999, Michael Manwaring, designer
More than 325 bronze plaques embedded in porcelain enamel pylons occur along a two-and-a-half-mile section of the waterfront on the southern edge of King Street and on the transportation platforms.

44. *M. Justin Herman Plaza*

44. M. Justin Herman Plaza
1971, Mario Ciampi/Lawrence Halprin
& Assocs/John Bolles
Foot of Market St.
Part of the Market Street Beautification Project, the plaza suffers some from its north orientation, but the daytime crowd enlivens the space as do frequent craft markets and entertainment. The fountain by Armand Vaillancourt used to have the double-decker freeway as a backdrop. Now that the freeway is gone, the array of angular concrete forms can no longer be joked about as a stockpile of spare freeway parts. The plaza's other sculptures are an equestrian statue of Juan Bautista de Anza by Julian Martinez, a gift from the governor of Sonora, Mexico, and a stainless steel and black epoxy sculpture by Jean Dubuffet titled *La Chiffonniere* stands near Embarcadero 4; Embarcadero 3 has a black cor-ten steel sculpture by Louis Nevelson. A list of other art works in the center's buildings is available.

45. *Landmark Building, gateway*

45. Landmark Building
1916, Bliss & Faville
1 Market St.
A huge Renaissance palace built to house the headquarters of the Southern Pacific Railroad Company but now under other ownership. Caesar Pelli designed the atrum's cagelike sculpture.

46. Audiffred Building

46. Audiffred Building
1889; 1980-81, William E. Cullen
1-21 Mission St.
Built by Hippolyte Audiffred to recall his native France, the building survived the 1906 fire but was gutted by another fire in 1980. It has since been rehabilitated.The nautical ornament on the ground floor cornice is a delightful reminder that the building was once right on the water.

47. Rincon Center

47. Rincon Center
1939-40, Gilbert Stanley Underwood
99 Mission St.

Rincon Towers
1989, Johnson Faim/Pereira & Assoc.
88 Howard and 101 Spear Sts.
Often called PWA Moderne, the minimalist Classicism employed by the Public Works Department is well represented here in symmetrical massing and a colonnade reduced to barely projecting piers capped by a narrow lintel. The WPA murals inside are notable. In 1989 the post office building became the frontispiece for a mixed use development that features a large, midblock atrium with a fountain by Doug Hollis that rains from the ceiling. The residential towers that front on Howard Street are handsome additions to the assortment of towers nearby.

47. Rincon Center, Entrance

48. 135 Main Street Building
1989, Robinson Mills & Williams
A disconcerting attempt at monumentality on the ground floor but very discreet above. Behind the building is a network of alleyways, some landscaped, that offer the pedestrian shortcuts.

48. 135 Main Street Building

49. YMCA
1924, Carl Werner
166 The Embarcadero
A handsome facade long hidden behind the demolished Embarcadero Freeway decks.

Bayside Plaza
1986, Tower Architects
188 The Embarcadero
Designed to reflect its waterside location; the folded metal fountain sculpture in front is by Ruth Asawa.

When Jasper O'Farrell made the city's first formal survey in 1847, he judged the existing street grid north of Market to be too limiting and made the blocks south of Market roughly four times as large. The large blocks encouraged the industrial use of the area's flatlands that began in the 1850s when foundries, shipyards, machine shops, and other heavy industries started up on the shore east of First Street.

The city's first working-class neighborhood–initially a tent city inhabited mainly by hopeful miners–stretched along Mission Street from First to Third Streets. Euphemistically called Happy Valley, the settlement occupied the vale between the sandy hills on Market and Howard Streets. A plank toll road constructed in 1850 ran from Kearny Street to Third Street and out Mission Street to the Mission Dolores. In 1852 the city's first public transit, the Yellow Line, used it as a route for horse-drawn, 18-passenger coaches. After 1869, when Second Street was cut through Rincon Hill, the rich began moving away, leaving the area to be industrialized. When the cable car made Nob Hill accessible in the 1870s, the social climbers left Rincon Hill for good. The hill itself was later leveled to serve as the springing point for the 1936 Bay Bridge linking San Francisco with the East Bay.

In 1854, the gas works at First and Howard Streets (later incorporated as Pacific Gas & Electric) gave the city gas lighting. Warehouses dominated the large blocks toward the bay, and shipyards lined Mission Creek. The yards produced vessels used, among other things, for transporting lumber and other building materials for the houses that began to carpet the streetcar suburbs of the Western Addition and the Mission district in the 1870s.

Until the area was destroyed by the fire after the 1906 earthquake, working class neighborhoods had expanded to fill in the alleys and back streets–some of which were named for madams of local reknown–along Missions and Howard Streets. After the fire the area rebounded with 41 new buildings erected along Mission, Third, and Jessie Streets. New Montgomery Street, which extended three blocks south of Market Street in the late 1860s, attracted tall office buildings that housed commericial uses in their ground floors.

Although development continued through the first decades of the 20th century, widespread unemployment in the 1930s brought deterioration to the area where much of the population of single men was unemployed. In 1954, despite the presence of some 4,000 residents and 700 businesses, the San Francisco Redevelopment Agency designated the district "blighted" to clear the way for the Yerba Buena Redevelopment Plan. Its focus was the Yerba Buena Center and Gardens, a three-block project extending from Market Street to Folsom between Third and Fourth Streets.

As the demolition of small hotels and lodging house removed people from the area, residents began to organize against the project. In 1969, the TOOR (Tenants and Owners in Opposition to Redevelopment) organization was granted a federal injunction that halted demolition of housing in the area until the redevelopment agency adopted a relocation plan and agreed to provide replacement housing. TOOR's own development corporation acquired four sites in the area and constructed 400 units of housing on each site.

Today the three blocks of Yerba Buena Center are the core of the 87-acre redevelopment area built up with museums, hotels, office buildings, and restaurants. No longer tied to Market Street the south-of-Market-area (SOMA) has stretched further along the Embarcadero; its large population is housed in multi-story and often multi-use buildings, many of which were built during the 1990s "dot.com" economic boom.

1. Hills Plaza *Spear and Harrison Sts.*
2. AboveNet Internet Service Exchange *465 Main St.*
3. Portside *Main and Bryant Sts.*
4. Bayside Village *Bayside Village Place*
   Housing *301 Bryant St.*
   Cape Horn Lofts *540 Delancey St.*
5. Delancey Street Center *600 The Embarcadero*
   Oriental Warehouse *650 Delancey St.*
6. S. F. Fire Department Pumping Station *698 2nd St.*
7. Maggini Warehouse *128 King St.*
8. Rincon Park
   SBC Park
   The Embarcadero 2nd to 3rd Sts.
9. Richard Sorro Commons *225 King St.*
   Avalon Building *255 King St.*
10. China Basin Building *185 Berry St.*
    Mission Bay Visitors Center *255 Channel St.*
11. Mission Place *Townsend 3rd to 4th Sts.*
12. Designers Lofts *200 Townsend St.*
13. Warehouse *301 Brannan St.*
14. South Park *2nd to 3rd Sts. Bryant to Brannan Sts.*
    Jack London Townhouses *86 South Park*
15. San Francisco Multi-Media Center *475 Brannan St.*
16. Studio/Residence *25 Zoe St.*
    Zoe Studios *49 Zoe St.*
17. Pacific Telephone Building *611 Folsom St.*
    Hawthorne Terrace *77 Dow Place*
18. San Francisco Museum of Modern Art *151 3rd St.*
    St. Regis Museum Tower Hotel *125 Third St.*
    California Historical Society *678 Mission St.*
19. Jessie Street Substation *222-226 Jessie St.*
    St. Patrick's Church *756 Mission St.*
    Aronson Building *700 Mission St.*
20. Yerba Buena Gardens *Mission and 3rd Sts.*
    Yerba Buena Center for the Arts *Mission and 3rd Sts.*
    Yerba Buena Theatre *Howard and 3rd Sts.*
    The Metreon *4th and Mission Sts.*
21. George R. Moscone Convention Center *Howard to Folsom Sts. 3rd to 4th Sts.*
    Moscone West Convention Center *4th and Howard Sts.*
22. Senior Activities Center *360 4th St.*
23. Yerba Buena Lofts *855 Folsom St.*
24. Dettner Printing Co. *835 Howard St.*
25. Old U. S. Mint *5th and Mission Sts.*
26. California Casket Co. *965 Mission St.*
27. Houses *271 Shipley St.*
28. SoMa Community Recreation Center *6th and Folsom Sts.*
29. Columbia Square Housing *Columbia Square St. and Folsom St.*
30. United States District Court of Appeals Building *7th and Mission Sts.*
31. Federal Office Building Complex *7th and Mission St.*
32. Koret of California *1130 Howard St.*
33. Ukranian Orthodox Church of St. Michael *345 7th St.*
34. Hallam Street Houses
35. Canon Barcus Community House *165 8th St.*
    SOMA Studios + 8th and Howard Apartments *1180-1190 Howard St.*
36. Magrun & Otter Co. *1235 Mission St.*
37. Solomon E T C offices *1328 Mission St.*
38. People's Laundry *165 10th St.*
39. Residential Lofts *1022 Natoma St.*
40. St. Joseph's Church *1415 Howard St.*
41. Jackson Brewery *1489 Folsom St.*
42. Jewelry Mart *999 Brannan St.*
43. The Galleria *101 Kansas St.*
    Showplace Square *Brannan St. between 7th and 8th Sts.*
44. Warehouses *650 7th St. and 6th and Bluyxome St.*
    Baker & Hamilton Warehouse *601-625 Townsend St.*

Previous page: Yerba Buena Theater

Steuart St.
Spear St.
Main St.
Beale St.
Fremont St.
Market St.
Mission St.
Drumm St.
Davis St.
Sutter St.
Post St.
2nd St.
New Montgomery St.
3rd St.
4th St.
5th St.
6th St.
7th St.
8th St.
9th St.
10th St.
11th St.
12th. St.
Howard St.
Folsom St.
Harrison St.
Bryant St.
Brannan St.
Townsend St.
King St.
Berry St.
Channel St.
Hooper St.
Irwin St.
Delancy St.
Bay Bridge
China Basin
Mission Creek Marina
Hallam St.
McAllister St.
Division St.
Alameda St.
15th St.
16th St.
80
280
N
1
2
3
4
5
6
7
8
9
10
11
12
13
14
15
16
17
18
19
20
21
22
23
24
25
26
27
28
29
30
31
32
33
34
35
36
37
38
39
40
41
42
43
44

1. Hills Plaza

2. AboveNet Internet Service Exchange

3. Portside

4. Bayside Village

1. **Hills Plaza (former Hills Brothers Coffee Factory)**
   1933, George Kelham; 1991-92, Whisler-Patri
   Spear and Harrison Sts.
   No longer an olfactory landmark for those crossing the Bay Bridge, this has become a much larger visual landmark with the addition of another building to create a mixed-use complex. Inside the building at 2 Harrison Street is the Gordon Biersch Restaurant Brewery designed by Interim Architects.
2. **AboveNet Internet Service Exchange**
   2001, SOM
   465 Main St.
   A 1940s warehouse rehabilitated to house computer technology with associated mechanical and electrical equipment and provide space for operations support, administration offices, and accessory retail. A vaulted, aluminum-clad roof covers the new penthouse for cooling towers and generators. The renovation includes a new entry, the replacement of all windows, and restoration of the concrete facade.
3. **Portside**
   1999, Tower Architects
   Main and Bryant Sts.
   Two residential buildings that dip under the freeway and borrow nautical imagery from their location near the waterfront and the Streamline Moderne mode.

South End Historic District

The South End Historic District, established in 1990, commemorates San Francisco's south waterfront district of warehouses and buildings dedicated to so-called heavy industry, which flourished from the mid-19th to the mid-20th century. The district's north, east, south, and west boundaries are Stillman, Delancey, King, and Ritch Streets–their names etched in bronze in the sidewalks of the district along with information about its history. Although a number of the structures that contributed to the district's importance are gone, many survive, Converted to light industrial use, they serve both the past and the present.

4. **Bayside Village and South Beach Marina**
   1990-91, Fisher-Friedman Assoc.;
   Land. Arch., Anthony Guzzardo
   Bayside Village Place
   Bayside Village has over 100 rental units per acre on an 8.6-acre site and is divided into three sections by a landscaped street and pedestrian mall. The interior circulation system conveys the sense of a village within the surrounding urban context, and the landscaping provides relief from the sameness of it all.

301 Bryant Street
1998, Tanner Leddy Maytum Stacy
A mixed-use building with 38 condominiums that makes good use of a difficult site abutting the Cape Horn Bluffs of Rincon Hill. Stair towers are used to create a tri-partite facade on Delancey Street; the building's glazed corners lighten the effect of the large mass and take advantage of the bay views.

4. 301 Bryant Street

Cape Horn Lofts
1907; 1998, Pfau Architecture
540 Delancey St.
The sign, Southend Warehouses, still visible on this landmark brick building reveals its original use. The conversion to a 16-unit liveork building required seismic upgrading of the brick shell and timber frame. A landscaped rooftop, mezzanine, and interior courtyard provide homeyness.

5. **Delancey Street Center**
1990-92, Backen Arrigoni & Ross
600 The Embarcadero
A remarkable achievement by an organization famous for social rehabilitation, this is a live-work complex with a large interior court and a lively and gracious appearance.

5. Delancey Street Center

Oriental Warehouse
1867; 1999 Fisher Friedman
650 Delancey St.
The oldest surviving warehouse on the south end of San Francisco's industrialized waterfront is now a brick shell infilled with metal-clad condominiums.

6. **S. F. Fire Department Pumping Station**
c.1920, Frederick H. Meyer
698 2nd St.
A handsome Classic Revival building that could have been mistaken for a Postmodernist design. The nearby 100 and 200 blocks of Townsend Street have some fine warehouses from the 1890s to the 1910s–224 and 264 Townsend are standouts. Fanciers of vintage industrial buildings will also find 310 and 350 Townsend Street worthing seeing.

6. S. F. Fire Department Pumping Station

7. **Maggini Warehouse**
c.1900
128 King St.
Another notable brick warehouse; others are nearby.

7. Maggini Warehouse

8. **Rincon Park**
2002, Olin Partnership/Cheryl Barton
The Embarcadero north of Pac Bell Park
A two-acre park made possible by the realignment of The Embarcadero after the 1989 earthquake. The GAP,

8. Rincon Park

whose 2002 corporate headquarters designed by Robert A. M. Stern & Associates stands across the street, donated the land. This green approach to the ball park is a setting for two large sculptures: Sea change by Mark di Suvero, a 60-foot high work of steel with a wind-activated top, 1995, and Cupid's Span, a bow and arrow of painted fiberglass and stainless steel also 60 feet high, by Claes Oldenburg and Coosje van Bruggen, 2002. The seating walls have an applique of bronze sea creatures designed by Ronnie Frostad to fend off skate-boarders.
The Muni Metro line along The Embarcadero has passenger shelters designed by Anna Murch with undulating, glass canopies atop branching columns.

SBC Park
2000, HOK Sport, Kansas City/
Michael Willis Architects
The Embarcadero, 2nd to 3rd St.
With 42,800 seats, a fenestrated arcade facing the bay, and parklike open spaces at each corner of the site this ball park makes the most of its waterside setting. The site was also advantageous because it did not entail disrupting the surrounding urban fabric. The design bows to baseball's past at Wrigley Field and is less exciting outside where it has a themed appear-

8. SBC Park

ance than inside where views of the bay as well as the spectators and the game itself offer real theater. Rumor has it that the wall toward the bay was lowered to offer the prospect of hitting a ball into the bay–who knows?

9. **Richard Sorro Commons**
2002, SMWM
225 King St.
100 units of subsidized housing for low income families in a pleasant, no-frills, U-plan building that includes a child-care center, a fenced courtyard, and a community center.

Avalon
2003, Fisher Friedman/HKS, engineers
255 King St.
250 units of studio to three-bedroom apartments in a glassy, high-rise tower with a commercial base that is appropriately located on a public transit corridor.

10. China Basin Building

China Basin

China Basin was also called Mission Bay because its water came from Mission Creek, which extended to the area of the Laguna de los Dolores near the Mission Dolores. The present site of the 303-acre Mission Bay development project begins at Pac Bell Park and extends south along the waterfront to 16th Street. In the 1860s the site was a railyard for the Southern Pacific RR Company and continued in this use for more than a century. In 1981, the company decided to sell its land and proposed a mammoth development to the City consisting of 9,000 housing units, 2100 hotel rooms, and some ten million square feet of commercial space. Grand plans came and went with the economic tides. In 1997 a redevelopment area was approved to create tax revenues, and the University of California in San Francisco (UCSF) decided to locate its Health Sciences campus at Mission Bay. The campus, located in the area near Third and 16th Sts, was designed by SOM. Development is on-going with several buildings in place and in progress at this writing.

11. Mission Place

10. China Basin Building
1922, Bliss & Faville; rem. 1973, Robinson & Mills
185 Berry St.
The office conversion of this enormous warehouse building, originally built for the Pacific Steamship Company, started a now well-established trend in this area.

Mission Bay Visitors Center
2000, SMWM
255 Channel St.
Occupying the shell of a 1960s tilt-slab warehouse, the visitors' center is a public gallery for the display of the master plan for the area and materials related to it and the extensive public process that accompanied it.

11. Mission Place
2004, SOM/HKS, engineers
Townsend 3rd to 4th St.
A four-acre, mixed-use development with more than 500 apartments above retail and office space, courtyards and gardens, and parking for 900 cars. The project was planned as an urban park with a mid-

12. Designer Lofts

block plaza separating the east and west sections. On Fourth, King, and Third Streets, ground floor retail, markets and restaurants serve the plaza. The full complement of residential amenities includes a social hall, fitness center, pools and spas.

12. **Designer Lofts**
    2003, Gary Edward Handel & Associates
    200 Townsend St.
    A colorful and well detailed building with 51 live/work units and ground floor commercial use.

13. Warehouse

13. **Warehouse**
    1909, Lewis Hobart
    301 Brannan St.
    A large brick warehouse complex with accents of Classical ornament on the entrance portal. Hobart was a prominent, early 20th century architect whose diverse practice produced Grace Cathedral, the Bohemian Club, and the Mills Tower, as well as a number of commerical and residential buildings. More notable warehouses from the 1880s, 1890s, 1900s can be seen at 615, 625, 660 Third St.

14. 86 South Park

14. **South Park**
    1856, George Gordon
    2nd St. to 3rd St., Bryant St. to Brannan St.
    An early upper-class residential development, South Park was a speculative tract laid out by an Englishman with similar London developments in mind. Though a row of the townhouses that were meant to encircle the elliptical drive was built, the whole project failed after the decline of Rincon Hill in the 1870s. The townhouses have disappeared, but the mid-block park still sparks memories and plans for recapturing its former promise.

    Jack London Townhouses
    1995, Levy Design Partners
    86 South Park
    Four residential units on a rectangular site in a building that masks its shape with bristling projections. The architects–conscientious to a degree not usually found in such developements–have made admirable use of non-toxic materials from renewable sources such as recycled newspaper for wall and ceiling insulation. Lightweight steel used for structural elements avoided the need for composite wood products. Alternative materials include cement board and slate, asphalt, and copper shingles.

14. Jack London Townhouses

15. **San Francisco Multi-Media Center**
    2000, Pfau Architecture
    475 Brannan St.

A c.1906 warehouse converted into unconventional loft-style work spaces. The two new floors with slanted walls and red metal cladding above the roof are devoted to information technology; they appear to be slipping down inside the building's core, perhaps symbolizing the collision of old technology with new. The additions also include an interactive entrance lobby, an elevator building systems core, an open-air landscaped courtyard. The different materials and forms create playfulness and attracts the eye.

15. San Francisco Multi-Media Center

16. Studio/Residence

1992, Tanner Leddy Maytum Stacy

25 Zoe St.

A small building on a narrow lot that combines inexpensive, maintenance-free industrial materials, carefully detailed in a minimalist format, to create simple, lofty spaces.

Zoe Studios

1997, Kotas/Pantaleoni

49 Zoe St.

Sixteen live/work lofts with an industrial look that suits this narrow back street.

17. Pacific Telephone Building

1972, McCue, Boone & Tomsick

611 Folsom St.

A well-detailed brushed-aluminum box for delicate and complex telephone switchgear. The program, which called for stringent environmental controls, resulted in the windowless paneled skin interrupted only by glazed sections for personnel circulation and lunchrooms.

17. Pacific Telephone Building

17. Hawthorne Place

18. San Francisco Museum of Modern Art

Hawthorne Place
2003, Kotas/Pantaleoni
77 Dow Place
A building with 83 condominium units that ends this short street with a colorful transparent facade.

18. San Francisco Museum of Modern Aart
1994, Mario Botta/Hellmuth Obata Kassabaum
151 Third St.
When Mario Botta was given his first U.S. commission in 1988 to design the SFMOMA he was mainly known in this country for his work in the Swiss region of Ticino where he had designed some small but striking cubistic houses that complemented the mountainous landscape. For San Francisco he enlarged these forms to create a large cubistic building that seems to have been dropped from the sky–to which its oculus still points. The museum-as-icon is not an unfamiliar building type, and Botta's example has earned acclaim as such. The ground floor plan followed the trend of enticing the public off the street with a restaurant and a book store. Beyond these amenities, the spacious atrium, invisible from the sidewalk, has yet to define itself in respect to its purpose; its main attraction is overhead where a steel bridge spans the drum of the oculus and translates the footsteps of those who cross it into ghostly patterns. Although the walls of the drum create an awkward circulation pattern on the fourth floor, the light-filled open space is a memorable feature. Additions to the interior are the Koret Education Center located on the third floor and designed by Leddy Maytum Stacy. Opened in 2002, the center has rooms for classes and lectures, an

18. San Francisco Museum of Modern Art

interactive learning lounge, and state-of-the-art audio/visual and data resource sytstems. The design is elegant, understated, and easy to use.

St. Regis Museum Tower Hotel
2004, SOM
125 Third St.
A 400-room luxury hotel with condominiums on the upper floor and a 20,000 sq. ft. Museum for the African Diaspora at the tower's base. The 1907 Williams Building, designed by Clinton Day, at the corner of Third and Mission Streets was incorporated into the fabric of the hotel. The tower tapers on Mission and Third Streets.

19 . St. Patrick's Church

19. California Historical Society

18. St. Regis Museum Tower Hotel

California Historical Society
1995, Rosekrans & Associates
678 Mission St.
The historic Builders' Exchange Building, designed in 1922 by Andrew K. Knoll, was rehabilitated for the offices, library, and galleries of the California Historical Society, which occupied the building in 1995.

19. Jessie Street Substation
1905, 1907, 1909, Willis Polk
222-26 Jessie St.
A landmarked brick box embellished with Classical ornament that will be part of the Jewish Museum now being designed by Daniel Liebeskind.

St. Patrick's Church
1872; int. rem., 1907, Shea & Lofquist
756 Mission St.

Aronson Building
1903, Hemenway & Miller
700 Mission St.
Two buildings that have survived the natural disasters and booms and busts of the SOMA district to remind us of its past.

Yerba Buena Gardens

Yerba Buena Gardens, fountain

Yerba Buena Gardens

Although the central block of the Yerba Buena Gardens redevelopment area was dedicated to culture and entertainment in the 1970s, a real plan for the central block was not created until the mid-1980s. The museum and theater buildings for the Center for the Arts were in built until the early 1990s, by which time many of the surrounding blocks had been developed privately. The San Francisco Museum of Modern Art had already acquired property on Third Street for its new building. The Redevelopment Agency's decision to have the YBG cultural facilities face the interior of the block placed the buildings' service areas on Third Street across from the entrance to the SFMOMA. The unfortunate consequence is that the SFMOMA attracts conventioneers and other pedestrians moving along Third Street between Market and Howard Street, while the YBC facilities have no welcoming entrances on Third Street. Indeed, for all its attractions, the central block seems more separated from than connected to it's urban context.

20. The Esplanade Gardens

1985, MGA Partners/Romaldo Giurgola

Originally intended to be a landscaped park open on its north and south sides to Mission and Howard Streets, the open space shrank to accommodate the northern addition to the Moscone Convention Center. Moscone North is underground but has an entrance lobby above ground that interrupts pedestrian traffic on Howard Street. The block's ground level was raised several feet above the surrounding sidewalks to allow for the height of the underground facility. A waterfall and upper terrace with cafes overlooking a reflecting pool mask the lobby's eruption on the garden side. The central greensward has acquired several features including a garden to lure butterflies and a pavilion for performing arts. It is withall a popular place. The Yerba Buena Center buildings were limited in size and materials by their location on top of the Moscone

20. The Esplanade Gardens

North addition. But the use of lightweight materials–tile and metal instead of stone and marble–give them a freshness appropriate to the new cultural complex.

a. **Center for the Arts**
1993, Fumihiko Maki & Assocs./Robinson Mills & Williams
Mission and Third Sts.
The museum exhibits works in all media and mainly serves the Bay Area's many arts organizations. Three different-sized galleries, a media center for film and video, and a multi-purpose space for the performing arts called The Forum occupy the building. Clad in corrugated aluminum siding, its effect is far from industrial. Rather it has an effortless elegance, typical of Maki's work, that is worth studying in detail.

20a. Center for the Arts

20a. The Center for the Arts

b. **Yerba Buena Theater**
1993, James Stuart Polshek
Howard and Third Sts.
The building is articulated to express the functions of its components. Different materials such as aluminum panels for the fly tower and proscenium, blue-black tiles for the auditorium, and glazed foyers, signal to the viewer what lies within. The auditorium has a high-tech tautness and excellent sightlines.

20b. Yerba Buena Theater

c. **Metreon**
1996, Gary Handel Associates/SMWM
Fourth St. from Mission St. to Howard St.
The Metreon was Sony's attempt to create an urban entertainment center in an enclosed mall that would lure people off the streets and trap them inside with food, music, movies, and shops. The building walls off one side of the park. While the entrances are uninviting and the circulation confusing, the rooftop terrace offers fine views of the urban surroundings that are ignored in the rest of the building.

20c. Metreon

20c. Metreon

20. George R. Moscone Convention Center

21. Zeum

21. Moscone West Convention Center

21. George R. Moscone Convention Center
1981; add. 1991, Hellmuth, Obata, Kassabaum, HOK; T. Y. Lin, structural engineer.
Howard St. to Folsom St., Third St. to Fourth St.
Moscone Center was the first project built on one of the three key blocks of the Yerba Buena Redevelopment Area. The original building was noted for the span of its below-grade exhibition halls, an engineering feat of the times. All major city convention centers are huge, and all expand over time. This one is no exception.

Zeum
2000, Adele Santos
4th and Howard Sts.
An entertainment complex with multiple attractions, mainly for youth: an historic carrousel, a playground, an ice-skating rink, an auditorium, and educational exhibits. The exterior suggests a village of varied materials and colors.

Moscone West Convention Center
2003 Gensler Architectural Design and Planning/ Michael Willis Architects/Kwan Henmi Architecture
4th and Howard Sts.
Departing from the image of a mausoleumlike concrete mound, the third Moscone Convention Center is a tall box with a saw-toothed, glazed curtain wall that wraps around the corner and allows the building to glow in the dark like a lantern. The vast size of the facility is not apparent, but the facts are that the foyer covers more than half an acre, and the top-floor ballroom can seat 3,500 people for dinner. Diller & Scofidio designed a media attraction for passersby in the form of a large screen for video projections attached to a rather heavy-handed vertical frame that slowly moves along the curtain wall above the sidewalk. The videos display action-in-progress inside the meeting rooms as well as pre-programmed segments that present behind-the-scenes activities in a somewhat surreal way. Times Square it's not, but it's a start.

22. Senior Activities Center
1925
360 4th St.
A residentially scaled Spanish Colonial Revival building that is a surprise in this area, fortunately put to good use.

23. Yerba Buena Lofts
2002, Stanley Saitowitz
855 Folsom St.
200 residential loft units with four floors of parking

embedded in the lower section of the building and ground-floor commercial spaces. The building extends 338 feet along Folsom Street. Designed as a concrete egg-crate, the projecting two-story glazed bays that alternate with balconies indicate the height of the interior spaces. The bays project above the roof to enliven the skyline. Although the design is unmistakeably contemporary, the rhythm of the 338-foot long elevation recalls San Franciso's traditional housing.

23. Yerba Buena Lofts

24. Dettner Printing Co.
1909, Coxhead & Coxhead
835 Howard St.
This architect's fondness for exaggerated detail appears here in the giant keystone over the entrance, perhaps the only opportunity afforded by the budget to add a little drama to a typically utilitarian building type. The metal-framed ground floor is handsome and well-proportioned.

26. California Casket Co.

25. The Old U.S. Mint

25. The Old U.S. Mint
1869-74, Alfred B. Mullet; 1976, Walter Sondheimer; 2007, Patri-Merker/Barry Howard & Assoc.
5th and Mission Sts.
Although this Tuscan-Doric temple was unfashionable when it was built, it was considered to be one of the best appointed mints in the country. Following a lengthy restoration, the mint opened as a museum in 1976 but closed again in the 1990s because of seismic shortcomings. Plans are underway to open it again for the Museum of the City of San Francisco and the Museum of American Money and the Gold Rush.

26. California Casket Co. office building
1909, Albert Pissis
965 Mission St.

28. SoMa Community Recreation Center

29. Columbia Square Housing

30. United States District Court of Appeals Building

An appropriately dignified Classical facade by one of the first practicing Bay Area architects trained at the Ecole des Beaux Arts in Paris.

27. Houses
1992, Sternberg Associates
271 Shipley St.
Six houses compressed on a small back street and arranced around a T-shaped entry court. Square bays with stepped parapets are clad in corrugated metal; walls are colored plywood with a diagonal pattern of battens.

28. SoMa Community Recreation Center
1991, Marquis Assoc./Omi Lang
6th and Folsom Sts.
A much-needed and well-designed facility that creates a neighborhood presence.

29. Columbia Square Housing
1996, Baker Vilar Architects/David Baker Associates; Delaney & Cochran, landscape architects
Columbia Square St. at Folsom St.
A 50-unit apartment complex with ground floor commercial use, the four story building on Folsom Street steps down to a smaller scale around the corner on Columbia Square. Here an entrance for residents opens to a courtyard garden and playground.

30. United States District Court of Appeals Building
1902-05, John Knox Taylor; 1931-33, George Kelham; 1995, SOM, Page & Turnbull,
7th and Mission Sts.
An opulent expression of federal authority in a Neo-Baroque style with grand interiors. The building was restored, seismically retrofitted, and enlarged by a team of architects headed by SOM and assisted by historic preservation architects Page & Turnbull. A 45,000 square-foot enclosed courtyard capped by a skylight and lined with offices was added, and the former inclosed post office was opened up as a public space. Although not visible from the street, the meticulous restoration and reconfiguration is a fitting tribute to an historic monument, the likes of which will probably not be seen again.

31. Federal Office Building complex
2005, Thomas Mayne
7th and Mission Sts.
A striking departure from the Classic Revival style of federal buildings exemplified by the Federal Courts across the street. The slender tower that stands at a right angle to the courthouse has a contemporary

elegance that is a welcome counterpoint to its older neighbor. The plaza and cafe provide urbanity in an area that deserves it.

32. Koret of California

c.1935; rem. 1972, Beverly Willis & Assoc.

1130 Howard St.

With its almost playfully fortified parapet, sunburst entrance, and other detail, this decorated box has the swank associated with the Art Deco period.

32. Koret of California

33. Ukrainian Orthodox Church of St. Michael

1906, S. Ardrio

345 7th St.

A twin-towered facade approached by a double-branching stair and flanked by palm trees, this oasis demonstrates that cultural institutions can endure even when ethnic enclaves have disappeared.

33. Ukrainian Orthodox Church of St. Michael

34. Hallam St. houses

34. Residential Lofts

34. Hallam St. houses

1991, Donald MacDonald & Assoc.

End of Hallam St.

Infill residential development on a very small scale with eye-catching, unconventional windows designed to pull light into tall, deep spaces.

Residential Lofts

2002, Siegel & Strain

10 Hallam St.

Nine units in a stuccoed box enlivened with galvanized metal cladding for bays and sawtooth roof monitors. Steel stairways visible inside a glazed entrance bay use seismic X-bracing as a design element.

35. Canon Barcus Community House

35. Canon Barcus Community House

2002, Herman & Coliver

165 8th St.

35. SOMA Studios + 8th & Howard Apartments

A housing facility sponsored by Episcopal Community Services that serves recently homeless families. Tenant service spaces and a childcare center are provided in the building along with a ground floor skills center at the corner of 8th and Natoma Streets. Townhouses with 2, 3, and 4 bedrooms frame three podium-level courtyards above the skills center and a 46-car parking garage; flats are on upper floors above circulation corridors. Varied forms of windows and balconies relieve the potential monotony of repetitive bay windows and give the design a lively and non-institutional character.

SOMA Studios + 8th & Howard Apartments
2003, David Baker & Partners/I. A. Gonzales Architects
1180-90 Howard St.
A large project with many financial backers and two types of housing: 88 small studios in one component and 74 family apartments in the other. The project also includes a 2,500 sq. ft. childcare center and 19,000 sq. ft. of retail. Different color schemes, materials, and forms distinguish the two parts.

36. Magrun & Otter Co.

36. Magrun & Otter Co.
1928, Bliss & Faville
1235 Mission St.
A fine display of the decorative possibilities of terra cotta.

37. Solomon offices

37. Solomon ETC/WRT offices
2000, Solomon ETC
1328 Mission St.
Live/work lofts that house the offices of the architects.

38. People's Laundry

38. People's Laundry
1906, J. Dolliver
165 10th St.
Originally the Lick Baths, this picturesque complex was built to serve those rendered bathless by the earthquake.

39. Residential Lofts
1992, Stanley Saitowitz
1022 Natoma St.
A decidedly non-contextual design, this early live/work building on a standard 25x80-foot SOMA lot has an exposed steel frame tied to its west wall that appears to slide through the building. Flanked by staircases, the floors project beyond the frame and are indicated by strip windows which, along with metal cladding, enforce the International Style-Modern character of the whole composition.

South of Market

40. St. Joseph's Church
1912, John J. Foley
1415 Howard St.
St. Joseph's imposing twin-towered, Neo-Baroque facade looms over this now largely industrial area, testifying to the Italian neighborhood that was once here. The Templo Calvario next door is an older Carpenter Gothic church, which has lost half its spire.

40. St. Joseph's Church

41. Jackson Brewery
c.1910; 1995 Siegel & Strain
1489 Folsom St.
An historic brewery converted to seven live/work units with streetside commercial space. The seismic bracing was kept invisible from the outside to preserve the building's original appearance. Inside, the brick walls, steel frames, and concrete ceilings were preserved.

41. Jackson Brewery

42. Jewelry Mart
1990, Tanner Leddy Maytum Stacy
999 Brannan St.
A triangular jewelry case with glass brick walls that marked a revival of popularity for this modernist material.

42. Jewelry Mart

43. The Galleria
c.1900; rem. 1973, Wurster, Bernardi & Emmons
101 Kansas St.
A spectacular joining of two brick warehouses by a large steel and glass atrium.

Showplace Square
1970s
Brannan St., between 7th and 8th Sts.
Two major buildings housing the showrooms of many local interior design firms.

44. Warehouses
c.1890
650 7th St., 6th and Bluxome Sts.

Baker & Hamilton Warehouse
1905, Albert Pissis; 2001, Leddy Maytum Stacy
601 Townsend St. at 7th St.
More noble brick storage palaces. A city landmark, 601 Townsend St. was rehabilitated for office use in 2001. The exterior retains its original appearance except for the addition of an elegant glazed canopy; the skylit interior light well was restored. The adjacent building at 625 Townsend St., completed in 2002, was designed to harmonize with the historic warehouse. The new building's transparent facade incorporates a terra cotta tiled "rain screen" separated from the wall to protect it from water damage.

43. Baker & Hamilton Warehouse

Mariposa
2002

Stretching from Mission Creek/ China Basin to Islais Creek, the Central Waterfront area was developed after the construction of the Long Bridge across Mission Bay in 1857. The bridge enabled the transportation of goods and materials from the south waterfront north to the piers near the city center. In 1862, John North's shipyard started operations near the present Pier 70. The Tubbs Cordage Co. followed in 1867; Tubbs St. marks its site. In 1883 the Union Iron Works moved from the early industrial area at the base of Rincon Hill to a site near Pier 70; in 1905 the plant was purchased by the Bethlehem Steel Co. After the steel works departed in the 1970s, the Port Authority took charge of the property.

The predominantly Irish workers in these industries settled in an area that included a now leveled promontory once called Irish Hill. In the 1930s the neighborhood became known as Dogpatch. "L'il Abner", a famous comic strip of the times, may have inspired the name.

In the decades after World War II heavy industry declined. Large-scale operations such as Bethlehem Steel and the American Can Companies began to close. In the 1970s. Artists and other urban pioneers moved into the industrial buildings and into Dogpatch itself. In the 1970s the area's best known agent of gentrification, the Esprit Company, began to produce stylish clothing and accessories in buildings that had belonged to the Acheson Topeka & Santa Fe Railroad. The main building at 900 Minnesota Street had housed a railroad spur as indicated by its curved wall on the southeast side. At the turn of the 21st century Esprit departed from the district, leaving behind Esprit Park, created for company employees and now a city park.

Dogpatch is considered the city's most intact turn-of-the-20th century working class neighborhood. Small houses and boardinghouses along with a school and the businesses that served the residents still stand. Today, street trees provide a green ambiance not present in the old days when fog caused residents to value sun more than shade. Dogpatch now resounds with the white noise of the freeway instead of the clang and bang of heavy industry. The 1000 block of Tennessee and the 900 block of Minnesota Streets offer streetscapes evocative of the neighborhood's earlier history.

On Third Street, the east boundary of Dogpatch, a light rail line to Cesar Chavez Street is slated for completion in 2006. Serving commuters to downtown, the line will bolster the out-migration of residents that began in the boom times of the 1990s beyond the south of Market area. Although the so-called dot.com bubble has burst, development of multi-unit, residential buildings continues. Reminiscent of the growth of the 19th century streetcar suburbs in the Mission district and the Western Addition, the residential loft buildings that have arisen along Indiana and 3rd Streets are many times the size of their antecedents in the 19th century inner-city suburbs and have greatly increased the area's population density.

Islais Creek at the south end of the Central Waterfront district is a man-made channel at the end of a freshwater creek originating in Glen Park. Industrial uses dominate the surroundings, but in recent years the efforts of the Friends of Islais Creek have produced two small parks on both sides of the Third Street Bridge, designed by the engineer Levon Nishkian. On the east side, a garden by Tony Bava has poplar trees around a circular lawn; the west side has Islais Landing, landscaped by Martha Ketterer of the Department of Public Works. Flowering shrubs and paths lead to the water's edge; a sign designed by Robin Chiang presents the history of the site. Plans to renovate the Copra Crane as a monument to labor are being carried out by retirees from local maritime unions.

Central Waterfront / Potrero Hill

4

1. Office Building *350 Rhode Island St.*
2. California College of the Arts *1111 8th St.*
3. MOST Building *80 Missouri St.*
4. Third Street Lofts *SW corner of 3rd and Mariposa Sts.*
5. Former Police Station *3rd and 20th Sts.*

   American Can Co. *3rd Ave. 20th St. to 22nd St.*
6. Pier 70/Bethlehem Steel Buildings *end of 20th St.*
7. Dogpatch Historic District *Tubbs Indiana Mariposa and 3rd Sts.*
8. Live/Work Lofts *1099-1207 Indiana St.*
9. Live/Work Lofts *1325 Indiana St.*
10. Live/Work Lofts *1415 Indiana St.*
11. Muni Maintenance Yard and Islais Creek Copra Crane *3rd St. and Cargo Way*
12. Crowell house *400 Pennsylvania St.*
13. Adams and Richards houses *300-301 Pennsylvania St.*
14. Live Oak School *Mariposa and Arkansas*
15. Potrero Heights/Goldman Building 2 *18th and Arkansas Sts.*
16. St. Gregory Nissan *De Haro and Mariposa Sts.*
17. House *610 Rhode Island St.*
18. Potrero Hill Neighborhood House *953 De Haro St.*
19. Victoria Mews *20th and Wisconsin Sts.*
20. Townhouse duplex *782 Wisconsin St.*
21. Streetscapes *559-609 Arkansas St. and 512-526 Connecticut St.*
22. San Francisco General Hospital *1001 Potrero Ave.*
23. Good Samaritan Family Resource Center *1290 Potrero Ave.*

Previous page: Third Street Lofts

Brannan St.
Townsend St.
Channel St.
Mission Creek Marine
280
Division St.
Alameda St.
6th. St.
China Basin St.
Hooper St.
15th St.
Irwin St.
8th St.
16th St.
17th St.
Mariposa St.
18th St.
19th St.
20th St.
Vermont St.
Kansaa St.
Rode Island St.
De Haror St.
Carolina St.
Wisconson St.
Arkansas St.
Connecticut St.
Missouri St.
Texas St.
Mississippi St.
Pennsylvania St.
Indiana St.
Minnesota St.
Tennesse St.
Third St.
Illinois St.
Hampshire St.
Potrero Ave.
22nd
Tubbs St.
23rd St.
101
25th St.
26th St.
Army / Cesar Chavez St.
Islais Creek
Napoleon St.
Jerrold St.
Evans Ave.
Cargo way
N
1
2
3
4
5
6
7
8
9
10
11
12
13
14
15
16
17
18
19
20
21
22
23

4

1\. Mixed-use Building Complex

2\. California College of the Arts, Montgomery Campus

3\. MOST Building

1. **Mixed-use Building Complex**
   2002, Pfau Architecture / Gordon H. Chong & Partners
   350 Rhode Island St.
   A block-size project with two four-story office buildings linked by a metal bridge but separated by a courtyard that provides a pedestrian connection to adjacent streets. The exteriors of the buildings are treated differently, giving the block a pleasantly varied appearance.
2. **California College of the Arts, Montgomery Campus**
   1999, Leddy Maytum Stacy/ARUP Engineers
   1111 Eighth St.
   This former Greyhound Bus maintenance depot, designed by Skidmore Owings & Merrill and built in 1951, was converted to house the multi-disciplinary program in the fine and applied arts and architecture of a venerable Bay Area educational institution based in Oakland. A variety of energy-conserving strategies, including rooftop solar collectors that deliver hot water to a radiant floor slab, were successfully used to temper the unobstructed interior space–400 feet long, 150 feet wide, and 30 feet high–so that a yearly base temperature of 65 degrees is maintained without a convenional heating system. The interior recalls the spatial drama of late Gothic churches.
3. **MOST Building**
   1987, Kotas/Pantaleoni
   80 Missouri St.
   The building's name is a play on its street address and the desire to make the "most" out of the site by putting two residential loft units above two ware-houses.

4\. Third Street Lofts

4. **Third Street Lofts**
   2002, Stanley Saitowitz
   3rd and Mariposa Sts., SW corner
   The most striking features of this building, which contains 38 residential units on Third Street and 8 on Mariposa St., are the metal vaults visible from Mariposa St. The vaults cover living spaces on mezzanines that float under a curved ceiling. The building's facade on Third Street adjoins other residential loft buildings that convey the contemporary look of the streetcar streetscape lined with multi-storied buildings with repeating, 15-foot high bays and balconies. A walk or drive around the area from Mariposa to Cesar Chavez Street and Third to Pennsylvania Street affords ample opportunity to study a variety of examples.

5. The American Can Company

6. Pier 70 + Bethlehm Steel 2

6. Administration and Bldg.#104

5. Former Potrero Hill Police Station

5. **Former Potrero Hill Police Station**
   1912, John Reid
   Third and 20th Sts.
   A Mission Revival building designed by the City Architect in a then fashionable style.

   The American Can Company
   c.1915 to c.1955
   Third St. between 20th and 22nd Sts.
   Converted to mixed-use in the 1970s, this two-block-long, concrete-framed industrial plant was built from stock company plans that were used for other company buildings across the country.

6. **Pier 70 + Bethlehem Steel 2: Administration and Bldg.#104**
   c. 1880s to c. 1920
   End of 20th St.
   The Union Iron Works moved here from China Basin in 1883. In 1905 the plant buildings were sold to Bethlehem Steel, which continued in operation until the 1970s. This is the most significant complex of industrial buildings from San Francisco's late 19th and

7. Former Irving Scott School

7. Condominiums and lofts

early 20th century industrial past. The neo-classical building on the left near the entrance to the site is the former Administration Building designed by Frederick H. Meyer in 1917. Next door is the Power House designed by Weeks & Day in 1912 and next in line is Building 104, an office/drafting building, designed by Percy & Hamilton in 1896. Across the way is the site's oldest building, the Machine Shop, which dates from 1868; its designer was Dr. D. E. Melliss, an engineer. Buildings 115 and 116 are former foundries. Unfortunately there is little hope of saving these survivors of the past due to the prohibitive costs of upgrading them to meet seismic standards and of remediating the toxicity of the site. If you are a fan of ghostly industrial sites, this one is well worth a visit.

7. **Dogpatch Historic District**
1870s to the present
Boundaries: Tubbs, Indiana, Mariposa, and Third Sts.

Former Irving Scott School
1895
1060 Tennessee St.

Row of cottages 1002-1012 Tennessee St.
1887-88
Built from a plan published by John Cotter Pelton, Jr. in the San Francisco Evening Bulletin between 1880 and 1883 and also in his book, Cheap Dwellings. The west side of the 900 block of Minnesota St. has a similar row of small houses from the 1880s.

7. Row of cottages 1002-1012 Tennessee St.

Condominiums and lofts
c. 1900, Land Development arm of the Atchinson Topeka & Santa Fe Railroad Company;
1993 remodeling, Pyatok Architects
701 Minnesota St. and Tennessee St.
Gutted In 1993, this handscome brick building

was infilled with 58 condominium residential loft units and four live/work units grouped around landscaped courts.

8. **Live/Work lofts**
   1998-99, Gary Gee
   1099-1207 Indiana St.
   20 rental lofts occupy this large building, which extend through the block to become 1011 Minnesota.

10. Indiana Industrial Lofts

8. Live/Work lofts

These units belong to the second generation live/work lofts and have a mezzanine floor in addition to the main living floor.

9. **Residential Lofts**
   2001, Leavitt Architecture
   1325 Indiana St.
   Forty-eight rental units in the loft format with an industrial vocabulary of materials. The building goes through the block to Minnesota St.

10. **Indiana Industrial Lofts**
    2001, David Baker & Partners
    1415 Indiana St.
    An early example of the live/work building type designed in an industrial aesthetic that suits the area.

11. **Islais Creek Motor Coach Maintenance and Operations Facility**
    2007, Robin Chiang & Co.
    Indiana St. at Cesar Chavez St.

Islais Creek Crane

Potrero Hill

Potrero Hill rises out of the flatlands between 16th and Cesar Chavez Streets and Highway 101. Potrero Avenue was once the eastern boundary of the Potrero Viejo, the old pasture of the Mission Dolores. Surrounded by freeways and industrial areas, the hill becomes residential as it rises. A few early settlers such as Captain Adams and Prentice Crowell, whose houses stand on Pennsylvania Street, saw the advan-

12. Prentice Crowell house

13. Adams house

15. Potrero Heights/Goldman 2

tages of this secluded hill and its fine weather. They settled on its bay side in the 1860s and 1870s. In the 1880s the hill was briefly known as Scotch Hill because of the many Scots who lived and worked in the Union Iron Works. After 1905 Russians were the largest immigrant group and remained so until the 1930s. No longer a backwater, Potrero Hill property is much sought after by urbanites appreciative of the spectacular views of downtown and the bay as well as the fine microclimate.

12. Prentice Crowell house

c.1870

400 Pennsylvania St.

Similar to the Richards house described below.

13. Adams house

1868

300 Pennsylvania St.

Richards house

1866

1301 Pennsylvania St.

Captain Adams bought this 13-acre tract in the 1860s, and probably built his home using an eastern carpenter's plan book. The Richards house seems, by comparison, very simple and chaste, having lost its entrance porch and its octagonal cupola, from which there would have been a fine view of the bay.

14. Live Oak School

2002, Bridges Architecture

1555 Mariposa St.

A former Hills Brothers coffee roasting facility converted into a private school, the complex retains its industrial character while presenting a pleasant public face.

15. Potrero Heights/Goldman 2

1995, David Baker & Partners; Jeffrey Miller, landscape architect

559-609 18th St.

Two early live/work buildings–one intended for artists –designed to reflect the industrial character of the area and built on a steep site over a collapsed railroad tunnel. The remarkable garden, located in the space between the two buildings, features segmental terraces that trace a serpentine path on the hillside atop the abandoned tunnel. The garden is open to the public.

16. **House**
1991, Daniel Solomon & Associates
610 Rhode Island St.
An intentionally gritty design using black asphalt shingles to allude to the industrial area down the hill. The enclosed metal fireplace box and flue enforce the symmetrical composition of this bi-lateral residence designed for two musicians.

16. 610 Rhode Island St.

17. **St. Gregory of Nyssa**
1995, John Goldman
500 De Haro St.
In both liturgy–based on 4th and 5th century Christian worship and its Jewish antecendents–and architecture, St. Gregory's congregation has sought cultural fusion. The building reflects such faraway sources as Russia's wooden Orthodox churches and Japan's castles and Shinto shrines. However, the most obvious influence is the regional Craftsman/Shingle style. The

17. St. Gregory of Nyssa

interior has two linked, octagonal spaces, each with its own accoustical system, devoted to the two liturgies celebrated in the church service. Painted icons of the "dancing saints" adorn the walls along with other artworks. All of this is worth seeing.

Pioneer Square & the Anchor Brewing Co.
c. 1915
Mariposa, Carolina, 18th Sts.
Industrial buildings, one converted to mixed use and one housing the city's most famous local brewery.

18. **Potrero Hill Neighborhood House**
1922, 1925, Julia Morgan
953 De Haro St.
Established in 1919 by the Presbyterian Church to serve the Russian immigrants settled on the hill. Morgan's reputation for designing small institutional

19. Victoria Mews

buildings won her the job. Others in this informal, shingle style include the Sausalito Womens Club. The Potrero Peace Park, 20th and De Haro St., is a terraced landscape with curving masonry retaining walls designed by Jeffrey Miller in 1997.

19. Victoria Mews
1979
20th and Wisconsin Sts.
Movie-set Victorian. Well done but best viewed from a distance, where the general mass merges with the older row housing in the hillside.

20. Townhouse duplex
1991, Kotas/Pantaleoni
782 Wisconsin St.
Painted schoolbus yellow, this back-to-back set of town houses expresses its great bay view.

20. Townhouse duplex

21. Vintage streetscapes of cottages and houses
1880s
559-609 Arkansas St.
1885
512-26 Connecticut St.

22. San Francisco General Hospital

23. Good Samaritan Family Resource Center

22. San Francisco General Hospital
1909-15, Newton Tharp, city architect; John Galen Howard/Frederick H. Meyer/John Reid, Jr.; 1976, Stone, Marraccini & Patterson
1001 Potrero Ave.
A huge campus of hospital buildings designed over a 50-year period. The progression from a varied vocabulary of materials and a relatively small scale to the inhuman scale of modern medical technology in concrete is obvious.

23. Good Samaritan Family Resource Center
1997, Mark Horton/Simon Martin-Vegue Winkelstein Moris
1290 Potrero Ave.
A varied group of building forms that houses 20 housing units and a 14,500 sq. ft. social services center that serves the community. An L-shaped plan on the corner lot made open spaces between the buidings possible.

The Mission district, one of the city's largest, has two fairly distinct sections. Although the eastern part has always had mixed industrial and residential uses–and originally large farms–the inner or western Mission grew in a more urban and residential way as a streetcar suburb. The mission itself, founded in 1776, was well sited on the banks of the Laguna de Manatial, which roughly covered the city blocks now bounded by 15th, Guerrero, 23rd, and Harrison Streets. The lake was fed by the Arroyo de Nuestra Señora de los Dolores, which gave the mission its name. The wisdom of the Franciscan padres, who founded the mission in the most benign part of what they regarded as a generally bleak and unfriendly peninsula, was ignored by the early Yankee settlers, who located their buildings by the cold and foggy bay because their ties were to trade, not agriculture. Although the mission's long decline following the Secularization Act of 1834 freed a great deal of land, the area was so remote from the new city center that it preserved its pastoral quality until the streetcar era began in the 1860s. Mission Street, originally the plank road that linked the mission with downtown, served as the main development channel. Once the streetcars began to run, the balmy climate attracted tourists. Roadhouses and an entertainment park, Woodward Gardens, at Mission and Duboce responded to their needs. From about 1870 to the early 1900s, the area filled up with single-and multi-family dwellings, many of which survive to make walking the best way to sightsee. Although it seems logical that the mulit-national population of Spanish-speaking people that now dominates the mission has been there from the beginning, the main national group from the streetcar era until World War II was Irish.

Several hills add variety to the relatively flat terrain. Dolores Park is a welcome green open space stretched along Dolores Street. John McLaren planted palm trees in the median strip after the 1906 fire in preparation for the 1915 Panama-Pacific International Exposition. Mission Street itself, one of the most colorful and lively of the city's major neighborhood shopping streets, is complemented by Valencia, 18th, and 24th Streets, which offer numerous eateries, markets, and shops.

The Precita Eyes and Mural Arts visitors center, 2951 24th Street, at Harrison Street, provides information and regular walking tours of murals in the district.

1. California Volunteers Memorial *Dolores at Market St.*
2. St. Frances Lutheran (St. Angsar) Church *152 Church St.*
3. St. Nicholas Russian Orthodox Church *2005 15th St.*
4. Church Street Terrace *350-360 Church St.*
5. Everett Middle School *Church St. at 16th St.*
6. Mission High School *18th and Dolores Sts.*
7. Mission San Francisco de Asis (Mission Dolores)

   Mission Dolores Basilica *16th and Dolores Sts.*
8. Former Notre Dame School *347 Dolores St.*

   St. Matthew's Lutheran Church *3281 16th St.*
9. Tanforan cottages *214 220 Dolores St.*
10. House *102 Guerrero St.*
11. Baha'i Center *170 Valencia St.*
12. Levi Strauss Factory and Playground *250 Valencia St.*
13. Armory *14th and Mission Sts.*
14. St. John the Evangelist Episcopal Church *1661 15th St.*
15. Duggan's Funeral Service *3434 17th St.*
16. 16th Street BART Station *16th St. and Mission St.*
17. Mission Plaza *2027 Mission St.*
18. The Lab/Camp Murals *2948 and 2940 16th St.*
19. House *65 Capp St.*
20. House *573 South Van Ness Ave.*
21. St. Charles School *18th and Shotwell Sts.*
22. Mission Neighborhood Center *362 Capp St.*
23. Women's Building *3543 18th St.*
24. Russian Orthodox Convent Our Lady of Vladimir *19th and Capp Sts.*
25. El Capitan Theatre *2361 Mission St.*
26. House *3755 20th St.*
27. McMullen house *827 Guerrero St.*

    Kershaw House *Guerrero and Liberty St.*
28. Liberty/Hill Historic District *Dolores 20th Mission 22nd Sts.*
29. Former St. John's Lutheran Church *3126 22 St.*
30. 900 block of South Van Ness Ave.
31. Double house *772-74 Shotwell St.*
32. Cesar Chavez Elementary School *825 Shotwell St.*
33. Apartments *1201 South Van Ness Ave.*
34. 700 block of Capp St.

    Mission Presbyterian Church *Capp and 23rd Sts.*
35. Mission Campus of City College; Downtown High School *22nd and Bartlett Sts.*
36. House *200 Fair Oaks Ave.*
37. Houses *1200 block Guerrero St.*
38. Horace Mann Middle School *3531 22nd St.*

    Mission Branch Library *24th and Bartlett Sts.*

    Houses *3300 block 23rd St.*
39. Frank M. Stone house *1348 S. Van Ness Ave.*

    House *1381 So. Van Ness Ave.*
40. Galleria de la Raza/Precita Eyes Mural Arts Center Murals *2857 and 2981 24th St./Balmy St.*
41. Houses *1200 block of Treat St.*
42. Houses *2733 and 2735 Folsom St.*
43. Houses *1100 block of Shotwell St.*
45. Holy Innocents Episcopal Church *455 Fair Oaks St.*
46. Apartments *26th St. and South Van Ness Ave.*

Previous page: Mission Dolores

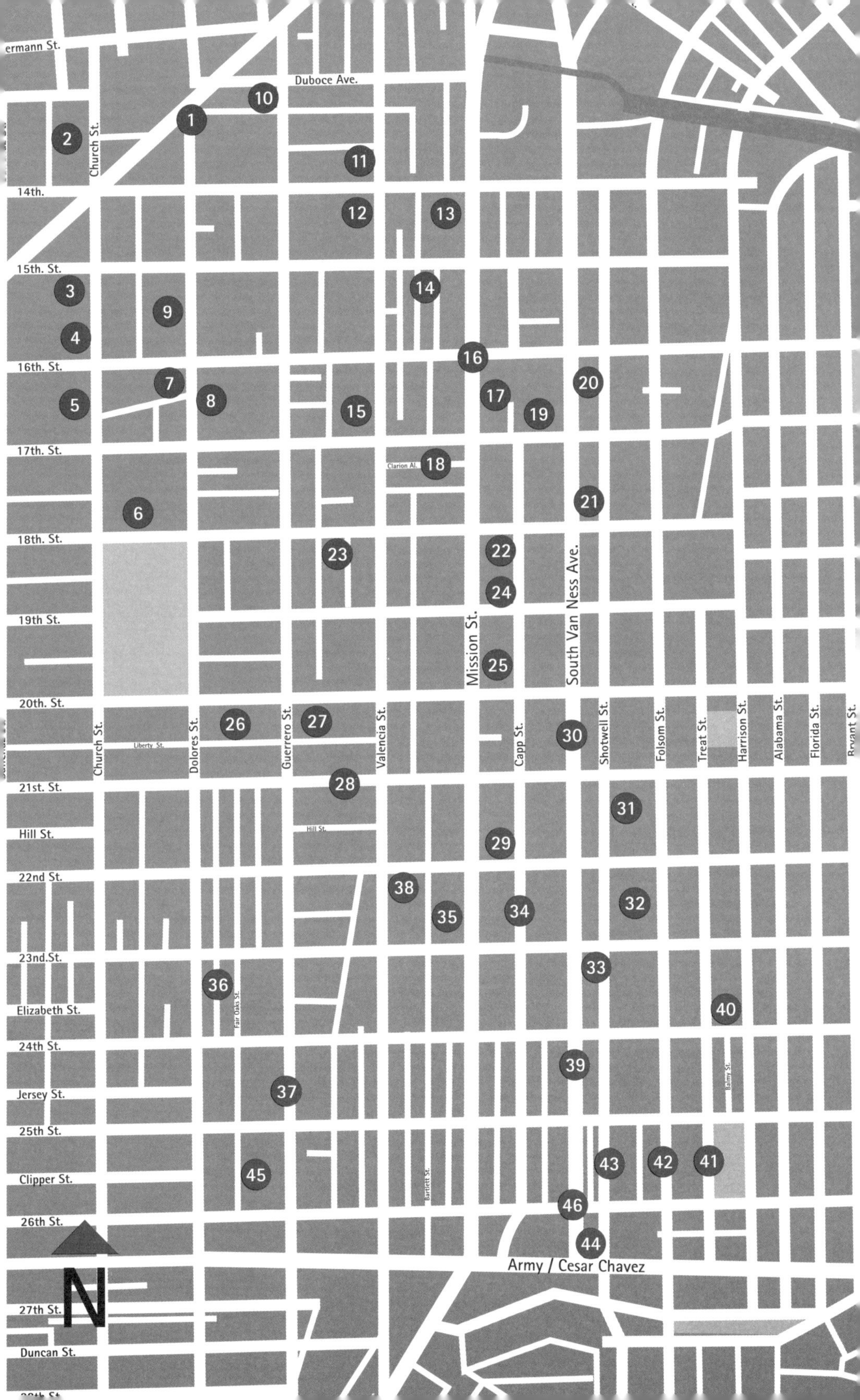

ermann St.
Duboce Ave.
Church St.
14th.
15th. St.
16th. St.
17th. St.
Clarion Al.
18th. St.
19th St.
Mission St.
South Van Ness Ave.
20th. St.
Church St.
Liberty St.
Dolores St.
Guerrero St.
Valencia St.
Capp St.
Shotwell St.
Folsom St.
Treat St.
Harrison St.
Alabama St.
Florida St.
21st. St.
Hill St.
Hill St.
22nd St.
23nd.St.
Elizabeth St.
Fair Oaks St.
24th St.
Balmy St.
Jersey St.
25th St.
Clipper St.
Bartlett St.
26th St.
Army / Cesar Chavez
N
27th St.
Duncan St.
1
2
3
4
5
6
7
8
9
10
11
12
13
14
15
16
17
18
19
20
21
22
23
24
25
26
27
28
29
30
31
32
33
34
35
36
37
38
39
40
41
42
43
44
45
46

5

1. California Volunteers' Memorial

3. St. Nicholas Russian Orthodox Cathedral

4. Church Street Terrace

6. Mission High School

1. **California Volunteers' Memorial**
   1906, Douglas Tilden, sculptor; Willis Polk, base
   Dolores at Market St.
   This fine equestrian statue by the city's greatest sculptor of outdoor works is perfectly placed at the head of Dolores Street's stately row of palms planted for the 1915 Panama-Pacific International Exposition. Gilbert Stanley Underwood's mighty fortress for the U. S. Mint of 1937 capped an existing bluff across Market Street.
2. **St. Frances Lutheran (St. Angsar) Church**
   1905-1907
   152 Church St.
   A stern Neo-Gothic church built for a Danish congregation.
3. **St. Nicholas Russian Orthodox Cathedral (former St. Luke's German Evangelical Church)**
   c. 1903
   2005 15th St.
   A Carpenter Gothic church with Russian orthodox accent atop its tower.
4. **Church Street Terrace**
   1981, Stephen Allen Roake
   350-60 Church St.
5. **Everett Middle School**
   1925, John Reid, Jr.
   Church St. between 16th and 17th Sts.
   Although the design has some elements of the Mission Revival Style, it also includes the Moorish-Byzantine mode. The lavish decorative detail testifies to the importance of urban public schools as neighborhood cultural institutions.
6. **Mission High School**
   1926, John Reid, Jr.; renovated 1972-78, J. Martin Rosse
   18th and Dolores Sts.
   A Mission district landmark that competes in prominence with the Mission Dolores Bascilica. The polychromed tile domes and fine Spanish Baroque detailing make this the most sumptuous of the city's public schools.
7. **Mission Dolores Basilica**
   1913
   16th and Dolores Sts.

   Mission San Francisco de Asis (Mission Dolores)
   1782; restored, 1918, Willis Polk
   These two make an eloquent pair. With its crude, stumpy columns marching up and down the gable, the humble mission bespeaks an altogether different time

and institution from the overwhelming Mission-style basilica next door. The mission church entrance was originally much lower to the ground; steps were added when Dolores Street was created and paved. The interior of the mission, restored by Polk, should be seen, but that of the basilica is disappointing. The time-worn cemetery with its lush vegetation blurs the harsh existence of the original mission population: 5,000 Indians were buried here. The original burial ground extended beyond what is now Dolores Street. The surviving cemetery has graves of prominent early Californians.

7. Mission Dolores Basilica

8. Former Notre Dame School

7. Mission San Francisco de Asis

8. **Former Notre Dame School**
   1907
   347 Dolores St.
   This graceful building, which housed the city's first girls' school, has a composite style that may be the result of the rebuilding of an already modified older structure. Its scale is complementary to the old mission.

   St. Matthew's Lutheran Church
   1901
   3281 16th St.
   A late Carpenter Gothic church.

9. **Tanforan cottages**
   c.1853
   214, 220 Dolores St.

10. 102 Guerrero St.

11. Baha'i Center

Two very early small cottages, one with a carriage house behind, preserve the look of the early Mission district.

10. House

1873, Henry Geilfuss; rest. 1980, Roy Killeen
102 Guerrero St.
A prominent, German-born architect, who designed residences for the affluent such as the Westerfield house at 1198 Fulton Street. The house listed here has a refined facade with distinctive, slender colonnettes dividing the windows.

11. Baha'i Center

1932, Harold Stoner
170 Valencia St.
A remarkable Art Deco design built for the Woodmen of the World.

12. Levi Strauss Factory & Playground

12. Levi Strauss Factory & Playground

1906; rest. 1970, Howard Friedman
250 Valencia St.
The starting place for all those blue jeans that have traveled the world, but are no longer made here.

13. Armory

1909, Woollett & Woollett
14th and Mission Sts.
This clinker-brick bastion was built in two phases. The first was a four-story building containing offices and other services; the second was a vaulted drill hall 60 feet high. Altogether the building has 70,000 sq. ft., which are no longer used for military purposes.

14. St. John the Evangelist Episcopal Church

1909
1661 15th St.
This church was apparently based on an English country church in the parish of Norwich. On the northwest corner of Valencia and 15th Streets is a handsome apartment house in a sophisticated urban mode.

15. **Duggans Funeral Service**
c.1900, Ernest Coxhead
3434 17th St.
Coxhead previews the Postmodernists in this interesting distortion of Classical elements.

15. Duggans Funeral Service

16. **16th St. BART Plaza**
1998-2003 renovation: Tom Richman,landscape architect; ceramic mural artists, Daniel Galvez, Jos Sances; metalwork railings: Victor Mario Zaballa, artist; Lawrence Berk, fabricator
NW corner16th and Mission Sts.
With 8,000 riders a day, this (heavily used) station was dangerously forlorn when BART and the Mission Housing Development Corporation hired Urban Ecology to engage neighbors and BART riders to renovate the plaza. The result is a colorful open space with artworks that evoke the culture and history of the neighborhood.

16. 16th St. BART Plaza

17. **Mission Plaza**
1981, Jorge de Quesada
2027 Mission St.
An early mixed-use residential and commercial development that still looks contemporary.

18. **The Lab/CAMP murals**
1984, Artists Collective; 1997, murals by CAMP
2948 and 2940 16th St.
An alternative exhibition space in a 1914 union hall founded by a group of interdisciplinary artists, CAMP, to show local work. Since 1992 the CAMP artists have also covered the walls of buildings on nearby Clarion Alley, which runs between Mission and Valencia Streets, with murals depicting a range of subjects.

19. **House**
1981, David Ireland
65 Capp St.
Known mainly for his process-oriented "conceptual" artworks in mixed media, Ireland has also worked with buildings. This dwelling, created for himself in an industrial aesthetic, has windows placed for looking out rather than in and a corrugated metal siding

19. 65 Capp St.

intended to discourage graffiti. The Capp Street Project had its first home here and was the setting for many outstanding installations by artists such as James Turrell. The building is now a private residence.

21. St. Charles School

22. Mission Neighborhood Center

23. Women's Building

24. Russian Orthodox Convent of Our Lady of Vladimir

20. 573 South Van Ness Ave.

20. House
c. 1890
573 South Van Ness Ave.
A grand and lonely Queen Anne House, restored and nicely painted.

21. St. Charles School
1875, Charles J. Devlin
18th and Shotwell Sts.
A wooden school in the Italianate style–a rare survivor from this period.

22. Mission Neighborhood Center
c.1900, Ward & Blohme
362 Capp St.
A residentially scaled community center in the Craftsman mode.

23. Women's Building
Established, 1980s; 1994 murals by Juana Alicia and Miranda Bergman
3543 18th St.
A building transformed into an eloquent billboard.

24. Russian Orthodox Convent of Our Lady of Vladimir
1914
19th and Capp Sts.
A decorated box with a festive quality built for the Emanuel Evangelical Church.

25. El Capitan Theatre

25. El Capitan Theatre
c.1930
2361 Mission St.
The scale of this combination theater and hotel with its abundant ornament testifies to the importance the Mission district had attained by the 1930s as a self-sufficient suburb with all the conveniences of downtown.

26. House
1889, Charles Shaner
3755 20th St.
Designed by an architect who mainly worked in Alameda. Other houses on this block are also notable.

27. McMullen house

27. McMullen house
1881; remodeled 1890, Samuel Newsom
827 Guerrero St.
The original house was enlarged and transformed by Newsom into a rather ponderous but inventive version of the Queen Anne style with a gambrel roof and exotic features such as the "moon gate" entrance, a Newsom hallmark.

28. 180 Liberty St.

28. 50 Liberty St.

28. Liberty/Hill Historic District
1870s to 1890s
Boundaries: Dolores, 20th, Mission, and 22nd Sts.
One of the city's best examples of a 19th-century residential district renovated and protected by neighborhood pride.

23–25 Liberty St.
1877

27 Liberty St.
1898, R. H. White

31 Liberty St.
1892, Julius E. Krafft

28. Liberty St.

28. Hill Street

29. St. John's Lutheran Church

30. 943 South Van Ness Ave.

37 Liberty St.
c.1875

49 Liberty St.
1870

58 Liberty St.
1876

70 Liberty St.
1870

109 Liberty St.
1870

159 Liberty St.
1878

3243-45 21st St.

3300 block 21st St.

3450 21st St.
O'Brien & Peugh

3367-69 21st St.

3371 and 3375 21st St.,
Albert Pissis

14-28 30 Hill St.
1878, The Real Estate Associates

25 Hill St.
1883, Charles Geddes

49 Hill St.
1885

77 Hill St.
1883

83-91 Hill St.
1884, T. J. Welsh
Italianate style on the even side and Stick style on the odd side.

29. **Former St. John's Lutheran Church**
1900
3126 22nd St.
The Carpenter Gothic facade has a strong linear quality and clearly expresses the building's original use as a church, now, a residence.

30. **Houses and apartments: 900 block of South Van Ness Ave.**

Charles Zimmermann house
1900, Robert Zimmermann
919 South Van Ness Ave.
Eclectic is hardly the word for this hodge-podge of styles well worth seeing.

John English house
1885, Peter Schmidt
943 South Van Ness Ave.

30. John Coop house

32. Cesar Chavez Elementary School

33. Apartments

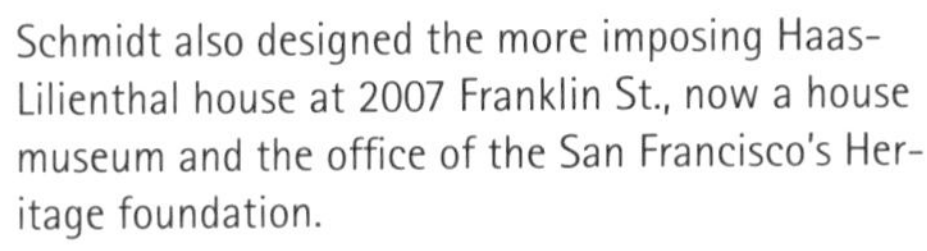

Schmidt also designed the more imposing Haas-Lilienthal house at 2007 Franklin St., now a house museum and the office of the San Francisco's Heritage foundation.

John Coop house
c. 1890
959 South Van Ness Ave.
The extravagant ornamental detail on this house probably came from Coop's San Francisco Planing Mill, once located near 5th and Brannan Sts. Other houses: 920, 989 and 1080-86 South Van Ness Ave., built in the same period, are also notable.

31. **Double house**
c. 1875
772-74 Shotwell St.
The twin-bay Italianate house at its best. The whole block is representative of this era of tract housing.

32. **Cesar Chavez Elementary School**
825 Shotwell St.
c. 1920; 1990, 1995, murals by Juana Alicia and Susan Kerk Cervantes.
A testimonial to the ability of painted images to transform a lacklustre building. For more about the Mission's murals see the introduction to this section.

34. *Mission Presbyterian Church*

35. *Mission Campus of City College*

37. *1200 block of Guerrero St.*

39. *1381 South Van Ness Ave.*

33. Apartments
c.1885
1201 South Van Ness Ave.
An unusual corner apartment house, with heavy gable hoods. The second floor was restored after a 1976 fire by San Francisco Victoriana, a local firm that has restored several 19th century buildings.

34. Houses
1889, T. J. Welsh
700 block of Capp St.
The east side has a nearly intact row of spec houses in the Stick style.

Mission Presbyterian Church
1890, Hamilton & Percy
NW corner of Capp and 23rd St.
A substantial shingle-style church with a fine tower.

35. Mission Campus of City College
Former Samuel Gompers High School
Downtown High School
1939, Masten & Hurd; 1995, Beverly Prior Architects/ Solomon ETC
22nd and Bartlett Sts.
The Valencia St. elevation of this streamlined Moderne building has striking rounded stair towers with glass brick.

36. House
1886
200 Fair Oaks St.
A Stick-style house.

37. Houses
1200 block of Guerrero St.
Among the many Victorian houses that line Guerrero Street. this block has an outstanding group. Note especially the towered mansion built by an Austrian immigrant at 1286, two double houses at 1259-65 with their original iron fences, the in-and-out facade of 1257, and an elegantly consistent Stick-Eastlake at 1253, and a fine corner commercial-residential building at 1201.

38. Horace Mann Middle School
1924, John Reid, Jr.; 1976, Hardison & Komatsu
3531 22nd St.
Another handsome school by John Reid; others nearby are: the Everett Middle School and Mission High School.

39. Frank M. Stone House
1886, Seth Babson
1348 South Van Ness Ave.

One of the state's first professionally trained architects designed this fine Queen Anne pile for a prominent San Francisco lawyer. The richly detailed interior is apparently intact. Other works by Babson include a house at 1920 Union Street. in Alameda and the mansions of Leland Stanford and William Crocker in Sacramento.

House
1884, Charles I. Havens
1381 South Van Ness Ave.

40. Mural Art on Balmy St.

40. Galleria de la Raza
2857 24th St.
The city's first exhibition space devoted to contemporary Hispanic art.

Precita Eyes Mural Arts Center and Balmy St.
2981 24th St.
Guide maps to the many murals that enliven building walls in the Mission district are available here along with information about the mural artists who work in the district. The nearby alley named Balmy St. is lined with murals depicting a range of subject matter.

41. Houses
1880s
2733, 2735 Folsom St.

43. House row 1100 block Shotwell St.

43. House row
c.1885
1110-28, 1136-38, 1140-42 Shotwell St.
A fine and fancy row.

41. House row
1890 and c.1885, John McCarthy
1200-02, 1232 and 1256 Treat St.
The first two buildings were built by an owner-developer who apparently wanted something fireproof for himself and so built this unusual brick Italianate. No. 1256 has some very fine ornament.

44. Apartments
c. 1910
26th and South Van Ness Ave.
An ourstanding Craftsman style apartment house in clinker brick and shingles, unusual in this area.

45. Holy Innocents Episcopal Church
c.1900, Ernest Coxhead
400 block of Fair Oaks St.
In his early practice Coxhead used the undulating shingled wall to great effect as exemplified in this small church. This block also has a notable collection of Victorian and Craftsman houses, and at the south end on 26th Street is a very nice Mission Revival hall.

This city area is notable for its architectural, social, and historical contrasts. For example, the San Francisco Civic Center, one of the noblest monuments of the turn-of-the-century City Beautiful Movement, borders on the Tenderloin, which has long been a damper to civic pride. North and west of the Civic Center is the Western Addition, one of the early 19th-century streetcar suburbs of the city and the location of the city's first redevelopment area. In the 1950s, 28 blocks of the Western Addition were completely razed in the cause of "urban renewal."

Known for decades as the Tenderloin, the area east of Van Ness Avenue was rapidly rebuilt after the 1906 fire with hotels and apartment blocks to re-house those who had been burned out and to accommodate the anticipated flood of visitors to the 1915 Panama-Pacific International Exposition. For a while after the expo closed this was a medium-to-high density residential area conveniently near downtown. Like all such districts, it was increasingly vulnerable to decline when the housing stock aged and automobile use increased the attractiveness of the outer suburbs. The renovation of small hotels in the Union Square and Civic Center areas, which began in the 1980s, has continued.

The 1858 Van Ness Ordinance created the Western Addition by extending the city's grid pattern of streets westward. To address the lack of city parks, the ordinance also designated the public squares of Jefferson, Alamo, Hamilton, and the so-called Hospital Lot, now part of Duboce Park. Hayes Valley, a 160-acre tract owned by Mayor Tom Hayes, lay between Alamo and Duboce Parks. Hayes' estate, which burned in 1872, included a pleasure garden with an art gallery and a concert hall; it may have set a precedent for the Civic Center.

Residential development in the Western Addition accompanied the laying of streetcar lines in the mid-19th century, creating a homogeneous middle-class suburb. However, in the aftermath of the 1906 earthquake and fire, dislocated downtown populations moved to the area in droves. Jews moved from the South-of-Market to the Fillmore area, and a small number of Japanese established "Little Osaka" nearby between Post and Sutter Streets. When the Japanese were relocated to detention camps in World War II, African-Americans from the southern states who came to work in Bay Area defense plants occupied the vacated buildings. In the 1960s the Japan Cultural Trade Center was built as the core of the first redevelopment area that sought to make amends for the Japanese relocation. Largely because of protests from preservationists and residents, subsequent redevelopment efforts stressed rehabilitation rather than removal so that the edges of the redevelopment area have merged with the rest of the district.

Pine Street is the northern boundary of the Western Addition. The Bush-Pine corridor was developed in the 1870s and 1880s when the cable and streetcar lines were extended westward. The small tracts on typically long narrow lots, 25 by 100 feet, were financed by the enterprising building societies of the building and loan associations. Some of the lots were even sold by lottery. When the automobile replaced rail transit to the western neighborhoods, the inner suburbs declined. As the demolition for the redevelopment area proceeded in the late 1950s, community protest increased and halted the destruction near Bush, giving a reprieve to buildings in the blocks covered here.

1. Houses *2200 block Pine St.*
2. Berge house *1900 block Webster St.*
3. Taylor house *1911 Pine St.*
4. Houses *1800 block Pine St. and 1700 block Gough St.*
5. Century Club of California *1355 Franklin St.*
6. Houses *2100 block Bush St. and 1-6 Cottage Row*
7. Stanyan house *2006 Bush St.*
8. Houses *2000 block Laguna St.*
9. Kokoro housing *1881 Bush St.*
   Green's Eye Hospital *1801 Bush St.*
10. Morning Star Church *1715 Octavia St.*
11. Houses 1700 and *1800 block Webster St.*
12. Thomas Payne house *1409 Sutter St.*
13. Regency Building *1320 Van Ness Ave.*
    Galaxy Theatre *Van Ness Ave. at Sutter St.*
14. Japanese Culture and Trade Center *Post St.-Geary Blvd. Laguna St.-Fillmore St.*
15. First Unitarian Church *1187 Franklin St.*
16. Castle Apartments *825 Geary St.*
    Alhambra Apartments *850 Geary St.*
17. St. Francis Square *Geary Expressway between Webster St. and Laguna St.*
18. Laguna Heights *85 Cleary Ct.*
    Laguna-O'Farrell Apartments *66 Cleary Ct.*
19. St. Mary's Cathedral *Geary Expressway at Gough St.*
20. St. Mark's Lutheran Church *1111 O'Farrell St. between Franklin and Gough Sts.*
21. Cadillac Showroom *1000 Van Ness Ave.*
22. Former Earle C. Anthony Packard Showroom *901 Van Ness Ave.*
23. Family Service Agency *1010 Gough St.*
24. F. C. Stadtmuller house *819 Eddy St.*
25. Cadillac Hotel *380 Eddy St.*
26. House *807 Franklin St.*
27. Former German Association building *601 Polk St.*
28. Tenderloin Community School *627 Golden Gate Ave.*

Previous page: San Francisco City Hall

29. State of California building complex
    Earl Warren Building
    Hiram W. Johnson Buildings *455 Golden Gate Ave.*
30. Federal Office Building *450 Golden Gate Ave.*
31. Former Motion Picture Studio *125 Hyde St.*
32. Hastings College of Law *198 McAllister St.*
    Law Center *200 McAllister St.*
33. William Taylor Hotel & Methodist Church *100-20 McAllister St.*
34. Friendship Village *Fillmore St. to Webster St. McAllister St. to Fulton St.*
    Former Holy Virgin Russian Orthodox Cathedral *858-64 Fulton St.*
35. The Civic Center *Franklin St. to McAllister St. Market St. to Hayes St.*
36. Chong-Moon Center for Asian Art and Culture *200 Larkin St.*
37. Federal Building *100 McAllister St.*
38. San Francisco Main Library *101 Larkin St.*
    Pioneers Monument *Fulton St. between Larkin and Hyde Sts.*
39. Orpheum Theatre *1192 Market St.*
    One Trinity Center *1145 Market St.*
40. Davies Symphony Hall *SW corner Van Ness Ave. and Grove St.*
41. Former New College of California *42-58 Fell St.*
42. Former High School of Commerce *135 Van Ness Ave.*
43. Former Masonic Temple *25 Van Ness Ave.*
44. San Francisco Conservatory of Music *50 Oak St.*
45. Zen Center *300 Page St.*
    Houses:
    294 Page St.
    273 and 287 Page St.
    251 Laguna St.
    395 Haight St.
46. Nightingale house *201 Buchanan St.*
47. San Francisco Lesbian Gay Bisexual Transgender Center *1800 Market St.*
48. Hermann Garden Cottages and minihouses *380-98 Hermann St. 498 Duboce St.*

Washington St.
Clay St.
Sacramento St.
California St.
Californ
Pine St.
Bush St.
Sutter St.
Post St.
Geary St.
Cleary Ct.
O'Farrell St.
Ellis St.
Eddy St.
Turk St.
Golden Gate Ave.
McAllister St.
Fulton St.
Grove St.
Hayes St.
Fell St.
Oak St.
Page St.
Haight St.
Duboce Ave.
Market St.
Mission St.
7th St.
8th St.
9th St.
10th St.
11th St.
12th. St.
Fillmore St.
Webster St.
Buchanan St.
Laguna St.
Octavia St.
Gough St.
Franklin St.
Van Ness Ave.
Polk St.
Larkin St.
Hyde St.
Leavenworth St.
a
b
c
d
1
2
3
4
5
6
7
8
9
10
11
12
13
14
15
16
17
18
19
20
21
22
23
24
25
26
27
28
29
30
31
32
33
34
35
36
37
38
39
40
41
42
43
44
45
46
47
49
N

6

2. Berge house

5. Houses, 1800 block of Pine St.

5. Houses, 2100 block of Bush St.

1. **Houses**

   2208 Pine St.
   1877

   2210 Pine St.
   1875

   2212 Pine St.
   1877

   2231 Pine St.
   1872

   2255 Pine St.
   1880, Samuel & Joseph Cather Newsom
   No. 2231 has a New England farmhouse look that suggests an earlier date than 1872, but the owners may just have wanted a simple house. No. 2255 by the Newsoms resembles their own house at 2129 California Street.

2. **Berge house**
   1884, B.E. Henrickson
   1900 Webster St.
   An unusual blind-window treatment, doubtless designed to enliven the side elevation while maintaining privacy, distinguishes the side of this elegant town house.

3. **Taylor house**
   1880, Wolfe & Son
   1911 Pine St.

4. **Houses, 1800 block Pine St. and 1700 block Gough St.**

   1837 Pine St.
   1890

   1843 Pine St.,
   1873

   1855 Pine St.
   1876

   1703 Gough St.
   1875

   1705 Gough St.
   1875

   1707 Gough St.,
   1885

   1709 Gough St.
   1875
   Two blocks of houses that exemplify the styles chosen by the city's late 19th-century speculative builders.

5. **Houses, 2100 block of Bush St.**
   2115-25 Bush St.
   1874, The Real Estate Assoc., builder

2103-07 Bush St.
1874

2100-02 Bush St.
1883, Samuel & Joseph Cather Newsom

2104 Bush St.
1884, Wolf & Son

The south side of the street has one of the best flat-front Italianate rows in the city. The whole block gives a good idea of the scale and character of tract development in this streetcar suburb by some of the most active real estate developers and builders of the last quarter of the 19th century.

1-6 Cottage Row
1882, John Nash, builder

All six cottages were built for $5,000 for shipping merchant Charles L. Taylor.

5. 1-6 Cottage Row

6. **Stanyan house**
1852
2006 Bush St.

Though it is well known that many prefabricated houses were shipped to San Francisco from New England during the Gold Rush era, this house is one of the very few that has been so identified. The interior has typical mid-century detail but is scaled down, as are the room sizes, to New England proportions. The exterior and interior detail was prefabricated in New England and sent around the Horn. The Stanyans, who owned the house from 1854 to 1974, replaced their large garden with the flats built on speculation in 1892. Then as now open space was vulnerable to real estate pressures.

6. Stanyan house (center building)

7. **Houses in the 2000 block of Laguna St.**

Odd side, Laguna St.
1889, William Hinkel

Even side, Laguna St.
1877, The Real Estate Assoc.

Two of the most entrepreneurial of the19th-century builder-developers created this harmonious street. The Real Estate Associates' simple Italianate houses gave way to fancier variations on the theme a decade or so later, as taste demanded more complicated frills.

8. **Kokoro housing originally built for the Congregation Ohabai Shalome**
1895, Moses J. Lyon; rehab. 2003
1881 Bush St.

An Hebraic-Victorian-Byzantine temple rehabilitated as assisted living units. Nearby at 1828-28 Pine Street is a fine row of 1870s houses.

8. Kokoro housing

8. Green's Eye Hospital

Green's Eye Hospital
1915, Frederick Meyer
1801 Bush St.
The gigantic eucalyptus trees in front of this reticent Classical building are said to have been planted by Mary Ellen "Mammy" Pleasant, San Francisco's mysterious and sinister madam, and housekeeper to Thomas Bell, whose mansion stood on this site.

9. Morning Star Church

9. **Morning Star Church**
c.1910
1715 Octavia St.
A tasteful design in the Japanese manner with fine terra-cotta tiles and decorative detail.

10 **Houses**

1717 Webster St.
1875

1737 Webster St.
1885, Samuel & Joseph Cather Newsom
One of the Newsoms minor masterpieces designed in the 1880s rectilinear style called Stick. The interlocking of ornament with form is particularly masterful. This is one of the houses restored under the auspices of the San Francisco Redevelopment Agency and the Foundation for San Francisco's Architectural Heritage. It was moved here from 773 Turk Street in 1975 to keep company with the fine group next door.

1771 Webster St.
1881

1781-87 Webster St.
1885

1809-11 Webster St.
1880

12. Galaxy Theatre

11. **Thomas Payne house**
c.1880, William Curlett
1409 Sutter St.
A candle-snuffer corner tower distinguishes this Stick Style house from those around it. Curlett was a prominent architect whose practice extended throughout the Bay Area.

12. **Regency Building**
1911, O'Brien & Werner
1320 Van Ness Ave.
This former Scottish Rite Temple is one of several designed by this firm. The Masons seem to have favored Florentine palaces around the turn of the century.

Galaxy Theatre
1986, Kaplan, McLaughlin, Diaz
Van Ness Ave. at Sutter St.

13. Century Club of California
1905; rem. 1914, Julia Morgan
1355 Franklin St.
A chaste Classic Revival facade, originally a private home that for two years after 1906 housed the State Supreme Court of California.

14. Japanese Cultural and Trade Center
1968, Minoru Yamasaki/Van Bourg Nakamura
Post St. to Geary Expressway, Laguna St. to Fillmore St.
Alas, this complex lacks the excitement of the 1960s architecture in Japan.

14. Japanese Cultural and Trade Center

15. First Unitarian Church
1887-89, George W. Percy; add. 1967-79, Callister, Payne & Rosse
1187 Franklin St.
Thomas Starr King, famous preacher and civic leader of the 1860s, was associated with this congregation; his tomb is in the churchyard. The church is a mixture of Romanesque and Gothic Revival elements. The contemporary concrete and redwood buildings used for offices and the church school form a remarkably harmonious complex that holds its own amidst the asphalt roadways around it.

16. Castle Apartments
c.1920
825 Geary St.

Alhambra Apartments
1914, James F. Dunn
850 Geary St.
Two of the more exotic examples of local apartment house architecture. The ever-inventive Mr. Dunn here turns his hand to Moorish styling.

16. Castle Apartments

17. St. Francis Square
1961, Marquis & Stoller
Geary Expressway between Webster and Laguna Sts.
The outstanding social success of Western Addition Renewal Area 1, this project was sponsored and subsidized by the Longshoremen's Union and had an income ceiling for residents. Its internal garden courts are attractive, and its simple architecture has worn well.

17. St. Francis Square

18. Laguna Heights
1963, Claude Oakland
85 Cleary Ct.

Laguna-O'Farrell Apartments
1960, Jones & Emmons
66 Cleary Ct.

19. St. Mary's Cathedral

22. Former Earle C. Anthony Packard Showroom

23. Family Service Agency

Two of the first center city projects by Joseph Eichler, a suburban developer famous for the architectural quality of his various housing tracts.

19. St. Mary's Cathedral
1971, Pietro Belluschi/Pier Luigi Nervi/ McSweeney, Ryan & Lee
Geary Blvd. at Gough St.
In 1960 after this site had been renewed with a supermarket, a fire completely destroyed the old cathedral on Van Ness Avenue. A quickly arranged trade demolished the year-old market, giving the Archdiocese a suitably prominent site in exchange for its Van Ness property. Four 190-foot-high hyperbolic paraboloids roof the 2,500-seat space over a base that houses various facilities including meeting rooms, a rectory, a convent, and, to the south, a parochial high school. The stained glass is by Gyorgy Kepes, the baldachino by Richard Lippold, and the organ was designed by Father Robert F. Hayburn.

20. St. Mark's Lutheran Church
1894, Henry Geilfuss
1111 O'Farrell St. bet. Franklin and Gough Sts.
A High Victorian Romanesque-Gothic church in red brick by an architect mostly known for his houses.

21. Former Cadillac Showroom
1923, Weeks & Day
1000 Van Ness Ave.
An elegant automobile palace adorned with docile bears, California's official animal.

22. Former Earle C. Anthony Packard Showroom
1927, Bernard Maybeck/Powers & Ahnden
901 Van Ness Ave.
The queen of the Van Ness Avenue automobile palaces, built for one of Maybeck's major clients. The red marble columns have unfortunately been painted white.

23. Former Family Service Agency
1928, Bernard Maybeck
1010 Gough St.
Maybeck's personal stamp on this Mediterranean-style building is evident in the handling of such elements as the spiral fire escape in its slot, the fenestration on the west facade, and the fence motif.

24. F. C. Stadtmuller house
1880, P. R. Schmidt
819 Eddy St.
A fine Italianate survivor of a time when this was a palm-lined street of single houses.

25. Cadillac Hotel
c. 1915; renovation Asian Neighborhood Design, 1992
380 Eddy St.
A successful adaptation of a once fashionable hotel to single-room occupancy by a firm that specializes in such work.

26. House
c.1875
807 Franklin St.
Another lonely Italianate survivor.

27. Former German Association
1913, Frederick H. Meyer
601 Polk St.
More or less straight from old Munich even down to the rathskeller in the basement. The California Culinary Academy now occupies the building.

28. Tenderloin Community School
1999, Joseph Esherick EHDD/Barcelon & Jang
627 Golden Gate Ave.
An appropriately colorful building with cheerful tilework by school children. A K-5 elementary school, child development center, community kitchen, and family resource center occupy the main part of the building; a medical-dental clinic is on a lower level. The design team headed by Esherick worked with the school district and the neighbors to create a model project for families and children.

29. State of California building complex
Earl Warren Building
(former California State Building)
1926, Bliss & Faville

Hiram W. Johnson State Office Building
1998, Skidmore Owings & Merrill with Page & Turnbull, historic preservation architects
455 Golden Gate Ave.
Two buildings fused into one to house the nation's largest state judicial system. The beauxartsian 1926 building, a competition winner, was the last addition to the Civic Center; it mainly housed the state supreme court. The seismic retrofitting that followed the 1989 Loma Prieta earthquake was accompanied by the construction of an adjoining 14-story state office building named for Hiram W. Johnson. Together the buildings have 130,000,000 sq. ft. and fill a city block. To minimize the mass of the much larger building its form was divided into vertical sections that step back as they rise. The top three floors are slightly rounded to give the building a distinctive cap. The exterior cladding of thin granite panels combined

29. State of California Building Complex

27. Former German Association

28. Tenderloin Community School

31. Motion picture studio

32. Law Center

34. Former Holy Virgin Russian Orthodox Cathedral

with concrete panels cast with crushed granite, quartz, and mica could not have been made for the earlier building. The interior has two ten-story atria in the east and west sections and a central atrium of seven stories atop the great hall on the main floor inside the Golden Gate Avenue entrance. Light is a major component of the interior design; glass walls permit it to flood the interior. The complex has the distinction of being the first state building completed through the award of a single contract for both architectural design and construction; some 35 firms comprised the HMS Design/Build corporation, formed specifically for this project.

30. **Federal Office Building**
1959, Albert F. Roller/Stone, Marraccini & Patterson/ John Carl Warnecke
450 Golden Gate Ave.
A lackluster blockbuster expressing all too well the contemporary scale of government.

31. **Motion picture studio**
1930, Wilbur Peugh
125 Hyde St.
A fine Art Deco facade. See also two former film depots of 1930 by the O'Brien Brothers at 245-51 and 255-59 Hyde. This area was once the center of the city's film industry.

32. **Hastings College of Law**
1950, Masten & Hurd; add. 1967, Gmathmey, Sellier & Crosby
198 McAllister St.

Law Center
1980, Skidmore Owings & Merrill
200 McAllister St.
Of this campus of modern buildings, the Law Center by SOM is the most recent and the most distinguished.

33. **William Taylor Hotel & Methodist Church**
1929, Miller & Pflueger/Lewis P. Hobart
100-20 McAllister St.

34. **Friendship Village**
1971, Buckley & Sazevich
Fillmore St. to Webster St., McAllister St. to Fulton St.

Former Holy Virgin Russian Orthodox Cathedral
1880
858-64 Fulton St.
Several 19th-century facades integrated into a varied site plan that has sympathetic shingled units around interior courts. On the same block is a several-times-recycled Gothic Revival church taken over by the Russians in 1930.

35. The Civic Center

1915-1981

Franklin St. to McAllister St., Market St. to Hayes St.

The Civic Center is not only a crowning achievement of City Beautiful Movement design in this country (along with the Washington Mall and the great turn-of-the-century fairs), but also the only really first-rate example of French High Baroque Revival carried out in detail. The City Hall itself is the jewel, inside and out. Don't miss the rotunda, which has ornament by Jean Louis Bourgeois executed by Paul Denville.

The Opera House, modeled on Garnier's Paris Opera, has a circulation system nearly as impressive. The Veterans Building, erected without a clear program, was later occupied on the upper floors by the San Francisco Museum of Modern Art, which moved to a new building in 1994. The other Civic Center buildings follow the general plan set forth by the advisory commission headed at first by John Galen Howard and later by Bernard Maybeck, and listing among its members Willis Polk, Ernest Coxhead, G. Albert Lansburgh, John Reid, Jr., Frederick H. Meyer, and Arthur Brown, Jr. The Civic Center has had a number of new additions over the years of varying quality; it continues to grow and to maintain its vitality.

35a. City Hall

35a. City Hall

a. City Hall

1915 (competition 1912), Bakewell & Brown; 1995-99, architects: Heller & Manus/Finger & Moy/Komorous-Towey; historic preservation architects, Carey & Co.; architects for the seismic upgrade, MBT Architecture.

Damage to the building by the 1989 earthquake was addressed by base-isolation. During this process new offices were added, and two light courts were uncovered for public use. The dome was also re-gilded and the exterior cleaned along with the scultureal groups by Henry Crenier.

35b. Opera House

35d. Civic Auditorium

36. Federal Building

b. **Opera House**
1932, Brown & Lansburgh
Opera House addition on Franklin St.:
1977, Skidmore Owings & Merrill

c. **Veterans Building and Herbst Theatre**
1932, Bakewell & Brown

d. **Civic Auditorium**
1915, John Galen Howard, Frederick Meyer & John Reid, Jr.; rem. 1964, Wurster, Bernardi & Emmons and Skidmore Owings & Merrill

36. Chong-Moon Center for Asian Art and Culture (former San Francisco main Public Library)
1916 (competition 1915), George Kelham; 2003, Gae Aulenti, HOK, LDA Architects, Robert Wong Architect, Page & Turnbull historic preservation architect
200 Larkin St.
The former Main Public Library building was rehabilitated to house the new Asian Art Museum, which moved here from its location in Golden Gate Park. Since the library building was part of the Civic Center Historic District, the architects were required to restore its historic fabric and retain its major spaces and its exterior unaltered. The areas open to change were mainly on the ground floor where two gloomy light wells were transformed into welcoming interior courts daylit by skylights with dramatic inverted gable forms. The 29,000 sq.ft. of gallery space for the permanent collection is located on the second and

36. Chong-Moon Center for Asian Art and Culture

third floors; spaces for temporary exhibitions are on the ground floor along with a resource room, classrooms, a cafe, and the museum store.

37. Federal Building
1936, Bakewell & Brown
Hyde and McAllister St.

A companion work to Bakewell & Brown's other Civic Center buildings with fine ornamental detail. The subsequent expansion of the federal government is more than obvious when this building is compared with its counterpart, #35.

39. Orpheum Theatre

38. San Francisco Main Library

38. San Francisco Main Library
1995, Pei Cobb Freed & Partners/Simon Martin-Vegue Winkelstein Moris
101 Larkin St.
The requirement for a contextual design to respond to the Beauxartsian Civic Center resulted in the application of stripped down classical motifs to the gridded surface of the west and north elevations of the new building. The product is neither fish nor fowl. The east and south elevations, which have a contemporary expression, are more successful. The interior is organized around a five-story skylit atrium.

Pioneers Monument
1894, Frank Happersberger
Fulton St. between Larkin and Hyde Sts.
A gift of James Lick, himself a pioneer, and a testimony to the days when monuments were conspicuously monumental.

39. One Trinity Center

39. Orpheum Theatre
1925, B. Marcus Priteca
1192 Market St.
Churrigueresque ornament applied over a glassy curtain wall. The city and the owners each thought the other would pay to have the blank back wall finished to match the character of the Civic Center-neither did.

One Trinity Center
1989, Backen Arrigoni & Ross
1145 Market St.

40. Davies Symphony Hall

43. Former Masonic Temple

45. 251 Laguna St.

45. 273 and 287 Page St.

40. Davies Symphony Hall
1981, Skidmore Owings & Merrill
SW corner Van Ness Ave. and Grove St.
An attempt to bridge the gulf between the French Classicism of the older Civic Center and today's architecture. The hemispherical projection on the east elevation is a balcony, which concert-goers may access during intermissions for spectacular city views.

41. New College of California
1932, Willis Polk
42-58 Fell St.

42. Former High School of Commerce
1909, Newton J. Tharp; 1926-27, John Reid, Jr.
135 Van Ness Ave.
The school was originally located on Grove Street, but in 1913 moved to Fell and Franklin Streets. In 1926-27 John Reid, Jr. designed the richly ornamented buildings on the rest of the block bounded by Fell, Franklin, Grove Streets, and Van Ness Avenue. The school closed in 1952, and the school district's central office occupied the building.

43. Former Masonic Temple
1910, Bliss & Faville
25 Van Ness Ave.
A pseudo Renaissance palazzo that provides a strong accent to this end of Van Ness Avenue.

44. San Francisco Conservatory of Music
1914, William D. Shea; 2005, SMWM
50 Oak St.
An historic building renovated and doubled in size. The contemporary addition has a 400-seat concert hall and recital halls seating 280 and 100 people.

45. Zen Center
1922, Julia Morgan
300 Page St.

Dietle house
1888, Henry Geilfuss
294 Page St.

Houses

273 and 287 Page St.
c.1875

251 Laguna St.
c. 1885

395 Haight St.
c. 1885
Well worth seeing, this cluster of buildings includes one of Julia Morgan's gracious institutional buildings,

originally designed for the Emanuel Sisterhood plus a Stick-style mansion by Geilfuss, and a varied group of other 19th century houses.

46. Nightingale house

46. **Nightingale house**
1882, John Marquis
201 Buchanan St.
A sprightly Stick-style cottage, perfect for a witch with a small family. Across the street at 201 Waller St. is a fine Mediterranean Revival style apartment house.

47. **San Francisco Lesbian Gay Bisexual Transgender Center**
2002, Cee/Pfau Collaborative
1800 Market St.
The 3,000 sf building has a curtain wall of tinted glass that lets it glow like a lantern at night; it has a cafe, conference rooms, and a gallery. The adjacent 1894 Fallon Building houses staff offices and a senior

48. Hermann Garden Cottages and minihouses

47. San Francisco Lesbian Gay Bisexual Transgender Center

center. It was originally built for the granddaughter of Joaquin Castro, the Governor of Mexican California, for whom the Castro district is named.

48. **Hermann Garden Cottages and minihouses**
1983-85, Donald MacDonald & Assocs.
380-98 Hermann St. and 498 Duboce St.
San Francisco's 1980s cottage revival movement was mainly the work of Donald MacDonald, who saw this house type as a solution to the problem of affordable housing. Although these minihouses contain ony about 600 square feet, they have lofts and high ceilings that add a feeling of spaciousness.

Since 1880 the boundaries of Chinatown proper have been California to Broadway and Kearny to Stockton Street. Grant Avenue, named for the general, was first called the Calle de la Fundacion; it connected the Mission Dolores to the Presidio. In 1835 the Englishman William Richardson drew a map showing his tent store at the intersection of the Calle and Clay Street, which ran downhill to the edge of the bay, then marked by Montgomery Street. By 1837 Richardson had built an adobe house called La Casa Grande; its location is marked by a plaque at 823 Grant. A sprinkling of other buildings soon followed that comprised the tiny port city called Yerba Buena.

The first Chinese, most of whom were from Canton (Kwangtung), came for the Gold Rush. Their numbers were sufficient to establish the hui-kuan, or district associations, whose memberships were based on common origin of place or family. Hui-kuan headquarters are Chinatown's most distinctive building type. Their mainland prototype consisted of a series of structures separated by courtyards. The most important component, the temple, stood at the end of the complex. Because this horizontal form was impossible in a dense urban location, the typical 19th-century commercial building was adapted for the purpose by stacking the components vertically. In this arrangement the temple occupied the top floor and became the most important part of the facade. These buildings are easily identified by their top floors, which have curving roof eaves and balconies with ritual bells, lanterns, and other trappings that are displayed on holidays. They are also likely to have the colors red, yellow, and green as part of their fabric. All three colors mean health, wealth, and good luck, making Chinatown the only neighborhood to have a color scheme.

By 1852 the Chinese had settled around the intersection of Dupont, as the Calle was renamed that year, and Sacramento, replacing the original French residents. The combination of discrimination at the mines and their diminishing payloads brought the Chinese back to the city where by 1860 they formed five percent of the population. In the 1860s they took over the manufacturing of footwear, clothing, and cigars. Their frugality and dedication to work did not endear them to the predominantly white male population.

Despite the inhumane treatment resulting from the anti-Chinese movement and the Chinese Exclusion Act of 1882, the Chinese persevered. When the 1906 fire razed Chinatown along with the rest of downtown, a group of merchants saw an opportunity to revamp the squalid, vice-ridden image caused by the district's gambling, opium, and prostitution dens; the alleys notorious for such pursuits, Waverly, Ross, and Spofford, were linked to the infamous Barbary Coast nearby. Whereas the pre-fire Chinatown was built mainly with undistinguished prefabricated wooden buildings, the post-fire "city-within-a-city" was reconstructed of durable brick. To lure tourists to this Oriental bazaar, the buildings were done up with architectural chinoiserie.

The gateway buildings, the Sing Chong and Sing Fat, at the intersection of Grant and California marked the beginning of the bazaar. At Jackson Street the market section began, and still does, except that its bustle spills over onto the neighboring streets. Sadly, the new building lacks the scale and naive theatricality of the old. But the vitality of the district is better expressed by its street life and festivals than its architecture.

1. Joice Street Steps
2. Ritz Carlton Hotel *600 Stockton St.*
3. Sing Chong Building *601-15 Grant Ave.*
   Sing Fat Building *717-19 Stockton St.*
   Old St. Mary's Church *Grant Ave. and California St.*
   Paulist Center of the West *600 California St.*
   St. Mary's Square *Grant Ave. and California St.*
4. Nam Kue School *765 Sacramento St.*
   Chinese Chamber of Commerce *728-30 Sacramento St.*
5. Association buildings *745 and 801-07 Grant Ave.*
6. Chinese Baptist Church *15 Waverly Pl.*
7. Chinese Consolidated Benevolent Association of the United States (Six Companies) *843 Stockton St.*
   St. Mary's Chinese Mission *902 Stockton St.*
8. Donaldina Cameron House *920 Sacramento St.*
9. Chinese Historical Society of America *940-50 Powell St.*
   YWCA Clay St. Center *965 Clay St.*
10. Commodore Stockton School Annex *Washington St. at Stone St.*
    Gum Moon Residence *940 Washington St.*
    Methodist Church *920 Washington St.*
11. Former Chinese Telephone Exchange *743 Washington St.*
12. Portsmouth Square *Grant Ave. to Kearny St. Clay St. to Washington St.*
13. Golden Gateway Redevelopment Project *Battery St. to The Embarcadero; Broadway to Clay St.*
    Phase 1 residential development *Jackson St.*
    Phase 1 town houses *Washington St.*
    Phase 2 residential development *Davis St. to Broadway*
14. U. S. Customs House *555 Battery St.*
15. Jackson Square *Jackson St. and Hotaling Pl. Montgomery and Sansome Sts. and Montgomery to Washington Sts.*
16. Original Transamerica Building 4 Columbus Ave. at Montgomery St.
17. Columbus Tower *Columbus Ave. and Kearny St.*
18. City Lights Books Store and Vesuvio's *235-253 Columbus Ave.*
19. St. Francis of Assisi Church *610 Vallejo St.*
20. Fugazi Hall 678 Green St.
21. Washington Square *Columbus Ave. to Stockton St. and Union St. to Filbert St.*
    Sts. Peter and Paul Church *666 Filbert St.*
22. Maybeck Building *1736 Stockton St.*
23. San Remo Hotel and Restaurant *2237 Mason St.*
24. Vanderwater Street buildings
25. House *210 Francisco St.*
    Telegraph Terrace *Grant Ave. and Francisco St.*
26. House *298 Chestnut St.*
27. House *281 Chestnut St.*
28. House *340 Lombard St.*
29. House *275 Telegraph Hill Blvd.*
30. Coit Tower *end of Telegraph Hill Blvd.*
31. Filbert Steps *Darrell Place Napiet Lane*
32. Apartment house *1360 Montgomery St.*
    Julius' Castle *end of Montgomery St.*
33. Houses
    1309, 1315 Montgomery
    25 29, 31 Alta St.
    287-289, 293 Union St.
34. Kahn house *66 Calhoun Terr.*
35. Ice Houses No.1 and No. 2 1265 *Battery and 151 Union St.*
36. Former Beltline Roundhouse *1500 Sansome St.*
37. Municipal buildings 111 Bay St.
38. Warehouses 1 Lombard St.
    Cargo West Warehouse *1105 Battery*
    Italian Swiss Colony Warehouse *1265 Battery St.*
39. Levi's Plaza *Battery St. to Sansome St. Union St. to Greenwich St.*

Previous page: View of Telegraph Hill from Levi's Plaza

San Francisco Bay
Jefferson St.
Beach St.
North Point St.
Bay St.
Francisco St.
Chestnut St.
Lombard St.
Greenwich St.
Filbert St.
Union St.
Green St.
Vallejo St.
Broadway
Pacific Ave.
Jackson St.
Washington St.
Clay St.
Sacramento St.
California St.
Pine St.
Bush St.
Sutter St.
Post St.
Geary St.
O'Farrell St.
Ellis St.
Eddy St.
Embarcadero
Columbus Ave.
Telegraph Hill Blvd
Alta St.
Calhoun St.
Commercial St.
Maiden Lane
Leavenworth St.
Jones St.
Taylor St.
Mason St.
Powell St.
Stockton St.
Grant St.
Kearny St.
Montgomery St.
Sansome St.
Battery St.
Front St.
Davis St.
Drumm St.
Main St.
Beale St.
Fremont St.
Market St.
Mission St.
2nd St.
New Montgomery St.
3rd St.
4th St.
Natoma St.
N
1
2
3
4
5
6
7
8
9
10
11
12
13
14
15
16
17
18
19
20
21
22
23
24
25
26
27
28
29
30
31
32
33
34
35
36
37
38
39

7

1. Joice Street Steps

2. Ritz Carlton Hotel

Entrance to Chinatown

3. Old St. Mary's Church & Sing Chong Building

1. **Joice Street Steps**
   One of the charming byways that contributes to San Francisco's Old World charm.
2. **Ritz Carlton Hotel**
   1909, LeBrun & Sons; 1913, Miller & Colmesnil/ Miller & Pflueger; 1991, Whisler-Patri Assoc.
   600 Stockton St.
   Monumental Roman-Renaissance grandeur in gleaming terra cotta. Originally built for an insurance company, the building has been successfully converted into a hotel.

Chinatown

The pagodalike towers of the two gateway buildings at Grant Avenue and California Street were designed to introduce the post-fire Oriental bazaar, originally much more exotic, that stretched along Grant Avenue. The colorful street lights topped with lanterns are a relic of the 1915 Panama Pacific Exposition. Old St. Mary's preceded this post-fire Chinatown by half a century. Although it too burned in 1906, the granite foundations from China and the brick and iron walls imported from the eastern U.S. survived. The church was soon restored, was remodeled and enlarged in the 1920s, burned again in 1969, and was again restored. St. Mary's academic Gothic Revival form was complemented in 1964 by the addition of a respectful but clearly contemporary brick rectory.

3. **Sing Chong Building**
   1908, T. Patterson Ross and A. W. Burgren
   601-15 Grant Ave.

   Sing Fat Building
   1908, T. Patterson Ross and A. W. Burgren
   717-19 California St.

   Old St. Mary's Church
   1853-54; 1907-09, Craine & England; 1969, Welsh & Carey
   Grant Ave. at California St.

   Paulist Center of the West
   1964, Skidmore Owings & Merrill
   600 California St.

   St. Mary's Square
   1960, Eckbo, Royston & Williams
   Statue of Sun Yat-Sen by Beniamino Bufano
4. **Chinese Chamber of Commerce**
   1912
   728-30 Sacramento St.

4. Nam Kue School

7. St. Mary's Chinese Mission

Nam Kue School
1925, Charles E. Rogers
765 Sacramento St.
A more traditional Chinese institutional building with a forecourt. The school was established to instruct Chinatown youth in Chinese culture.

5. **Association Building**
c.1915
745 Grant Ave.
A fancy rendition of the association building type. Across the street at 736-38 Grant is the Chinese World (newspaper) building of 1907.

Soo Yuen Benevolent Association Building
1907-19, Salfield & Kohlberg
801-07 Grant Ave.
An unusual interpretation of the association building type that wraps around the corner lot in an imaginative way with a tripartite facade and a graceful balcony.

6. **Chinese Baptist Church**
1887, G.H. Moore; rebuilt 1908, G. E. Burlingame
15 Waverly Pl. at Sacramento St.

7. **Chinese Consolidated Benevolent Association of the United States (Six Companies)**
1908
843 Stockton St.
This building for the six hui-kuan, which banded together in the 1860s to battle legal and extra-legal actions against their members, is a strong expression of the association type commonly found in Chinatown.

St. Mary's Chinese Mission
c.1906,
902 Stockton St.

Waverly Pl., Spofford St., and Ross Alley
The blocks between Stockton and Grant and Sacramento and Jackson are laced with alleys once notorious for gambling and other vices that contributed to Chinatown's lurid past. Today they are less colorful. At 36 Spofford is a modest building designed by Charles M. Rousseau and built in 1907 for the Chee Kung Tong, the Chinese Freemasons. For six years it was a major center of Sun Yat Sen's revolutionary movement. After 1906 Waverly Place was lined with three- and four-story association buildings. Two architecturally interesting ones that remain are at the Washington Street end; another particularly colorful example is the 1911 Sue Hing Benevolent Association at nearby 125-29 Waverly Place.

8. Donaldina Cameron House

10. Commodore Stockton School Annex

10. Gum Moon Residence

10. Methodist Church

8. **Donaldina Cameron House**
   1908, Julia Morgan; rem. 1940s; add. 1972, E. Sue
   920 Sacramento St.
   In 1873 the Presbyterian Church set up a foreign mission to serve San Francisco's Chinese. After the original hall burned in 1906, a new one was built on the present site and officially named for its famous director in 1942. The architect was rightly favored by many eleemosynary institutions; she knew how to design practical buildings that had dignity and presence.

9. **Chinese Historical Society of America (Former Chinatown Women's YWCA Residence Hall)**
   1932, Julia Morgan
   940-50 Powell St.

   YWCA Clay Street Center
   1931, Julia Morgan; 2001, Barcelon & Jang
   965 Clay St.
   Two facilities designed concurrently by Morgan, for some years the official YWCA architect for the western region. The first, a severe, elongated Tuscan villa, is now for senior citizens; the latter, an active social center, is more stylistically adventuresome and has an urbane yet residential scale and plan.

10. **Commodore Stockton School Annex**
    1924, Angus McSweeney; rem. 1974-75, Bruce, Wendell & Beebe
    Washington St. at Stone St.
    A handsome blend of Mediterranean and Oriental imagery.

    Gum Moon Residence
    1912, Julia Morgan
    940 Washington St.

    Methodist Church
    1911, Clarence Ward
    Grant Ave. at Washington St.
    The Protestant missions in Chinatown were largely devoted to rescuing Chinese girls from prostitution. They were run by dedicated women of enormous energy. Their favorite architect, Julia Morgan, was of the same stripe. This understated Florentine villa was the residence for the original Methodist Church next door, also designed by Morgan, which burned in 1906, and was replaced by the present building, designed in 1911 by Clarence Ward.

11. **Bank of Canton (former Chinese Telephone Exchange)**
    1909
    743 Washington St.

The site of San Francisco's first newspaper, the California Star, later became the home of the country's only Chinese telephone exchange. Outmoded by the 1950s, the exchange closed and the building interior was remodeled for its new occupant, the Bank of Canton.

12. Portsmouth Square

12. Portsmouth Square

Once the plaza of the Spanish colonial port town of Yerba Buena, renamed San Francisco in 1847. By 1844 the first official building, a customs house, was built at the northwest corner of the plaza. In 1846 Captain Montgomery raised the American flag here and named the plaza Portsmouth Square after his U.S. Navy sloop. At the time of the Gold Rush the square acquired the set of hotels and gambling houses that, along with the customs house, were vital to the town's economy. As the city center moved southward and the mining industry ceased to be the city's economic base, the square declined in civic importance and finally became a city park. In 1963 a split-level park with garage below, designed by Royston, Hanamoto & Mays, reshaped the square. Various monuments, including one to Robert Louis Stevenson designed by Bruce Porter and Willis Polk in 1897, were reinstalled. A plaque giving the history of the square is by the stair from the upper to the lower level.

13. Golden Gateway Redevelopment Project, Phase 1 residential development

13. Golden Gateway Redevelopment Project

Battery St. to the Embarcadero; Broadway to Clay St.
Urban renewal plan
1957, Skidmore Owings & Merrill

Phase 1 residential development

1961-63, garages, point towers & town houses
Wurster Bernardi & Emmons/DeMars & Reay
Jackson St.

Phase 1 town houses

1961-63, Anshen & Allen; Sasaki Walker Assoc., Washington St.

13. Golden Gateway edevelopment Project, Phase 2 residential development

Phase 2 residential development

1981-82, condominiums, Fisher-Friedman
Davis St. to Broadway

This first major downtown housing development, a Redevelopment Agency project, replaced the city's produce market with slab towers and a neat, suburban village of town houses. In 1981-82 Fisher-Friedman designed the final residential increments of the project, which has pleasant interior courts, commercial space on the ground floors and parking below

15. Hotaling Building

15. Hotaling Building & Hotaling Annex West

grade. By now both blocks of housing have become period-pieces, but their existence has contributed greatly to the urbanity of this part of town.

14. U.S. Customs House
1906-11, Eames & Young
555 Battery St.
Although most of the post-fire buildings downtown used stone sparingly, usually in combination with less expensive terra cotta, the federal government built for the ages, as in this Customs House building. Handsome decorative detail using patriotic symbols of authority enriches the exterior. The interior has generous public spaces, a handsome stairway and other fine details.

15. Jackson Square
Jackson St. bet. Montgomery and Sansome Sts., Hotaling Pl., and Montgomery to Washington St.
The city's first official Historic District and the only group of downtown business buildings to survive the 1906 earthquake and fire. Except for the elaborate, prefabricated cast-iron and cast-stone facades of the Hotaling buildings, which housed a wholesale liquor business, the buildings are relatively simple; the sharp change in scale from the adjacent financial district buildings heightens the 19th-century character of the historic district.

Building
400-01 Jackson St.
A post-1906 rebuilding of a c.1882 office structure.

Ghirardelli Building
1853
415-31 Jackson St.

Tobacco and coffee warehouse
1861
435-41 Jackson St.

Jackson Hotaling Annex East
c.1860
443-45 Jackson St.

Hotaling Building
1866
451-61 Jackson St.

Hotaling Annex West
c.1860
463-73 Jackson St.

Building
432 Jackson St.
Rebuilt after 1906 from rubble of other buildings.

Solari Building, East-Larco's Building
1866
470 Jackson St.

Bank of Lucas Turner & Co.
1853, Keyser & Brown after a design by Reuben Clark
498 Jackson St. to 804 Montgomery St.
Now the home of the west coast's premier architectural bookstore, William Stout's Architectural Books.

15. Golden Era Building

15. Bank of Lucas Turner & Co.

15. 701 Jackson St.

Golden Era Building
1852
732 Montgomery St.
Mark Twain and Bret Harte were among the contributors to The Golden Era, an early literary magazine.

Genella Building/Belli Annex
1851
728-30 Montgomery St.

Belli Building-Langerman's Building
1851
722-24 Montgomery St.

Burr Building
1859-60
530 Washington St.

Barbary Coast

Nearby on the corresponding blocks of Pacific Avenue was the Barbary Coast, once the city's major vice center. After many ups and downs it vanished in the post-World War II era. The buildings were rebuilt after 1906 to their pre-fire scale. The area has some sensitive rehabilitations of old buildings for new uses. One Jackson Place, remodeled by Lloyd Flood in 1964, was downtown's first conversion of warehouses into an interior shopping mall.

Varennes St. in North Beach

16. Original Transamerica Building

17. Columbus Tower

18. City Lights Books Store

North Beach

The name North Beach refers to the sand beach that bordered the bay west of Telegraph Hill before the shoreline was extended about four blocks by fill and bounded by a sea wall constructed between 1881 and 1913. At the foot of Powell was Harry Meigg's 2,000-foot wharf and amusement park, the location of Abe Warner's famous Spider Palace where the cobwebs were so thick that they were said to support human weight. Besides bath-houses and other facilities for swimming and healthful recreation, the area was home to a number of prominent citizens before the 1860s when Rincon Hill replaced it as the zone of "better residence." A number of industries took advantage of the waterside location. Of the ten breweries located there by 1876, only the old Malting House on Francisco between Mason and Powell Streets survives. North Beach was long the local equivalent of New York's Greenwich Village. Over the years its ethnicity has changed from Italian to mostly Chinese.

16. Original Transamerica Building

1911, Charles Paff; 1915 remodel by O'Brien & Werner, Italo Zanolini

4 Columbus Ave. at Montgomery St.

A wedding cake building that reveals terra cotta's ability to rival stone in the rendering of decorative detail. Originally two stories high, the top story was added later. First called the Fugazi Banca Popolare, the company began in 1859 as John Fugazi's travel agency with banking on the side.

17. Columbus Tower

1905, Salfield & Kohlberg; rem. 1959, Henrik Bull

Columbus Ave. and Kearny St.

An eye-catching landmark for those coming downtown, the building is owned by Frances Ford Coppola.

18. City Lights Books Store and Vesuvio's

1913, rem. 1918, Italo Zanolini

235-53 Columbus Ave.

Two social landmarks of the Beat Generation era, City Lights was the country's first all-paperback bookstore, as well as a principal hangout for the literati, including Allen Ginsberg, Jack Kerouac, Kenneth Rexroth, Lawrence Ferlinghetti, the owner, and many other notable beatniks. Across the alley, Vesuvio's was an extension of this memorable scene. Though most of the other gathering places have passed on, a few, such as the Cafe Trieste, survive along upper Grant Avenue

19. St. Francis of Assisi Church

19. **St. Francis of Assisi Church**
1860, rem. 1913, C. J. I. Devlin
610 Vallejo St.
The exterior of this church, including the towers, survived the 1906 fire and was incorporated into the present structure. This was the city's first parish church after the Mission Dolores; it was founded by the French community. Stylistically, it is related to Old St. Mary's.

20. **Fugazi Hall**
1912, Italo Zanolini
678 Green St.
John Fugazi, donor of Fugazi Hall, was also the founder of the Transamerica Company. He competed with two other Italian bankers, A. P. Giannini and Andrea Sbarbaro, but eventually all three combined to create the giant Bank of America. Fugazi gave this cultural and community center in perpetuity to the Italian community.

21. Sts Peter and Paul Church

21. **Washington Square**
Columbus Ave. to Stockton St., Union to Filbert St.
Blighted by unkempt cemeteries in its first decade, this early rectangular plot was leveled in the 1860s and became a favorite place to promenade after Montgomery Avenue, renamed Columbus in 1909, was cut across one corner of it in the 1870s. Lillie Coit's monument to the Volunteer Fire Department, sculpted

21. Washington Square

by Haig Patigian and installed in 1933, and the 1879 statue of Ben Franklin are in the Square. In 1958 Lawrence Halprin & Associates and Douglas Baylis designed the present landscape, which is so sympathetic to its surroundings and to the activities of the square that it seems as though it had always existed.

Sts. Peter and Paul Church
1922-24, Charles Fantoni; 1939, John A. Poporato
666 Filbert St.

22. Maybeck Building, Former Telegraph Hill Neighborhood Association

24. Vandewater Street Buildings

25. House, 210 Francisco

25. Telegraph Terrace

This Italianesque Gothic Revival church anchors the square claiming it as the traditional center of the Italian community. The original design, perhaps derived from Orvieto cathedral, called for a large mosaic for the central facade. This scheme was abandoned in 1939 when Poporato was commissioned to finish the church. One of its high moments came when Cecil B. DeMille featured it in his 1923 silent film, *The Ten Commandments.*

22. Maybeck Building, Former Telegraph Hill Neighborhood Association
1908-09, Bernard Maybeck; add. 1913, 1928; rem. 1940s, John Kelly; add. 1980s, AGORA
1736 Stockton St.
An historic neighborhood center founded by Alice Griffith, a pioneering social worker, the building's alpine chalet style was often used by Maybeck. The many alterations of form and use have preserved the attractive courtyard.

23. San Remo Hotel and Restaurant
c.1915; rem. 1978, Monte Bell
2237 Mason St.
A pleasant and understated remodeling that enhances the old North Beach character of this building.

23. San Remo Hotel and Restaurant

24. Vandewater Street Buildings

No. 15
1974, Jerry Weisbach

No. 33
1981, Donald MacDonald

No. 55
1981, Daniel Solomon & Assoc.
A North Beach alleyway with several recent buildings which give it a past-to-present character.

25. House
1981, Baken Arrigoni & Ross
210 Francisco St.

Telegraph Terrace
1984, Backen Arrigoni & Ross
Grant and Francisco Sts.
Contemporary eclectic Mediterranean styling picturesquely composed and well sited.

27. 281 Chestnut St.

26. **House**
1929
298 Chestnut St.
More typical of 1920s Mediterranean mansions in Pacific Heights and St. Francis Wood.

27. **House**
1999, Leddy Maytum Stacy
281 Chestnut St.
Set high above the street to catch the views the house is divided into narrow slices of parallel space with exterior materials chosen to complement the formal design and weather naturally.

28. 340 Lombard St.

28. **House**
2000, Jim Jennings
340 Lombard St.

29. **House**
1942, Gardner Dailey
275 Telegraph Hill Blvd.

30. **Coit Tower**
1934, Arthur Brown, Jr.
End of Telegraph Hill Blvd.
This emblematic landmark occupies the site of the first west coast telegraph, a semaphore, which in 1849 connected Point Lobos at the ocean entrance to the Bay with Point Loma, as the hill was then called. By 1853 an electromagnetic line took its place. The next landmark, a castlelike observatory built in 1882, burned in 1903. In 1929 Lillie Coit, a local heroine with a penchant for firefighting, died, leaving the city a bequest for beautification. A monument was commissioned from Arthur Brown, Jr., principal architect of the San Francisco Civic Center; it was designed by Henry Howard, son of John Galen Howard, who worked in Brown's office. The result, popularly decoded as a stylized hose nozzle, may also be seen as a de-Classified column because of its fluted shaft and missing capital. The recently restored interior features WPA murals by several artists; it is well worth a visit.

30. Coit Tower

31. **Filbert Steps, Darrell Place, Napier Lane Residence**
Below Pioneer Park, where Coit Tower stands, Filbert becomes a flight of steps. No. 351 is a building that exemplifies early Bay Area Modernism in its cubistic form. The Montgomery Street landscaping was for many years the personal effort of Grace Marchant,

32. 1360 Montgomery St.

whose contribution is commemorated by a plaque. A cluster of houses from the 1860s and 1870s is at 228 and 224 Filbert and across the way on the two pedestrian lanes, Darrell Place and Napier Lane. As of this writing the dates of the Napier Lane houses are: No. 10, 1875; No.15, 1884; No. 16, 1872; No. 21, 1885; No. 22, 1876, and No. 32-34, 1890, but remodeled. No. 36 Darrell Place is a condominium building by Ace Architects intended as an homage to Bay Regional architecture. A flight of wooden steps leads down the precipitous hillside. The hill's scarred flanks bear witness to the quarrying operations that chipped away at its base for years until stopped in 1903. Among other uses the quarried rock became fill for the Embarcadero.

32. 1360 Montgomery St.

32. Apartment house

1937, J. S. Malloch, builder
1360 Montgomery St.

One of the city's best examples of the Style Moderne, this was the luxurious apartment building featured in the 1946 Humphrey Bogart, Lauren Bacall movie *Dark Passage.*

Julius' Castle

1922, Louis Mastropasqua
End of Montgomery St.

One of the hill's most colorful landmarks.

32. Julius' Castle

33. Houses

1309, 1315 Montgomery St.
1860s

25, 29 Alta St.
c.1870

31 Alta St.
1852

287-89 Union St.
1850s

293 Union St.
1860s

Although most of Telegraph Hill's buildings are post-1906, two clusters of houses on the eastern flank of the hill reveal what it looked like in its early period. The simple wood-frame buildings of almost miniature scale resemble the prefabs shipped from New England to this Yankee outpost. Few have escaped alterations, but they have a time-bound quality that matches their setting.

34. Kahn house

34. Kahn house

1939, Richard Neutra
66 Calhoun Terrace

A rare northern California example of the European International style by its southern California master.

35. The Ice Houses No. 1 & No. 2
1914; rem. 1970, Wurster Bernardi & Emmons
1265 Battery St., 151 Union St.
The first of many conversions of old warehouses to new uses that have enlivened the area with often inventive designs melding the old and the new. A pleasant walk down Battery Street, the verge of the original waterfront, will reveal many more.

36. Former Beltline Roundhouse
1914; rem. 1985, Tower Architects
1500 Sansome St.
A pleasant conversion into offices of the only railway roundhouse that ever stood on the Embarcadero.

37. Municipal Buildings
c.1925
111 Bay St.
Handsome proto-modern buildings that play a background role for the beginning of an important street.

38. Warehouse
c.1900; rem. 1980, Hellmuth, Obata & Kassabaum
1 Lombard St.
An extensive interior remodeling of one of the fine warehouse buildings in the north Embarcadero district.

Cargo West Building
1879
1105 Battery St.

Italian Swiss Colony warehouses
1903, Hemenway & Miller
1265 Battery St.

39. Levi's Plaza
1982, Helmuth, Obata & Kassabaum/Howard Friedman /Gensler & Assoc.; Lawrence Halprin, land. arch.
Battery St. to Sansome St., Union St. to Greenwich St.
A benchmark in corporate headquarters design, this lowrise complex of brick buildings is scenographically composed to enhance the view of Telegraph Hill and even incorporate it as borrowed scenery. The site plan integrates the buildings with the landscaped plaza and provides a sweeping suburban park across Battery Street that is the most luxuriously appointed corporate front yard in town. The fountains are the latest in Lawrence Halprin's line of Sierra mountainscape tours de force.

38. Warehouse

38. Italian Swiss Colony warehouses

38. Warehous

39. Levi's Plaza

Only a few people ventured to live on the knoblike hill that rose up sharply west of the burgeoning city of the 1850s and 1860s. Rincon Hill first to the south was the prime residential neighborhood and remained so until Andrew Hallidie invented the cable car, which ran up Clay Street in 1873 and up California Street in 1878. Thereafter the hill was called Nob, perhaps because of its shape, but also, allegedly, because the first hill climbers were called "nabobs" (a word once applied to Europeans who got rich in India). The Big Four: Charles Crocker, James C. Flood, Mark Hopkins, and Collis P. Huntington, who controlled the all-powerful railroads, the Comstock Bonanza kings, and other assorted millionaires built a stand of mansions redolent of instant wealth that, with few exceptions, were leveled in the fire that followed the 1906 earthquake. The survivors were the brownstone mansion that belonged to James C. Flood, and the Fairmont Hotel that was still under construction when the disaster struck. The hill's first owners have been perpetuated in hotel names–the Mark Hopkins, the Fairmont, and the Stanford Court–and various relics of the pre-fire scene. One such remnant is the impressive Sierra granite wall contributed by the engineers of the Central Pacific Railroad in the mid-1870s that surrounds the block on which the mansions of Mark Hopkins and Leland Stanford stood. Elegance did not depart the hilltop with the nabobs after the fire. The hotels, town houses, and Grace Cathedral preside over one of the city's truly urbane areas. Yet the hill is much larger than its illustrious center; the overall population is mixed both ethnically and economically, as the reader who follows this tour will see.

One of the city's most homogeneous stands of apartment houses occupies the downtown slopes of Nob Hill. Since most of them were built within a few years after the 1906 fire, the buildings convey the fashionable streetscape of that time. Although their names may be unfamiliar today, the architects were among the post-fire decades' most active practitioners. The viewer will note thematic variations on styles that are difficult to classify. The basic vocabulary of decorative detail is Classical, but there is also a sprinkling of the curvaceous floriate forms associated with Art Nouveau. A few contemporary designs have been pieced into the old fabric. A walk up and down Pine, Bush, and the cross streets in this district will be particularly rewarding to those for whom architectural sightseeing is a typological game.

Russian Hill was so named because some graves allegedly containing the bones of Russian sailors were discovered there in the 19th century. Whether or not any Russians ever set foot on the hill is still in doubt, but the name is secure. Both historically and architecturally this is one of the city's richest areas, worth exploring at leisure. The 1000 block of Vallejo marks the hill's 360-foot summit–also a high point of architecture. While those who wished to lord it over downtown lived on Nob Hill, a bohemian aristocracy inhabited the more rustic slopes of Russian Hill, where the Livermore family had a farm and orchard and where lived such writers as Ina Coolbrith, Bret Harte, and Charles Warren Stoddard, known collectively as the Golden Gate Trinity. Coolbrith, state poet laureate, lived at Taylor and Vallejo, where there is now a tiny park named for her. Helen Hunt Jackson also lived and died on the hill's eastern brow. Perhaps because it was so sparsely built and because there were wells, a few enclaves escaped the 1906 fire. The largest of these is a woodsy block bounded by Green, Taylor, Broadway, and Jones. Tucked in here and there on its slopes are some very early, nearly invisible houses. Out of respect for the occupants' privacy we list only the visible ones, a considerable treasure trove.

1. Apartment houses
900 block of Pine St.
2. Apartment houses
1100 block of Pine St.
3. Marie Antoinette Apartments
1201 Pine St.
French Flats *1250 Pine St.*
4. Cathedral Apartments
1201 California St.
5. Grace Cathedral *California St. between Taylor and Jones Sts.*
6. Masonic Memorial Temple
1111 California St.
7. Huntington Hotel
Nob Hill Center Garage
Town house
Morsehead Apartments
1000 block of California St.
8. Town house
831-49 Mason St.
9. Pacific Union Club
Huntington Park
1000 block of California St.
10. Mark Hopkins Hotel
Stanford Court hotel
900 block of California St.
11. Fairmont Hotel *950 Mason St.*
12. Brocklebank Apartments
Park Lane Apartments
1000 block of Mason St.
13. The Nob Hill
1190 Sacramento St.
14. Apartments
1230 and 1242 Sacramento St.
15. Apartments
1202-06 and 1201-19 Leavenworth St.
16. Apartments
1425-29 and 1417-27 Clay St.
17. Apartments
1135-41 Taylor St.
18. Apartments
1200 block of Taylor St. and 1200 block of Washington St.
19. Row of flats
1314-30 Taylor St.
Hillgate Manor
1360-90 Taylor St.
20. Cable Car Barn and Museum
1201 Mason St.
21. House *1476 Pacific Ave.*
22. Nuestra Señora de Guadalupe
908 Broadway
23. Russian Hill Place
1000 block Vallejo St.
24. Alhambra Theatre *Polk St. between Union and Green Sts.*
25. Apartments *1101 Green St.*
26. Houses *1000 block of Green St.*
27. House *1110 Green St.*
28. Macondry Lane
29. Houses
900 block of Union St.
1800 block of Mason St.
30. Fannie Osborne Stevenson house
1100 Lombard St.
31. House *65 Montclair Terrace*
32. Wright house *950 Lombard St.*
33. House *998 Chestnut St.*
House *805-07 Chestnut St.*
34. San Francisco Art Institute
800 Chestnut St.
35. Walters house *2475 Larkin St.*
36. Houses and apartments
800 block Francisco St.
37. Houses *2423, 2455 Leavenworth St.*
38. Cottage row *2540-59 Hyde St.*
39. Terraced houses
737 757-63 765 Bay St.
40. National Maritime Museum
680 Beach St. at Polk St.
41. Ghirardelli Square *Polk St. to Larkin St. Beach St. to North Point St.*
42. Hyde St. Pier (San Francisco Maritime Historical Monument)
end of Hyde St. at Jefferson St.
43. Haslett Warehouse *NE and SE corner Hyde and Beach St.*
The Cannery
2801 Leavenworth St.

Previous page: Grace Cathedral

Jefferson St.
Beach St.
Embarcadero
North Point St.
Bay St.
Francisco St.
Vanderwater St.
Chestnut St.
Lombard St.
Greenwich St.
Telegraph Hill Blvd
Filbert St.
Union St.
Green St.
Vallejo St.
Broadway
Pacific Ave.
Jackson St.
Washington St.
Clay St.
Commercial St.
Sacramento St.
California St.
Pine St.
Bush St.
Sutter St.
Post St.
Maiden Lane
Geary St.
O'Farrell St.
Columbus Ave.
Van Ness Ave.
Franklin St.
Polk St.
Larkin St.
Hyde St.
Leavenworth St.
Jones St.
Taylor St.
Mason St.
Powell St.
Stockton St.
Waverly St.
Grant St.
Kearny St.
3rd St.
N
1 2 3 4 5 6 7 8 9 10 11 12 13 14 15 16 17 18 19 20 21 22 23 24 25 26 27 28 29 30 31 32 33 34 35 36 37 38 39 40 41 42 43

1. 900 block of Pine St.

3. Marie Antoinette Apartments

3. French flats

1. **Apartment houses, 900 block of Pine St.**

   900-08 Pine St.
   1915, Rousseau & Rousseau

   901-23 Pine St.
   1911, Sitler Bros., builders

   955 Pine St.
   1911, Rousseau & Rousseau

   961 Pine St.
   1912, James F. Dunn

   985-95 Pine St.
   1909-11, Cunningham & Politeo

2. **Apartment houses, 1100 and 1200 blocks of Pine St.**

   1111 Pine St.
   1909, C. O. Smith

   1145 Pine St.
   1912, Charles J. Rousseau

   1155 Pine St.
   1913, F. S. Holland

   1163 Pine St.
   1913, Rousseau & Rousseau
   Two block's worth of exemplary post-1906 earthquake and fire apartment houses.

3. **Marie Antoinette Apartments**
   1909; 1201 Pine St.

   French flats
   1919, James F. Dunn
   1250 Pine St.
   The entrance composition of the first building is truly eye-catching; the second is one of the half dozen or so often-flamboyant exercises in French Art Nouveau that Dunn built in various parts of the city.

4. **Cathedral Apartments**
   1930, Weeks & Day
   1201 California St.
   This firm designed two of the largest apartment buildings on the top of Nob Hill, as well as two of the major hotels. Although the work is more competent than exciting, its consistency and restraint help knit this otherwise not very coherent assemblage of buildings together.

5. **Grace Cathedral Complex**
   Between Taylor and Jones Sts.
   This complex of buildings occupies the site of the Charles Crocker mansion. After the mansion was destroyed in 1906, the family gave the property to the Episcopal diocese, which commissioned the English architect George Bodley for a design that

was set aside for lack of funds. Lewis P. Hobart's design for the church was constructed in two phases; construction stopped again in 1941, and the building was finally completed in 1964. Constructed of reinforced concrete for seismic reasons, the exterior surface was bush-hammered to give it a more stone-like quality and is now much admired. On its completion in 1964, replicas of Ghiberti's bronze doors from the Cathedral Baptistry in Florence, Italy, were installed at the new east end. The stained glass in the west end is by the Charles Connick Studios in Boston, while that in the east end is by Gabriel Loire of France and the Willet Studios in Philadelphia. Tours of the interior are given several times a week. The Cathedral School is neatly shoehorned into its restricted site and its rooftop playground is an architectural feature. Damage from the 1989 earthquake resulted in a 1990 plan by Wm. Turnbull Associates for a new Chapter House and courtyard east of the cathedral and a labyrinth set near the new entrance stairway on Taylor Street. The additions were completed in 1995.

5a. Grace Cathedral

5a. Grace Cathedral

5a. Grace Cathedral

Grace Cathedral
1928-33, 1936-41, Lewis P. Hobart;
1961-1964, Weihe, Frick & Kruse
California St. between Taylor and Jones Sts.

Diocesan House
c.1912, Austin Whittlesey
1051 Taylor St.

Cathedral Close, Chapter house, and Labyrinth
1995, Wm. Turnbull Assoc.

Cathedral School
1965, Rockrise & Watson; 1995 addition,
Wm. Turnbull Assoc.
1275 Sacramento St.

5b. Diocesan House

5c. Cathedral Close, Chapter house, and Labyrinth

7 & 8. Morsehead Apartments and Town houses

6. **Masonic Memorial Temple**
   1958, Albert Roller
   1111 California St.
   A gleaming white monumental mass that, if it does nothing else, firmly anchors one corner of the hilltop.

7. **Huntington Hotel**
   1924, Weeks & Day
   1075 California St.

   Nob Hill Center Garage
   1956, Anshen & Allen
   1045 California St.

   Town house
   1911, George Schasty
   1021 California St.

   Morsehead Apartments
   1915, Houghton Sawyer
   1001 California St.
   Though quite different in style and scale, these four buildings go together very well. The hotel epitomizes discretion and taste, and the garage is, for the times, remarkably deferential to its old neighbors. Schasty's town house is a welcome transplant from New York, while Sawyer's apartment house, also reminiscent of Paris, turns the corner gracefully by means of its baroque cornice and balconies.

8. **Town houses**
   1917, Willis Polk
   831-49 Mason St.
   An urbane row that continues the spirit of good taste and deference to its neighbor buildings.

9. Pacific Union Club

9. **Pacific Union Club (orig. James Flood mansion)**
   1886, Augustus Laver; 1908-12, Willis Polk/D. H. Burnham & Co.; 1934, George Kelham
   1000 California St.

Because it was built of Connecticut brownstone and not wood, Flood's mansion survived the 1906 fire that devastated the more ostentatious homes of his neighbors. When the gutted shell was to be restored as the new home of the Pacific Union Club, William Bourn, Willis Polk's great patron who was on the building committee, got him the commission. Polk's sensitive remodeling, which consisted of adding wings and altering the top floor, improved the proportions and changed the architectural character from that of a dry, tightly drawn 19th-century town house to a more free and gracious Neoclassical 20th-century manor house. The interiors, accessible only to members, are the quintessential image of a gentleman's

9. Huntington Park, looking east

9. Huntington Park, looking west

9. Huntington Park

club. The bronze fence surrounding the property is the city's finest; Flood allegedly employed one man just to polish it. West of the club is Huntington Park.

Huntington Park

The David Colton house stood here until Collis P. Huntington purchased the land and gave it to the city after 1906. This oasis features a replica of the Tartarughe Fountain in Rome. To sit in the park on a sunny day is to feel on top of the world.

10. Mark Hopkins Hotel

1925, Weeks & Day; 2002, restoration of entrance canopy and lobby, Architectural Resources Group
999 California St.

The city's most flamboyant Stick Style palace occupied this site before the fire. Commissioned by Mark Hopkins, the pinnacled pile was really for his wife, who inherited it when Hopkins died in 1878. In 1893, she gave it to the San Francisco Art Association (now the Art Institute), which occupied it until it burned in 1906 and subsequently sold it to purchase the Institute's present site on Russian Hill. The hotel

10. Mark Hopkins Hotel

10. Mark Hopkins Hotel, entrance

11. Fairmont Hotel, rear view

is in the simplified Gothic Revival style of the 1920s and is notable for its site plan, which incorporates a drive-in entrance court, and for the 1936 rooftop lounge designed by Timothy Pflueger, the Top of the Mark, long the most famous cocktail lounge in town and ancestor of many hoteltop restaurants.

Stanford Court

1911, Creighton Withers; rem. 1972, Curtis & Davis
905 California St.

The California Street Cable Car line was started by Leland Stanford as a tidy investment that could also, if he wished, transport him to his door. After 1906 a luxury apartment house with an inner court replaced his palace. It was converted at great expense

11. Fairmont Hotel

to a luxury hotel, but somehow the low-ceilinged court does not convey a sense of the grandeur one anticipates.

11. Fairmont Hotel

1906, Reid Bros.; rest. 1907, Julia Morgan;
tower add. 1962, Mario Gaidano; 2001, restoration of lobby and interior remodeling, Gensler Assoc./ Page-Turnbull preservation architect
950 Mason St.

James G. Fair, a Comstock silver king, owned the property, but his daughter, Tessie Fair Oelrichs, built the hotel, which was on the verge of opening when the 1906 disaster struck. Julia Morgan restored and completed the interior, but Dorothy Draper is rumored to have designed the lobby appointments, including the wonderful carpet. The Fairmont and the Pacific Union Club are the two most complementary structures on the hill, the one huge and light, the other compact and dark. Despite the much larger size and Neo-Baroque grandeur of the hotel, its scale does not diminish the importance of the former mansion.

Inquire at the hotel desk for the location of the Reid Brothers rendering of the hotel with terraced gardens that were never built. A corridor along the south side of the hotel leads to the rooftop garden replete with palm trees that offers a fine view of the city.

12. Park Lane Apartments

12. Brocklebank Apartments
1926, Weeks & Day
1000 Mason St.

Park Lane Apartments
1924, Edward E. Young
1100 Sacramento St.
The drive-in court of the Brocklebank echoes that of the Mark Hopkins on the other side of the Fairmont and provides a protected circulation zone along this side of the hill. The Moderne-style Park Lane Apartments provide a counterbalancing mass for the Brocklebank.

14. 1230, 1242 Sacramento St.

13. The Nob Hill
1958
1190 Sacramento St.
A slender apartment tower that preserves the scale of the hilltop.

14. Apartments
1916, Arthur Laib
1230, 1242 Sacramento St.
Parisian influence is very strong in these two finely detailed apartment houses in a particularly choice block. The incongruous tiled roof on No. 1242 was probably a later remodeling.

14. The Chambord Apartments

The Chambord Apartments
1921, James F. Dunn; 1985, rest., Marquis & Assoc.
1298 Sacramento St.
Often cited for its kinship with the work of Antonio Gaudi, this apartment building owes its swelling forms to an unusual floor plan in which oval living rooms are stacked in the corners of the building and expressed in the bowed-out balconies. In 1985 the floriate ornament originally omitted from the exterior was copied from the architect's drawings and applied to the balconies.

15. 1202-06 Leavenworth St.

15. Apartments

1202-06 Leavenworth St.
c.1911, Charles McCall

1201-19 Leavenworth St.
1908-09, James F. Dunn
McCall's design for this brown-shingled apartment house was for years attributed to Julia Morgan because of its resemblance to Morgan's rural-suburban residential buildings in Berkeley. Across the

16. 1425-29 Clay St.

17. 1135-41 Taylor St. at Pleasant St.

18. 1232 Washington St.

19. Row of flats

street is an example of Dunn's pre-Francophile style in a Classic Revival apartment house that rambles on and on up the block.

16. Apartments

1425-29 Clay St.
1907, G. H. Osterbeck, builder

1417-27 Clay St.
1909

17. Apartments
1908, Bakewell & Brown
1135-41 Taylor St. at Pleasant St.
A restrained shingled block designed as a home and studio for the artist Emil Pissis. Oddly enough, the most formal elevation is up the hill on the side street.

18. Apartments, 1200 block of Taylor St.

1224 Taylor St
1914, Austin Whittlesey

1250 Taylor St.
1911, U. E. Evans

1255-57 Taylor St.
1915, Falch & Knoll

Apartments

1224 Washington St.
1909, Charles Whittlesey

1232 Washington St. (1315 Taylor)
1910, Henry C. Smith
No. 1224 Washington St. is strongly influenced by contemporary Parisian apartment design. Charles Whittlesey favored the Pueblo Revival style, as can be seen in 1232 Washington St., which also fronts on Taylor St. Next door at No. 1234-54 is a vigorous example of the Craftsman style.

19. Row of flats
1910, Arthur J. Laib
1314-30 Taylor St.
Clearly a more modest budget dictated this row of Mission Revival flats than Laib's more Parisian apartments.

Hillgate Manor
1923, Henry Gutterson
1360-90 Taylor St.
An agreeable way of planning a moderate-sized apartment building that gives the occupants the amenity of a garden court and the passersby a visual treat. This type of building in the city appears to have been a rare commission for Gutterson–more's the pity.

20. Cable Car Barn and Museum
c.1910
1201 Mason St.
This is the last cable car powerhouse in operation in the world and worth a visit both for the machinery and for the museum collection, which includes the original Clay Street cable car. Hallidie was an English-born inventor and engineer who came to San Francisco during the Gold Rush era and produced the west coast's first wire cable, the first step in the invention of the cable car. Both a building and a plaza are named for him.

21. 1476 Pacific Ave.

21. House
2003, Leddy Maytum Stacy
1476 Pacific Ave.
A facade with an abstract, minimalist composition nicely balanced between glazed and wooden sections. The six floor levels are not apparent on the exterior.

22. Nuestra Señora de Guadalup

22. Nuestra Señora de Guadalupe
1906,1912, Shea & Lofquist
908 Broadway
Once the parish church for the city's Latin quarter, this lovely landmark still evokes the Mediterranean world.

23. 1000 block Vallejo St., Russian Hill Place, Florence St. and Ina Coolbrith Park
Willis Polk designed the double access ramp that leads to the 1000 block of Vallejo St. in 1914, the year the Livermore family commissioned him to design the houses at 1, 3, 5, and 7 Russian Hill Place, built in 1916. The plan of the block is scenographic, with the ramps converging on a central access to the heart of the block, while the flanking side streets, Russian Hill Place and Florence Street, are lined with houses that define a keyhole view and shield the block's interior. Polk's Russian Hill Place houses make two important contributions: on the Jones Street side they form a subtly articulated wall closing off the street and on the upper side they become cottages lining a brick-paved country lane. Polk's use of overscaled Classical detail is particularly effective here. No. 1085 Vallejo by Charles McCall and Nos. 35, 37, and 39 Florence Street by Charles Whittlesey (c.1920) depart from Polk's variations on the Spanish Mediterranean theme. Whittlesey's are Pueblo Revival, but they perform the same functions as Polk's designs in regard to their relationship to the street.

23. 1, 3, 5, 7 Russian Hill Place

23. 30, 35, 37, 39 Floence St.

The interior of the block was once quite open. The Hermitage condominiums by Esherick Homsey Dodge & Davis–designed with great respect for their famous

23. Hermitage Condominiums

23. Polk-Williams house

24. Alhambra Theatre

25. 1101 Green St.

setting–occupy the sites of two famous brown-shingle houses that were demolished for a fortunately never realized high-rise scheme. Still recalling the early context of the hill are the Marshall houses at 1034 and 1036, two of three gable-roofed, brown-shingled reminders of New England farmhouses. They were built by a parishioner of Joseph Worcester, pastor of the Swedenborgian Church, whose rustic cottage once stood at the end of the row. The Livermore house on the back of the lot at 1045 dates from 1865. Willis Polk remodeled it around 1891, and Robert A. M. Stern designed significant additions and alterations in 1990-the entrance is now on Florence. A landmark of the Second Bay Region Tradition is the Polk-Williams house at 1013-19. Willis Polk designed it for his family, which, at the time it was built in 1892, included his father, mother, brother, and wife. The client for this double house was a painter, Mrs. Virgil Williams, whose husband had founded the California Institute of Design. Polk apparently waived the commission in exchange for the eastern frontage of the lot. The shingled facade does not divide neatly in two parts, but rather suggests a street row in a medieval village. The old saw about the house with the Queen Anne front and the Mary Ann behind fits well here. The building's back end tumbles down the hillside, taking advantage of the slope to add layers of space. Polk's studio was on a lower rear level. The interior of the house is a remarkable sequence of vertically organized spaces.

At the head of the Vallejo Street steps leading down to Mason is Ina Coolbrith Park.

24. Alhambra Theatre
1930, Miller & Pflueger
Polk St. bet. Union and Green Sts.
Moorish was but one of several exotic styles used for early movie palaces; this is San Francisco's only example.

25. Apartments
c.1925, H. C. Baumann
1101 Green St.
One of Baumann's several Neo-Churrigueresque apartment blocks with a nicely detailed lobby. Those who live on the upper floors have fine views!

26. Houses, 1000 block of Green St.

1088 Green St. (former firehouse)
1907

1085 Green St
1966, Joseph Esherick

1067 Green St. (Feusier Octagon)
1857; add. 1880s

1055 Green St.
1866; rem. 1916, Julia Morgan

1045 Green St.
1880s

1039-43 Green St.
1880s

26. 1067 Green St. (Feusier Octagon)

Except for 1085 this is a rare group of survivors of the 1906 fire; the flats, No. 1039-43, were moved here after the fire. The Feusier Octagon, like the octagonal house occupied by the Colonial Dames, was inspired by Orson Fowler's tract on healthful living, *A Home for All.* The added Mansard roof made it fashionable in the 1880s.

27. House
2003, Stanley Saitowitz
1110 Green St.

26. 1039-43 Green St.

This 1960s house retained its envelope but had its interior totally remodeled and the stucco cladding replaced with synthetic wood siding painted a dark grey. The tower element, glazed with channeled glass, has an elevator and stair as well as habitable spaces. There are five levels and a north-facing terrace with sweeping views.

28 Macondray Lane

A walk down this two-block pedestrian street on the steep north face of Russian Hill will make you want to move right in–unless both your soul and your feet are flat. Macondray Terrace, the 1981 condominiums by Hood Miller Assoc. deserve praise for sensitive siting, planning, use of materials, and compatibility with a difficult site.

27. 1110 Green St.

29. Houses, 800 and 900 blocks of Union St.

858, 864, 873 Union St.
1910-12, John A. Poporato

811 Union St.
1912, Charles Fantoni

887 Union St.
1917, Paul DeMartini

901 Union St.
1907, Righetti & Kulh

29. Houses, 900 blocks of Union St.

919, 920 Union St.
1907, 1917, John A. Poporato

927, 953, 988 Union St.
1909, 1907, John A. Poporato

940 Union St.
1922, Louis Traverso

30. Fannie Osborne Stevenson house

962 Union St.
1917, Rousseau & Rousseau

1800 block Mason St.
1909-11, Paul J. DeMartini
and Louis Traverso
(except Nos. 1834-38, Biglietto & Trevia)
Italian architect-builders had lucrative practices in this neighborhood after the 1906 fire. These blocks are representative of the kind of multi-unit buildings that were considered adequate for the neighborhood population of the time, but today represent priceless investments.

30. Fannie Osborne Stevenson house
1900, Willis Polk; later add.
1100 Lombard St.
Additions have made a hodgepodge of this house, but

30. Lombard Street wiggle

the client, widow of Robert Louis Stevenson, and the architect, a staunch member of San Francisco's Bohemia, validate its claim to importance.

Lombard Street wiggle
Designed in the 1920s as an alternative to the scary grade that drivers encounter on Filbert Street two blocks away, this may be San Francisco's most famous

street. On any given day photographers cluster at the top or bottom of the block and fashion models-both humans and automobiles-often appear. The gardens in the median strip are communally owned and cared for.

31. 65 Montclair Terrace

31. House
1938, Gardner Dailey
65 Montclair Terrace
An example of Gardner Dailey's personal adaptation of the European International style.

32. Wright house
1907, Willis Polk
950 Lombard St.

33. 998 Chestnut St.

33. House
1948, John Funk
998 Chestnut St.
The cubistic geometry of this Californian International Style shows off to advantage on this spectacular site. The ten-year old photograph was included to show what the now tall tree hides.

34. San Francisco Art Institute

34. San Francisco Art Institute
1926, Bakewell & Brown;
add. 1970, Paffard Keatinge Clay
800 Chestnut St.
Two versions of exposed concrete, each highly successful in its own way. The older building is a stripped-down but gracious Mediterranean Revival building cast as a monastery complete with cloister. The contemporary addition is in Le Corbusian beton brut with rooftop elements treated as sculpture and walls articulated with the master's work in mind. Don't miss the Diego Rivera mural inside the older building.

House
1927, B. F. Wayne
805-07 Chestnut St.
A very sensitive site plan for this house, which combines traditional Mediterranean Revival elements with nontraditional materials such as industrial steel sash windows.

35. Walters house

35. Walters house
1951, Wurster, Bernardi & Emmons
2475 Larkin St.
This large town house is handled with a splendid disregard for formality. Its casual exterior covers an interior of great dignity and spatial interest, organized to take maximum advantage of the view.

36. 898 Francisco St.

36. Houses and apartments, 800 block of Francisco St.

800 Francisco St.
c.1940, James Hjul, engineer

825 Francisco St.
before 1854, R. C. Ruskin; rem. several times

864 Francisco St.
1912, John Galen Howard and Mark H. White

Patigian house
1914, Ward & Blohme
898 Francisco St.

This block has a remarkably varied group of houses ranging from one of the city's oldest at 825, through almost every architectural period and style.

36. 800 Francisco St.

37. Houses
c.1926, Winfield Scott Wellington
2423, 2455 Leavenworth St.

Were these houses stuccoed, their cubistic geometry would reveal their modernity. Shingled and weathered, they blend in perfectly with their context.

38. Cottage row

38. Cottage row
c.1900, Lucius Solomon, builder
2540-50 Hyde St.

An engaging gable-roofed row.

39. Terraced houses

39. Terraced houses
1850s; rem. 1937, William W. Wurster
757-63, 765 Bay St.

House
1937, William W. Wurster
737 Bay St.

The first group is beautifully sited to step down the hill; their studied simplicity is typical of early Wurster houses.

40. National Maritime Museum
1939, William Mooser, Sr. & Jr.
680 Beach St. at Polk St.

Looking appropriately like an oceanliner's superstructure, this streamlined Moderne landmark houses

40. National Maritime Museum

40. National Maritime Museum

historical material on west coast shipping, including a fine collection of models and photographs. The murals are by Hilaire Hyler and Sargent Johnson. Originally designed to serve as a bath house, it was converted to a museum in 1951. A walk out to the end of the curving breakwater that protects Aquatic Park provides a great view of San Francisco.

41. Ghirardelli Square

41. Ghirardelli Square

42. Hyde Street Pier

41. Ghirardelli Square
1860-1916

Tower Building
1915, William Mooser; rem. 1962-67,
Wurster, Bernardi & Emmons,
Lawrence Halprin, landscape architect
Polk St. to Larkin St., Beach St. to North Point St.
Deservedly one of the city's great tourist destinations, this collection of old (and one new) brick buildings originally housed the Ghirardelli Chocolate Company. It was taken over and remodeled into restaurants and shops by developer William Matson Roth as an almost non-profit venture. The fountain is by Ruth Asawa.

43. Argonaut Hotel, former Haslett Warehouse

42. Hyde Street Pier (San Francisco Maritime Historical Monument)
End of Hyde St. at Jefferson St.
Administered by the state, the pier has a fascinating collection of old vessels open for visits.

43. Argonaut Hotel, former Haslett Warehouse
1907-09; rehab. 2003, Kaplan McLaughlin Diaz
NE and SE corners, Hyde and Beach Sts.
Built by the California Fruit Canners Association, this timber and brick warehouse once housed the largest fruit and vegetable cannery in the world.

43. The Cannery, Interior Court

The Cannery
c.1909 ; rem. 1968, Joseph Esherick & Assoc.
2801 Leavenworth St.
An old warehouse was gutted and given a new interior structure to house shops and restaurants on three levels with an interior court.

Though the city annexed Pacific Heights as part of the Western Addition in the early 1850s, by the turn of the century it was a neighborhood in its own right. Previously the hollow north of the ridge was called Golden Gate Valley, an appropriately pastoral name for the vegetable and dairy farms that dotted the landscape. The Laguna Pequeña by the bay shore drew the first settlers because of its fresh water supply from springs. Here laundries and dairy farms flourished, the latter so much so that by the 1870s the area was called, as it is today, Cow Hollow. By this time the heights above began to be built up with more pretentious homes whose owners, unable to find space in other fashionable areas of the city, were attracted by the splendid views. However, they were not pleased by the barnyard odors from Cow Hollow; in 1891 the city shut down the dairy industry and assigned prisoners the task of filling the lagoon with sand from the nearby dunes. Even so, Cow Hollow remained a zone of modest residences compared to the more prestigious Pacific Heights.

During the fire that raged for days after the 1906 earthquake, the Army Corps of Engineers dynamited Van Ness Avenue to stop the blaze because it was the first natural break in the terrain. The resulting destruction of the mansions that lined the boulevard permitted retailers to relocate their businesses along the cleared avenue and transform the street from a prime residential use to the commercial strip it remains.

Today Pacific Heights is one of the city's most varied residential areas with houses of every size and pretension and a remarkable collection of churches and temples. The main commercial strip along Union Street has numerous shops and restaurants catering largely to the upper-class neighborhood around it as does the other shopping area along Chestnut in the Marina. Fillmore is the main north-south shopping artery spanning Pacific Heights and the Western Addition; it was leveled before 1915 to enable the construction of a light rail line to transport people to the grounds of the 1915 Panama Pacific Exposition. Because of the steepness of the slope down to the north from the ridge, most of the great mansions have spectacular views of the Golden Gate and Marin County. It is wise to plan walking tours in an east-west direction–although there are some steep surprises even here–and to travel north and south in a car with good brakes.

9

Pacific Heights / Inner Marina

1. Houses *California and Franklin Sts.*
   First Church of Christ Scientist *1700 Franklin St.*
2. Trinity Church *1666 Bush St. at Gough St.*
3. Houses *1911-21 Sacramento St.*
4. Atherton house *1976 California St.*
   Tobin house *1969 California St.*
5. Houses *2018-26 California St.*
6. House *2151 Sacramento St.*
7. Houses *2100 block California St.*
8. Houses *2245 and 2212 Sacramento St.*
9. Barreda house *2139-41 Buchanan St.*
10. Temple Sherith Israel *California and Webster St.*
11. Houses *2200-2300 blocks Webster St.*
12. Houses 2500 block *Washington St.*
13. Spreckels Mansion *2080 Washington St.*
14. House *2004 Gough St.*
15. Haas-Lilienthal House *2207 Franklin St.*
16. Greenlee Terrace Apartments *1925-55 Jackson St.*
17. Whittier House *2090 Jackson St.*
18. Apartment house *2411 Webster St.*
19. Calvary Presbyterian Church and the Christian Education Building *Fillmore and Jackson Sts.*
20. Leale House *2475 Pacific Ave.*
21. Apartment houses *2300 block of Pacific Ave.*
22. Bourne House *2550 Webster St.*
23. Talbot-Dutton House *1782 Pacific Ave.*
24. Houses *2414-24 and 2340 Gough St.*
25. Houses
    2201 Broadway
    2151 Bradway
26. Houses 2209 and *2256 Van Ness Ave.*
27. Apartment complex *1737-57 Vallejo*
    Burr house *1772 Vallejo St.*
28. Flood Mansion (First) *2120 Broadway*
    Hamlin School *2129 Broadway*
29. Two apartment buildings *1945 1955 Broadway*
30. Convent of the Sacred Heart/ Hammond Mansion *2252 Broadway*
    James L. Flood Mansion (second) *2222 Broadway*
    Joseph T. Grant Mansion *2200 Broadway*
31. Apartment complex *2255-63 Vallejo St.*
32. Leander Sherman House *2156 Green St.*
33. Flats *1950-80 Green St.*
34. Golden Gate Valley Library *Green and Octavia Sts.*
35. House *1641 Green St.*
36. Apartment house *2415 Franklin St.*
37. The Octagon/National Society of Colonial Dames *2645 Gough St.*
38. Holy Trinity Orthodox Cathedral *Van Ness Ave. and Green St.*
39. Vedanta Society-old temple *2963 Webster St. at Filbert St.*
40. Marina Middle School *3500 Fillmore St.*
41. Apartment House *3650 Fillmore St.*
42. Apartment Houses *1600 block of Beach St.*
43. Former San Francisco Gas Light Company *3640 Buchanan St.*
44. Heritage Retirement Community building *3400 Laguna St.*
45. Fort Mason Bay St. *Van Ness Ave. to Laguna St.*

Previous page: Apartments at 2415 Franklin St.

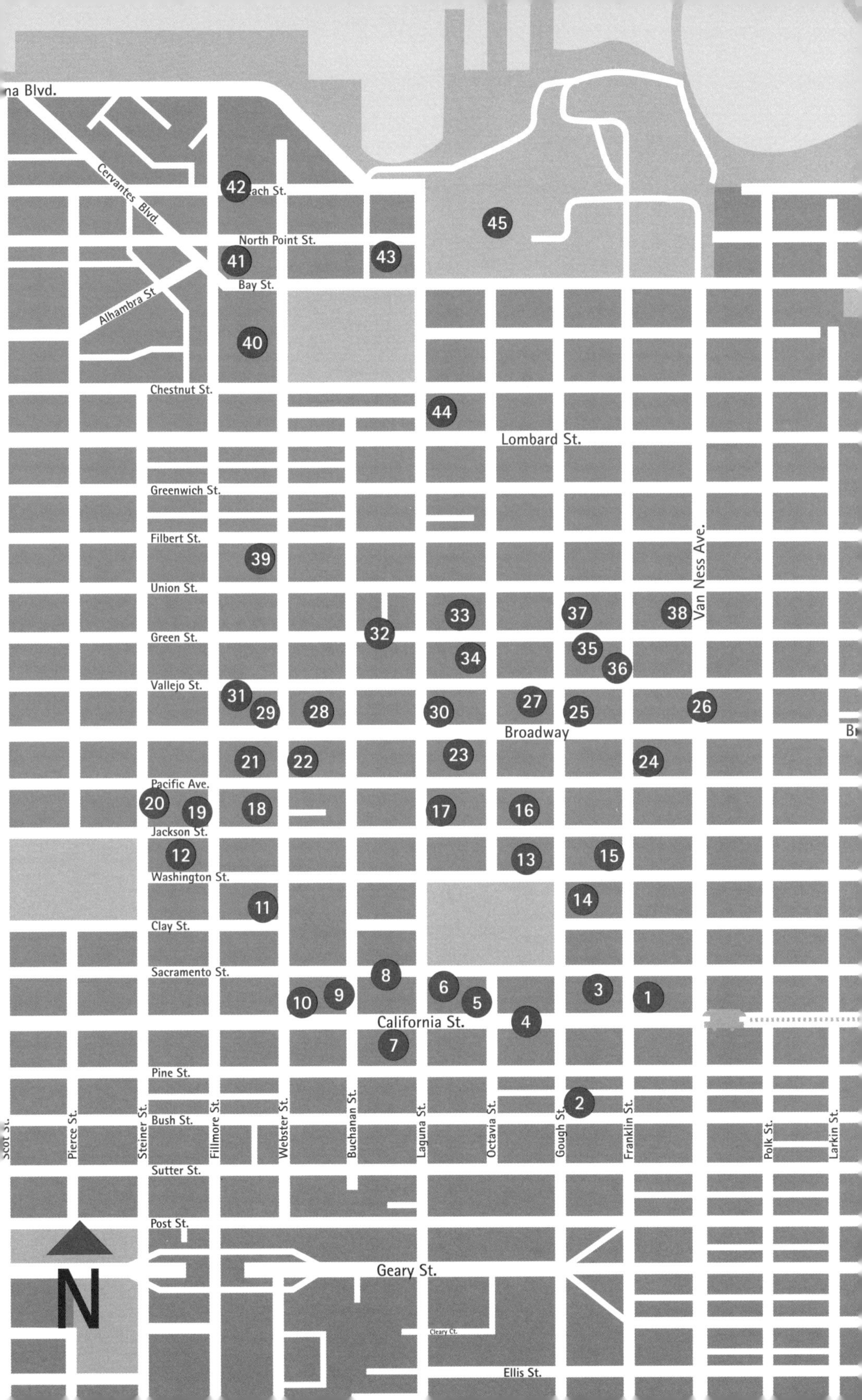
na Blvd.
Cervantes Blvd.
Beach St.
North Point St.
Bay St.
Alhambra St.
Chestnut St.
Lombard St.
Greenwich St.
Filbert St.
Union St.
Green St.
Vallejo St.
Broadway
Pacific Ave.
Jackson St.
Washington St.
Clay St.
Sacramento St.
California St.
Pine St.
Bush St.
Sutter St.
Post St.
Geary St.
Cleary Ct.
Ellis St.
Van Ness Ave.
Scot St.
Pierce St.
Steiner St.
Fillmore St.
Webster St.
Buchanan St.
Laguna St.
Octavia St.
Gough St.
Franklin St.
Polk St.
Larkin St.
N
1
2
3
4
5
6
7
8
9
10
11
12
13
14
15
16
17
18
19
20
21
22
23
24
25
26
27
28
29
30
31
32
33
34
35
36
37
38
39
40
41
42
43
44
45

1. Wormser-Coleman house

2. Trinity Church

4. Atherton house

3. Five houses

1. **Wormser-Coleman house**
   1876; rem. 1895, Percy & Hamilton
   1834 California St.
   Lilienthal-Pratt house
   1876
   1818-20 California St.
   Coleman house
   1895, W.H. Lillie
   1701 Franklin St.
   Bransten house
   1904, Herman Barth
   1735 Franklin St.
   If you come from downtown this corner announces Pacific Heights as an area of stately mansions. The families were related, which permitted the last house to be oriented toward a communal south garden. The styles range from full-blown Queen Anne on the corner to Georgian Revival at 1735.
   First Church of Christ, Scientist
   1915, Edgar Mathews
   1700 Franklin St.
   Polychromed terra cotta and varicolored brickwork enrich this otherwise staid Lombard-Gothic Revival church. The interior is worth seeing.
2. **Trinity Church**
   1893, A. Page Brown
   1666 Bush St. at Gough St.
   A massive fortresslike church, the large square tower is open to the interior.
3. **Five houses**
   c.1870-1895
   1911-21 Sacramento St.
   A widely varied group, ranging in style from Italianate to early Classic Revival, in an area otherwise largely consisting of apartment buildings.
4. **Atherton house**
   1881-82, Moore Bros., Charles Tilden, builders
   1990 California St.
   House
   1883, Schmidt & Havens
   1976 California St.
   Two of California Street's most exuberant Victorians, showing the transitions from Italianate to Stick-Eastlake and Queen Anne. The Atherton house was enlarged and brought up to date a decade after it was built (the date 1881 appears over a pair of upper-story windows). The California Street addition completely changed the orginal house and gave it the scale of a rural Queen Anne villa that appears to be

almost bursting out of its site. In 1923 Charles J. Rousseau, member of an important family of architects, bought the house, which served as home to his heirs for more than 50 years.

Tobin house
1913, Willis Polk
1969 California St.
Half of a Gothic double house Polk designed for the de Young sisters, one of whom moved away from the city and never built her half.

7. 2175-87 California St.

5. **Houses**
1880-90
2018-26 California St.
A striking series–no two alike. No. 2026 was updated after the 1906 fire with curved glass windows in the front bay and the addition of carved panels below the cornice.

6. **House**
1881; rem. c.1910
2151 Sacramento St.
Willis Polk allegedly remodeled this house, which was briefly the home of Arthur Conan Doyle.

7. 2151 California St.

7. **Houses**

2129 California St.
1882, Samuel & Joseph Cather Newsom

2145-49 California St.
1882, Samuel & Joseph Cather Newsom

2151, 2159 California St.
1880s

2165 California St.
1882, McDougall & Sons

2175-87 California St.
1879
The first two houses by the Newsom brothers have distinctive decorative detail. Note the strapwork in the spandrel of No. 2129 and the flat-sawn cut-out forms on No. 2145. Nos. 2151 and 2159 have the kind of elegance associated with the Hinkels, No. 2165 has urns and garlands. This is an unusually cohesive row on a stretch of California Street rich in late 19th century houses.

7. 2129 California St.

8. **Georgian Revival house**
1903
2245 Sacramento St.

House
1895, A. Page Brown
2212 Sacramento St.
A huge Colonial Revival box including the requisite Palladian window.

8. 2212 Sacramento St.

10. Temple Sherith Israel

Mansion Hotel
1887
2220 Sacramento St.
A house in transition from Queen Anne to Colonial Revival that has suppressed its towers.

9. **Barreda house**
1880; rem. 1904, Willis Polk
2139-41 Buchanan St.
Fernando Barreda was minister from both Spain and Peru to the Court of St. James and the U.S. This was remodeled by Polk when he married Barreda's daughter.

11. 2239-53 Webster

10. **Temple Sherith Israel**
1905, Albert Pissis; 1999, restored, int. remodeled, RMW
California and Webster Sts.
A neo-Byzantine design, monumental in scale and effect.

11. **Italianate row houses**

2209-35, 2239-53 Webster St.
1878-79, Henry Hinkel

2244-50, 2315-17 Webster St.
1878-79, The Real Estate Assoc.
This fine row by the oldest of this famous family of five brothers is part of a historic district that extends along Webster from Jackson to Clay. Of the 25 houses included in the district, 12 are by Henry Hinkel and five by the Real Estate Associates, his competitors. Other builders are also represented. Since all the houses were built between 1878 and 1880, the street has a rare homogeneity for the period.

11. 2315-21 Webster St.

12. **Houses**

Brown-shingled double house
c.1900
2576 Washington St.

Stick Style houses
1887
2527, 2531 Washington St.

Italianate house
1879
2560 Washington St.
This block has a good range of older houses, from the exuberantly painted Queen Anne house at No. 2527, to the handsome dark-shingled double house at No. 2576.

13. Spreckels Mansion

13. **Spreckels Mansion**
1913, MacDonald & Applegarth
2080 Washington St.

A French palace for French Alma de Bretteville Spreckels, for whom Applegarth also designed the Palace of the Legion of Honor in Golden Gate Park.

14. House
1889, T. C. Matthews & Son
2004 Gough St.
A Queen Anne house with plaster reliefs affixed to the facade like patterns appliqued on a Victorian sampler.

14. 2004 Gough St.

15. Haas-Lilienthal house
1886, Peter R. Schmidt
2007 Franklin St.
One of the great monuments of the city's Victoriana, this queen of Queen Anne villas is owned by the Foundation for San Francisco's Architectural Heritage and is open for tours. (Call 441-3000 for information.) These two families were among the founders of the city's influential Jewish community and were related to the owners of the cluster of houses at California and Franklin streets.

15. Haas-Lilienthal house

16. Greenlee Terrace Apartments
1913, Arthur J. Laib
1925-55 Jackson St.
A densely packed complex in the picturesque Mission Revival style.

17. Whittier house
1894-96, E. R. Swain & Newton J. Tharp
2090 Jackson St.
Imported brownstone and a design that recalls the early work of McKim, Mead & White contribute to the eastern look of this rather somber mansion.

17. Whittier house

18. Apartment house
c.1915, James F. Dunn
2411 Webster St.
Dunn's Francophilia varied from the tasteful to the extravagant, as demonstrated here.

18. 2411 Webster St.

19. Calvary Presbyterian Church
c.1900

Christian Education Building
1979, Robinson, Mills & Williams
Fillmore and Jackson Sts.
This church was built using materials from the original church, which stood on Union Square (demolished c.1898). The recent school building provides continuity from past to present.

20. Leale house
c.1853
2475 Pacific Ave.
One of the few remaining early dairyfarm houses, this one had its facade modernized c.1875.

22. Bourn house

25. 2201-2151 Broadway

21. Apartment house
c.1930
2340 and 2360 Pacific Ave.
Fine examples of Art Deco styling.

22. Bourn house
1896, Polk & Polk
2550 Webster St.
This compact clinker-brick townhouse with bold Classical detailing was designed for the president of the Spring Valley Water Company for whom Polk also designed two great estates: Filoli, near Woodside, a few miles from the city, and the so-called Empire Cottage at his Empire mine near Grass Valley.

23. Talbot-Dutton house
1875; add. 1905
1782 Pacific Ave.
An elegant Italianate house that was a wedding present from a lumber tycoon to his daughter. In 1905, a matching wing was added that created the unusual double-bay facade.

23. Talbot-Dutton house

24. House row
1895, George Hinkel
2414 and 24 Gough St.

25. Houses
1914, G. Albert Lansburgh
2201-2151 Broadway
Two more handsome brick mansions. Lansburgh's design is notable for its restraint and its strong geometry.

26. Houses
2209 Van Ness Ave.
1901

2256 Van Ness Ave.
1908, Moses Lyon
Two remnants of the stand of stately homes that lined

Van Ness Avenue before it was dynamited to stop the 1906 fire following the earthquake.

27. Apartment group
1920s
1737-57 Vallejo St.
The city's only version of the once popular period-revival-style Norman farmhouse compound. The site plan is similar to Craftsman apartment groups of the same period.

27. James L. Flood Mansion (First)

27. Apartment group

29. Two apartment buildings

Burr house
1875, Edmund M. Wharff; remodeled 1941, William W. Wurster
1772 Vallejo St.

28. James L. Flood Mansion (First)
1900-01, Julius E. Krafft
2120 Broadway

Sara Dix Hamlin School
1965, Wurster, Bernardi & Emmons
2129 Vallejo St.
The imposing Mannerist mansion on Broadway is backed by Wurster, Bernardi & Emmons's simple and straightforward classroom building below.

29. Two apartment buildings
c.1925, H. C. Baumann
1945, 1955 Broadway
Baumann designed so many Churrigueresque apartment buildings all over the city that they have become a distinctive part of its architectural image. Two more are up the hill at 2070 and 2090 Pacific. (Note also the Classical details of the house at 1905 Broadway.)

30. Convent of the Sacred Heart (former Andrew Hammond Mansion)
1905
2252 Broadway

31. 2255-63 Vallejo St.

34. Golden Gate Valley Branch Library

30. James L. Flood Mansion (Second)

James L. Flood Mansion (Second)
1912, Bliss & Faville
2222 Broadway

Joseph D. Grant Mansion
1910, Hiss & Weekes (N.Y.)
2200 Broadway
Over the years this school has acquired three of the city's most imposing houses, of which the Italian Renaissance palazzo by Bliss & Faville is the prize.

31. Apartment complex
1909, Stone & Smith
2255-63 Vallejo St.
The Craftsman style lent itself to picturesque massing of buildings for interesting off-street courts.

32. Leander Sherman house
1879
2156 Green St.
Built by the founder of the city's leading music store, this house with a Mansard roof has a three-story music room where Paderewski, Schumann-Heink, and Lotta Crabtree (a next-door neighbor), among others, performed.

33. Flats
1875
1950-80 Green St.
This early row of apartments was moved here in 1891. The present front was originally the back.

34. Golden Gate Valley Branch Library
c.1910, Coxhead & Coxhead
Green and Octavia Sts.
This terra-cotta-clad branch library shows Ernest Coxhead in a less inventive format than his other, more free-wheeling works that draw on Classical sources.

35. House
1940, William W. Wurster
1641 Green St.
A classic Wurster house that demonstrates that unpretentious design can be assertive.

35. 1641 Green St.

36. Apartments
1915, James F. Dunn
2415 Franklin St.
One of the most elegant of Dunn's essays in this imported Belle Epoque style.

36. 2415 Franklin St.

37. The Octagon/National Society of Colonial Dames
1857; rem. 1953, Warren Perry
2645 Gough St.
Orson Fowler's best selling book, A Home for All, or *The Gravel Wall and Octagonal Mode of Building*, first published in 1849, was the inspiration for about seven octagonal houses in San Francisco. Only two remain, and of the two only this one preserves most of its original appearance despite being moved across the street and remodeled. Now a museum, it is open to the public.

37. The Octagon/National Society of Colonial Dames

38. Holy Trinity Russian Orthodox Cathedral
1909
1520 Green St.
One of the city's many notable wooden vernacular churches, this one replaces an earlier church destroyed in 1906.

38. Holy Trinity Russian Orthodox Cathedral

37. Vedanta Society

39. Vedanta Society
1905, Joseph A. Leonard
2963 Webster St. at Fillmore St.
The structure makes for a delightful meeting of the mysterious East and the uninhibited West.

42. 1695 Beach St.

42.1627-29 Beach St.

43. Former San Francisco Gas Light Company

40. Marina Middle School
1936, George W. Kelham/William P. Day
3500 Fillmore St. at Bay St.
One of the few large-scale public schools built in the Depression–the Moderne-style decorative detail is notable.

The Marina
The Marina was developed after the 1915 Panama-Pacific International Exposition with apartment houses, double and single houses, and flats. The dominant styles are the Mediterranean Revival modes from Spanish to French, and the Modernistic or Moderne styles, which use the vocabulary of stylized ornament associated with Art Deco. In general, simplified planar forms with ornament restricted to openings and edges, a pastel palette, and a uniform height and scale contribute to the homogeneity of the district. Although the first impression may be one of sameness, there is considerable variation from the bay to Chestnut Street. The district is very walkable.

41. Apartment house
1933, Richard R. Irvine
3650 Fillmore St.

42. Apartment houses

1600 Beach St.
1936, Richard R. Irvine

1695 Beach St.
1931, Richard R. Irvine

Double house
1935, S.A. Colton
1627-29 Beach St.

1633-37 Beach St.
1939, Oliver Rousseau

43. Former San Francisco Gas Light Company
1893
3640 Buchanan St.
This brick Richardsonian block is the lone survivor of a former gasworks. It has a walled garden and a handsome interior space.

44. Heritage Retirement Community
1924-25, Julia Morgan
3400 Laguna St.
Julia Morgan designed a number of buildings for benevolent organizations; they are notable for their logical plans and quiet dignity. The Heritage organization was founded as a refuge for homeless Gold Rush children. This dignified building has an L-plan with a pleasant and protected south-facing garden court.

44. Heritage Retirement Community

45. Fort Mason,Quarters 3, Moody house

45. Fort Mason, Bay level

45. Fort Mason, Bay level

45. Fort Mason

Bay St., Van Ness Ave. to Laguna St.

The Spanish armed Black Point, or Punta Medanos, as they called it, with a few guns in 1797. By 1822 only one was left. Although the point was declared a U.S. military reservation in 1850, the Army did not occupy it until the Civil War. In the meantime several houses were built by squatters, the most famous of whom was John C. Fremont, whose house was demolished in 1864 for a Civil War gun battery. Although they have since been altered, three other houses do remain from the pre-Army days. They form an irregular row north from the gate on Bay Street as follows: Quarters 2, Brooks house, 1855; Quarters 3, Moody house, 1855; Quarters 4, Haskell house, 1855

In 1877 the larger residence just south and east of these was built as the commanding general's house; it was later converted to an officers' mess. The other buildings on the upper level are mostly WPA Mission Revival structures. One of them houses a youth hostel. The fort was used for coast defense batteries until the turn of the century, but its most important function was as port of embarcation for overseas forces from 1912 through the Korean War. Today, the piers on the lower level that served this function have a new life as the Fort Mason Center, home to a variety of cultural venues, including: the Craft and Folk Art Museum, SF MOMA's rental gallery, the Museo Italo Americano, and the Magic Theatre. A number of non-profit organizations have offices in the buildings. Directories for the various activities are available in the main office. The waterside part of the former fort is accessible from Marina Boulevard. The entire site is now part of the Golden Gate National Seashore and is under the direction of the National Park Service.

San Francisco's drive to rise phoenix-like from the ashes of 1906 coincided with the completion of the Panama Canal. The splendiferous 1915 Panama Pacific International Exposition celebrated both events. The site, located on the bay between Black Point and the Presidio, was created by a massive tidal land-fill project carried out by the Army Corps of Engineers. The Exposition was the last of the great fairs to be planned and designed in the Beaux-Arts Classical style initiated by the 1893 Columbian Exposition in Chicago.

According to Louis Christian Mullgardt, author of *The Architecture and Landscape Gardening of the Exposition,* "The arrangement of this Exposition is distinctive because of its Court Composition. Eight Palaces seemingly constitute a single structure, containing five distinct courts or places for large public gatherings, which are open to the sky." The Expo's Architectural Commission was composed of Willis Polk, chairman; Clarence Ward; W.B. Faville; George W. Kelham; Louis C. Mullgardt of San Francisco; and McKim, Mead & White; Carrere & Hastings; and Henry Bacon of New York. John McLaren was in charge of landscaping, Karl Bitter and A. Stirling Calder of sculpture, Jules Guerin of color and decoration. A Department of Travertine Texture was created to supervise the composition of colored surface materials in order to unify the buildings and sculpture. While the most spectacular structure was Mullgardt's glittering Tower of Jewels, the entire complex reveled in the consumption of energy through spectacular night illumination and fireworks displays.

The much loved Palace of Fine Arts was the only structure to survive the expo's closing. The Marina–as the greensward bordered by walks and roadways that skirted the bay was called–remains; its name was given to the district as a whole following the demolition of the fairgrounds. What replaced the great stucco palaces of the Expo was a stuccoed Mediterranean village with scenographic charm but no great architectural distinction. Italians were the neighborhood's first residents.

10 Pacific Heights / Outer Marina

1. St. Dominic's Church *Bush and Steiner Sts.*
2. Rose Court *2607 Pine St.*
3. Houses *1703-19 Broderick St.*
4. Ortman Schumate house *1901 Scott St.*
5. Selfridge house *2615 California St.*
6. Row houses *2837-73 Clay St.*
7. Apartment house *2971-73 Clay St.*
8. Cottage Row *2910 California St.*
9. Cottages *1805-17 Baker St.*
10. Pacific Heights townhouses *1900 block of Lyon St.*
11. House *3100 Clay St.*
12. Swedenborgian Church and related buildings *2100 block of Lyon St. and 3204 Washington St.*
13. Former firehouse *3022 Washington St.*
14. Howard house *2944 Jackson St.*
15. Waldorff School *2938 Washington St.*
16. Apartment house *2874-76 Washington St.*
17. Houses *2600 block of Jackson St.*
18. Houses *2415-21 Pierce St.*
19. Houses *2600 block of Pacific Ave.* Burr house *1772 Vallejo St.*
20. Houses *2500 block of Divisadero St.*
21. Houses *2800 block of Pacific Ave.*
22. Houses *3000 block of Pacific Ave.*
23. Houses *3100 block of Pacific Ave.*
24. House *2330 Lyon St.*
25. Napthaly house *2960 Broadway*
26. House *2901 Broadway*
27. Houses *2800 block of Broadway*
28. House *2660 Divisadero St.*
29. Houses *2700 block of Vallejo St.*
30. Perry house *2530 Vallejo St.*
31. Casebolt house *2727 Pierce St.*
32. Houses *2421 and 2423 Green St.*
33. House *2633 Green St.*
34. House *2960 Vallejo St.*
35. Houses *2500 and 2600 blocks of Lyon St.*
36. House *2508 Green St.*
37. House *2516 Union St.*
38. House *2460 Union St.*
39. St. Mary the Virgin Episcopal Church *2301 Union St.*
40. St. Vincent de Paul Church *Green and Steiner Sts.*
41. Double house *2056-58 Jefferson St.*
42. Palace of Fine Arts *Baker St. at Beach St.*

Previous page: Palace of Fine Arts

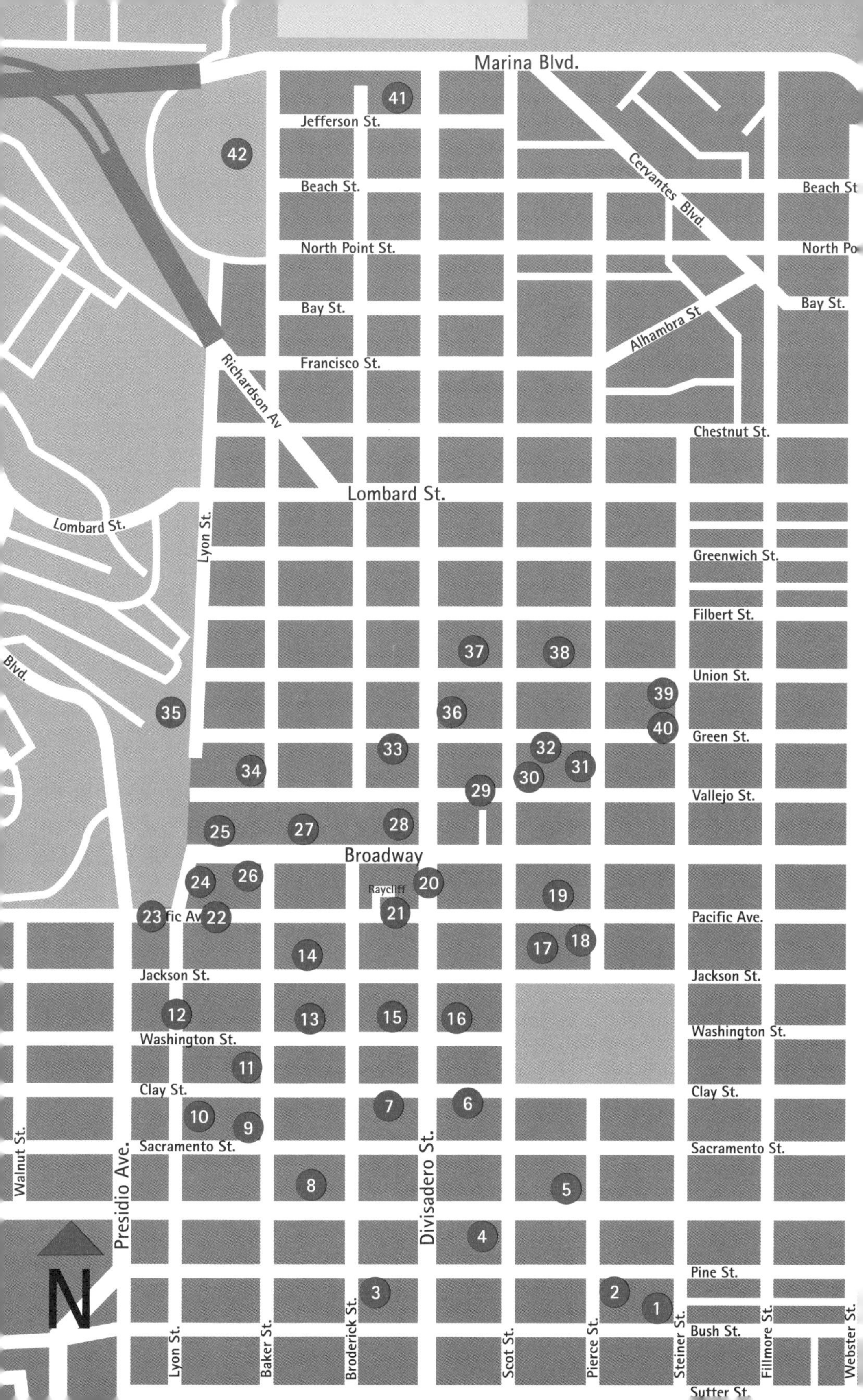

Marina Blvd.
Jefferson St.
Beach St.
Beach St
Cervantes Blvd.
North Point St.
Bay St.
Bay St.
Alhambra St.
Francisco St.
Richardson Av
Chestnut St.
Lombard St.
Lombard St.
Lyon St.
Greenwich St.
Filbert St.
Union St.
Green St.
Vallejo St.
Broadway
Raycliff
Pacific Ave.
Jackson St.
Jackson St.
Washington St.
Washington St.
Clay St.
Clay St.
Sacramento St.
Sacramento St.
Walnut St.
Presidio Ave.
Divisadero St.
Pine St.
Bush St.
Sutter St.
Lyon St.
Baker St.
Broderick St.
Scot St.
Pierce St.
Steiner St.
Fillmore St.
Webster St.
N
1
2
3
4
5
6
7
8
9
10
11
12
13
14
15
16
17
18
19
20
21
22
23
24
25
26
27
28
29
30
31
32
33
34
35
36
37
38
39
40
41
42

10

1. St. Dominic's Church

2. Rose Court

4. Ortman-Schumate house

1. **St. Dominic's Church**
   1927, Arnold S. Constable; 1992 rest. and seismic upgrading, Esherick Homsey Dodge & Davis
   2390 Bush St. at Steiner St.
   Academic Gothic revival, well executed throughout. Concrete buttresses were added for seismic bracing after the 1989 earthquake.
2. **Rose Court**
   (former Mary Ann Crocker Old Ladies Home)
   1890, A. Page Brown; 2001, AND (Asian Neighborhood Design)
   2607 Pine St.
   A Queen Anne/Shingle style building that recalls the early work of McKim, Mead & White, whose New York office Brown worked in before coming to California. Fire destroyed part of the original building, but it continued in use as a school until seismic upgrading was required after the 1989 earthquake. In 2001, the addition of a third story and other alterations completed the conversion of the building to affordable housing with a childcare unit.
3. **Houses**
   1883, Charles Hinkel, builder
   1703-19 Broderick St.
   Although they show a transition from Italianate to Stick style, these seven houses were built at the same time by the ubiquitous Hinkel family.
4. **Ortman-Schumate house**
   1870
   1901 Scott St.
   A great San Francisco landmark in the Italianate style, this freestanding house with elaborate gardens gives a hint of what this part of the city looked like in the 1870s.
5. **Selfridge house**
   c.1878; int. remod. 1930s, Julia Morgan
   2516 California St.
   Selfridge built both this house and 2603-13 California St.

   1900 block of Pierce St.
   Fine rows of Italiante houses.
6. **Row houses**
   1875, The Real Estate Assoc., builders
   2637-73 Clay St.
   A vintage row of Italianate houses from this very successful, 19th century design-build firm.
7. **Apartment house**
   c.1900
   2971-73 Clay St.

A Queen Anne apartment house that has some very impressive Classical ornament.

8. Cottage row

8. **Cottage row**
   1989, Kotas/Pantaleoni
   2910 California St.
   Fine condominiums designed to look like cottages marching up a side street.
9. **Five cottages**
   c.1890
   1805-17 Baker St.
   Small-scale streetscapes like this one were handled with real grace by Victorian builders.
10. **Pacific Heights town houses**
    1979, Daniel Solomon & Assoc.
    1900 block Lyon St.
    Contemporary Shingle style condominiums that fit very well into the old neighborhood.

11. 3100 Clay St.

11. **House**
    1897, McDougall & Son
    3100 Clay St.
    An elaborate towered Queen Anne house in transition to the Colonial Revival style. Across the street at 3101 Clay is an apartment house with an amazing cornice.
12. **Swedenborgian Church**
    1894, A. Page Brown
    2107 Lyon St.
    A beloved landmark of the early Craftsman era, this church brought together the talents of A. Page Brown, the architect; Bruce Porter, who sketched the original design and did the stained glass; Bernard Maybeck; and A.C. Schweinfurth, who did the drawings in Brown's office. The prime mover behind the project was the Rev. Joseph Worcester, pastor of the church,

12. Swedenborgian Church

13. Former Engine Company 23 Firehouse

14. Howard house

and friend and patron of the artists and architects who fostered the Bay Area branch of the California Arts and Crafts Movement. The garden provides an appropriate introduction to the church. The church interior is a living room with a roof supported by untrimmed madrone tree trunks and a great brick fireplace. The stained-glass windows by Porter are complemented by William Kerth'slandscape paintings. The pegged wooden chairs with seats and backs of woven rushes that Brown or Maybeck may have designed were credited by Gustav Stickley as the inspiration for Mission furniture. Rarely have nature and architecture been so well integrated.

Two nearby buildings associated with the church are at 2121 Lyon Street, designed in 1894 in Brown's office to be the parsonage, and the parish house, 3204 Washington Street, designed by G. W. Percy and Willis Polk in 1900.

Flats
c.1905, Edgar Mathews
2106-10 Lyon St.
An appropriately Craftsman group of flats across from the Swedenborgian Church.

13. **Former Engine Company 23 Firehouse**
1893
3022 Washington St.
This churchlike Victorian firehouse with its hose-tower steeple has become a studio-residence.

14. **Howard house**
1939, Henry T. Howard
2944 Jackson St.
One of the best of the city's few examples of the streamlined Moderne style of the 1930s.

15. **Waldorff School**
1987, Tanner Leddy Maytum Stacy
2938 Washington St.

16. 2874-76 Washington St.

17. 2600 Jackson St.

16. **Apartment house**
c.1905, Edgar Mathews
2874-76 Washington St.
The many-dormered roofscape is the eye-catching element of this shingled apartment.

17. **House**
1894, Willis Polk
2622 Jackson St.
Probably Polk's first major independent commission, this sandstone house has his characteristic rather heavy and spare application of Classical detailing.

House
1897, Ernest Coxhead
2600 Jackson St.

19. 2698 Pacific Ave.

18. **Houses**
c.1910, Edgar Mathews
2415-21 Pierce St.

19. **House**
1904, Sidney B. Newsom & Noble Newsom
2698 Pacific Ave.
The sons and successors to the original Newsoms, who designed often flamboyant High Victorian houses, here follow the turn-of-the-century trend to Classicism.

House
1937, William W. Wurster
2600 Pacific Ave.

20. 2560 Divisadero St.

20. **House**
1939, William W. Wurster
2560 Divisadero St.
A simplified Regency-Revival house with well-proportioned massing. Wurster appears to have favored brick for his traditional houses and wood for the more informal ones.

21. 1 Raycliff Ter.

House
1990, Esherick Homsey Dodge & Davis
2550 Divisadero St.

House
c.1930, Paul Williams
2555 Divisadero St.
A rare northern California work by Williams, one of the country's first prominent black architects, who practiced in Los Angeles and exported this narrow bit of Hollywood Regency style to San Francisco.

21. 2800 Pacific Ave.

21. 2810 Pacific Ave.

22. 3095 Pacific Ave.

21. **Houses by two generations of prominent San Francisco architects:**

1 Raycliff Ter.
1951, Gardner Dailey

2889 Pacific Ave.
1890, Arthur Brown, Jr.

2870 Pacific Ave.
1937, Wurster, Bernardi & Emmons

2830 Pacific Ave.
1910, Albert Farr

2820 Pacific Ave.
1912, Willis Polk & Co.

2810 Pacific Ave.
1910, Albert Farr

2800 Pacific Ave.
1899, Ernest Coxhead

22. **House**
1959, Wurster, Bernardi & Emmons
3095 Pacific Ave.
A late Wurster, Bernardi & Emmons boxy design, more mannered than Wursteer's 1930s work as in No. 33.

House
1953, Joseph Esherick
3074 Pacific Ave.
In his third San Francisco town house Esherick spaced four-by-fours across the facade to express the structural module of the frame. Compare this very restrained structural decoration with the 19th-century designers' elaboration of structural members as surface ornament in the so-called Stick Style houses.

23. 3198 Pacific Ave.

23. House
1912, Ernest Coxhead
3151 Pacific Ave.
The exigencies of hillside sites encouraged inventiveness in plan and massing. When combined with fine traditional detail, as in Coxhead's work, the products were truly original houses that did not present themselves as such.

House
1892, Samuel Newsom
3198 Pacific Ave.
An outstanding example of the plasticity often achieved by wrapping the curved and angled forms of houses that mixed Queen Anne and Colonial Revival style elements with shingles.

24. 2330 Lyon St.

24. House
c.1920
2330 Lyon St.
A rambling Mediterranean style house with an arcaded entrance court on the uphill side. In plan, if not in style, this is kin to the post-World War II ranch house.

25. Napthaly house
1913, Willis Polk
2960 Broadway
A delightful pink Mediterranean villa.

26. House
1926, Henry Smith
2901 Broadway
An example of determined Neoclassicism prevailing over almost all odds. Perched on a cliff, this Renaissance palace is approached by a complicated ramp from below.

27. House
1900, Willis Polk
2880 Broadway
A Neoclassical manor house that recalls the London work of the English architect John Nash.

28. 2660 Divisadero St.

29. 2795 Vallejo St.

31. Casebolt house

House
1913, Walter Bliss
2898 Broadway
An elaborate Dutch-Colonial manor house that contrasts wonderfully with Polk's pastel palace next door.

28. **House**
1938, John E. Dinwiddie
2660 Divisadero St.
A lone example in San Francisco of the residential work of this prominent local 1930s Modernist. The canted, boxed window was later imitated by tract builders so often that it became a cliche.

29. **Houses**
c.1905
2727, 2737 Vallejo St.
House
1938 Wurster, Bernardi & Emmons
2795 Vallejo St.
A pair of dark-shingled houses of the First Bay Tradition, and what was originally a dark Wurster, Bernardi & Emmons box. The stairway is indicated to the outside world by a diagonal across the hall window.

30. **Perry house**
1925, Warren Perry
2530 Vallejo St.
A quiet shingled house, more academically "eastern" than most local work. Warren Perry succeeded John Galen Howard as the second supervising architect of the University of California campus in Berkeley.

31. **Casebolt house**
1865-66
2727 Pierce St.
Set back in the center of the block, this great Italianate was once the manor house of Cow Hollow. Henry Casebolt, a Virginia blacksmith who arrived and made his fortune during the Gold Rush era, used salvaged ship timbers for much of his mansion's structure. The white wood exterior was once speckled with dark tones to mimic stone, which, for eastern pioneers, was a classier material.

32. **Two houses**
1893, 1895, Ernest Coxhead
2421, 2423 Green St.
The quiet exterior of Coxhead's own house at No. 2421 conceals an ingenious interior, with a long glazed entrance gallery on the west side running from a high-ceilinged living room on the street to the

dining room on the rear garden. The master bedroom on the upper floor has a select view through the corner bay window

36. 2508 Green St.

33. **House**
1939, William W. Wurster
2633 Green St.
One of Wurster's few overt nods toward what was then the new International style.

34. **House**
1950, Joseph Esherick
2960 Vallejo St.
This shingled house carries on the Cow Hollow tradition of rus in urbe. The south court below street level creates an inviting entrance for visitors.

35. 2601 Lyon St

35. **Houses**
c.1920
2517-25 Lyon St.
1912, S. G. Holden
2535-37 Lyon St.
1915, William F. Knowles
2545-47 Lyon St.
c.1920
2601 Lyon St.
A Spanish-Mediterranean enclave perched on the Presidio wall. No. 2601 is a handsome terminus for Green Street.

36. **House**
1901, Edgar Mathews
2508 Green St.
A half-timbered Craftsman house, whose mate to the left is almost certainly also by Mathews, a prolific designer of shingled houses and apartments in Pacific Heights.

38 2460 Union St.

40. St. Vincent de Paul

37. House

1890, A.C. Schweinfurth; int. remod. 1955, John Funk
2516 Union St.
A simplified Colonial Revival house of quiet distinction by an architect who belonged to the group of architects who forged the Bay Area's first regional approach to design.

38. House

c.1872; rem. 1892, Mooser & Cuthbertson
2460 Union St.
An Italianate house updated with a Mansard roof to produce an odd piece of eclecticism.

39. St. Mary the Virgin Episcopal Church

1891; rem. 1953, Warren Perry
2301 Union St.
The courtyard fountain is fed by one of the springs that nourished Cow Hollow's early dairies. The informal shingled church also reflects the area's pastoral past. Warren Perry's sympathetic remodeling shifted the entrance from Steiner to Union Street.

40. St. Vincent de Paul

1916, Shea & Lofquist
Green and Steiner Sts.
The exaggerated scale of the fake half-timbering, the gabled gambrel roofs, and the tower of this huge church make it unusual among the many Roman Catholic churches designed by this firm in the city. It is stylistically related to the smaller-scale San Anselm's in San Anselmo.

41. Double house (Dr. William Schiff house)

1937, Richard Neutra & Otto Winkler
2056-58 Jefferson St.
Neutra's International-Style vocabulary of form and materials displayed here in a steel and glass facade with standard industrial window sash. Like the Kahn house on Telegraph Hill, this design had almost no influence in the Bay Area.

42. Palace of Fine Arts, 1915 Panama Pacific International Exposition

Bernard Maybeck
Baker St. at Beach St.
In 1915 Louis C. Mullgardt, who designed the other showpiece of the PPIE, the Tower of Jewels, described the Palace's design as "a free interpretation of Roman forms and a purely romantic conception, entirely free from obedience to scholastic precedent. Its greatest charm has been established through successful composition; the architectural elements have been

arranged into a colossal theme...into which the interwoven planting and the mirror lake have been incorporated in a masterful way." Until 1962 the crumbling stucco original of this beloved relic of the Exposition survived in the melancholy state that

44. Palace of Fine Arts, 1915 Panama Pacific International Exposition

Maybeck himself said was the right mood for the fine arts. Then, thanks largely to the generosity and persistence of Walter Johnson, who matched the funds raised by the city, it was restored in concrete. The exhibition building behind the rotunda was given a new life as a home for the Exploratorium, an auditorium, and other cultural activities. Plans are now being made to restore the pergola and exhibition building along with the lagoon, but completion dates are unknown at this writing.

Alamo Square, the counterpart of Alta Plaza in Pacific Heights, is a focal point of the westward part of the Western Addition. This high plaza is a true breathing space surrounded by a prime collection of the kind of late 19th-century houses that fill the blocks of the area stretching westward to Golden Gate Park. South of the Panhandle is the once-notorious Haight-Ashbury district, the haunt of generations of flower children since the 1960s.

Before the development of the streetcar suburbs began, these sparsely populated western lands were dairy farms and ranches. William Crocker, one of the so-called Big Four of the Southern Pacific Railroad, owned large tracts of land here along with other wealthy citizens. After the Southern Pacific ran the first cable car line out Haight Street from Market Street to Stanyan Street in 1883, the area developed rapidly in part because of the tourist traffic to Golden Gate Park and the Chutes, a typical 19th-century amusement park. As more streetcar lines were laid both on the flat streets and on the hills, more blocks were built up with houses. The disproportionate number of 1890s Queen Anne-style structures in the district testifies to the peak of the boom. As the area filled apartment houses and flats were built in the transitional styles from Queen Anne to Colonial and Classic Revival after the turn of the century. The acute housing shortage after the 1906 disaster caused the conversion of many of the huge single and two-family houses to multiple-unit buildings. The more transient post-1906 population brought about a decline in status for the area. As the single-family population got into their automobiles in increasing numbers and moved to the western suburbs, the area's character changed even more. At the end of the post-World War II suburban expansion period the district housed a mixture of members of the Beat Generation, blacks displaced by urban redevelopment in the nearby Western Addition, and others who had either been long-time residents or who had moved in to take advantage of the low rents. Recent decades have witnessed gentrification, which has raised the visual quality of the district and increased the possibilities for serendipity in architectural sightseeing, eating, and shopping.

11

Haight / Western Addition

1. Amancio Ergina Village *Scott, O'Farrell, Pierce, and Ellis Sts.*
2. Beideman Place *Eddy St. to O'Farrell St. Scott St. to Divisadero St.*
3. Holy Cross Parish Hall *1822 Eddy St.*
4. House *1825 Turk St.*
5. House *1671 Golden Gate Ave.*
6. Andreozzi house *1016 Pierce St.*
7. Missionary Temple house row and apartments *1400 block Golden Gate Ave.*

   Flats *1400 block Golden Gate Ave.*
8. Apartments *1300 block McAllister St.*
9. Houses 700 block Broderick St.
10. Houses

    1255 Fulton St.

    1201 Fulton St.

    1198 Fulton St.
11. House *809-811 Pierce St.*
12. Houses *900 block Steiner St.*
13. Houses

    700 Steiner

    900 block Grove St.
14. Houses *800 block Fillmore St.*
15. Brahma Kumaris Meditation Center *401 Baker St.*
16. House 1588 Fell St.

    House *301 Lyon St.*

    Former Southern Pacific Hospital *Baker and Fell Sts.*
17. Ohloff House *601 Steiner St.*
18. Houses *400 block Shrader St.*
19. Apartments *1899 and 1907 Oak St.*
20. Alonzo McFarland house *400 Clayton St.*
21. Phelps house *1111 Oak St.*

    Mish house *1153 Oak St.*
22. House *1901 Page St.*
23. House *1777 Page St.*
24. Houses *1500 block Page St.*
25. Houses *1400 block Page St.*
26. Haight Ashbury Children's Center *1101 Masonic St.*
27. Apartments *1390-92 Page St.*
28. Former telephone exchange *865 Page St.*
29. Houses *500 block Cole St.*
30. Flats *1677-81 Haight St.*

    Commercial building *1660 Haight St.*
31. All Saints Episcopal Church *1350 Waller St.*
32. House row *1214-56 Masonic Ave.*
33. House row *142-60 Central Ave.*
34. Apartments *91 Central Ave.*
35. Houses *1000 block Haight St.*
36. Apartments *135-39 Pierce St.*
37. Haight Street Lofts *625 Haight St.*
38. Houses *800 block Ashbury St.*
39. Casa Madrona Apartments *110-16 Frederick St.*
40. Houses *1400 block Masonic Ave.*
41. House *1526 Masonic Ave.*
42. Richard Spreckels mansion *737 Buena Vista Ave. West*
43. Apartments *555 Buena Vista Ave. West*
44. Norma Talmadge house *439 Roosevelt Way*

Previous page: View of downtown from Alamo Square

Sutter St.
Post St.
Geary Ex.
Parker Ave.
O'Farrell St.
Terra Vista Ave.
Ellis St.
Eddy St.
Turk St.
Golden Gate Ave.
McAllister St.
Fulton St.
Grove St.
Hayes St.
Fell St.
Oak St.
Page St.
Haight St.
Waller St.
Beulah St.
Fredrick St.
Carl St.
Parnassus Ave.
Grattan St.
Alma St.
Rivoli St.
17th. St.
Masonic Ave.
Divisadero St.
Central St.
Lyon St.
Baker St.
Brodrick St.
Scott St.
Pierce St.
Steiner St.
Fillmore St.
Cole St.
Clayton St.
Downey St.
Asbury St.
Buena Vista West
Buena Vista Ave. East
Hill Ave.
Roosevelt Park
Clifford Terr.
States St.
Roosevelt Way
Hermann St.
Duboce Ave.
Noe St.
Sanchaz St.
Church St.
14th.
Henry St.
15th. St.
Castro St.
Market St.
16th. St.
18th. St.
19th St.
20th. St.
Liberty St.
21st. St.
Douglass St.
Eureaka St.
Diamond St.
Collingwood St.
N
1
2
3
4
5
6
7
8
9
10
11
12
13
14
15
16
17
18
19
20
21
22
23
24
25
26
27
28
29
30
31
32
33
34
35
36
37
38
39
40
41
42
43
44

1. Amancio Ergina Village

5. 1671 Golden Gate Ave.

1. **Amancio Ergina Village**
   1985, Daniel Solomon & Assoc.
   Scott, O'Farrell, Pierce, and Ellis Sts.
   One of the best of the subsidized housing projects built in the Western Addition redevelopment area, this 72-unit cooperative is both contemporary and compatible with the late 19th-century neighborhood around it.
2. **Beideman Place**
   c.1875-95
   Eddy St. to O'Farrell St., Scott St. to Divisadero St.
   Beideman Place town houses
   1989, Daniel Solomon and Assoc./John Goldman
   A mixed group of late l9th-century houses, three were moved here in 1976 and offered for sale by the Foundation for San Francisco's Architectural Heritage. The street also has a group of sympathetic contemporary town houses.
3. **Holy Cross Parish Hall**
   1854
   1822 Eddy St.
   The city's oldest church, on the exterior, is this simple frame building, formerly St. Patrick's. Originally built on Market Street where the Palace Hotel stands today, it was part of St. Ignatius College, founded by the Jesuits as the city's first institution of higher education. It was moved here in 1873 and remodeled in 1891 as a parish hall.
4. **House**
   1895, Henry W. Cleaveland
   1825 Turk St.
   A Queen Anne house of noble proportions on a large lot.
5. **House**
   c.1880
   1671 Golden Gate Ave.
   Moorish was stylish for firehouses and apartment buildings, but this seems to be the only Moorish house around.
6. **Andreozzi house**
   1886, John W. Dooley, contractor
   1016 Pierce St.
   A representative 1880s house with fine decorative detail.
7. **Missionary Temple, house row, and apartments**
   1892-c.1900
   1400 block Golden Gate Ave.

Flats
1884, John P. Gaynor
1400 block Golden Gate Ave.

Chateau Tivoli
1892-c.1900, William Armitage
1057 Steiner St.

The Classic Revival building at 1455 resembles a branch library. Next to it are some amazing c.1890 castellated Queen Anne apartment houses and across the street there is a row of speculative flats built in 1884 for $30,000.

7. 1400 block Golden Gate Ave.

7. Chateau Tivoli

8. **Apartments**
c.1900
1300 block of McAllister St.

A splendid row of late chateauesque Queen Anne flats. Across the street at No. 1347 is one of James F. Dunn's elegant Parisian Belle Epoque designs. One wishes Mr. Dunn had had a block to himself somewhere. In any case, this is worth seeing for its complexity and contradiction.

8. 1347 McAllister St.

9. **Houses**
1895, Cranston & Keenan, contractors
700-18, 701-11 Broderick St.

There is nothing like the Queen Anne style for bringing plasticity and rhythm to a streetscape. Plaster decorative motifs like those on 707 and 714 could be ordered by the piece from various catalogs of architectural decoration.

10. **Houses**

1255 Fulton St.
c.1895

Another Queen Anne to delight the eye of the visitor.

1201 Fulton St.
c.1895, Edgar Mathews

A cottage inspired by the English Arts and Crafts Movement, which drew inspiration from medieval building types like the Cotswold cottage.

10. 1201 Fulton St.

10. Westerfield house, tower

Westerfield house
1889, Henry Geilfuss
1198 Fulton St.
Geilfuss's style is particularly marked by a linear or modular organization of the elevations emphasized by vertical decorative wood strips. This so-called San Francisco Stick or Strip style is a variation on the eastern style that developed as a more direct but complicated expression of a building's invisible structural frame as exterior decoration.

12. 908 Steiner St.

10. Westerfield house

11. **House**
1894, A. J. Barnett
809-11 Pierce St.
And another fine Queen Anne house.

12. **House**
1888
908 Steiner St.
In 1967 this house became the first and most famous of a wave of rainbow-colored paint jobs. Since then fashion's wheel has turned and quiet colors reflect current taste. Who knows when the wheel will turn again?

Houses
910, 915, 921 Steiner St.
c.1895, Martens & Coffey

The Archbishop's Mansion
1904, Patrick Shea
1000 Fulton St.
An elegant exercise in the Classical Revival mode with a French touch in the Mansard roof. On the interior a huge hall has a curving three-story stairway that leads to the 15 bedrooms and a sitting room. The dining-room seats 50 guests. The house was designed for Archbishop Patrick Riordan and is now a bed-and-breakfast, which seems quite appropriate.

12. The Archbishop's Mansion

13. **Houses**
1890s
710-720 Steiner St. and 900 block of Grove St.
A rich and varied stand of houses, some built on speculation and others designed for affluent clients. Nos. 710-20 Steiner (1894-95), developed by Matthew Kavanaugh, are among the city's most published "painted ladies." No. 940 Grove, on the corner of Steiner (1895, Pissis & Moore), had an addition in 1971 by Beebe & Hersey. No. 814 Steiner dates from 1895, and No. 850, by T. Patterson Ross, dates from 1899. The Koster mansion at No. 926 Grove (1897) was designed by Martens & Coffey in the early Classic Revival style. No. 975 Grove sports a California golden bear on the chimney, while No. 957 (1886), designed by Samuel and Joseph Cather Newsom, cost all of $5,000.

13. 710-705 Steiner St.

14. **Houses**
1895, Martens & Coffey
820, 833-35 Fillmore St.
More examples of late Queen Anne exuberance.

15. **Brahma Kumaris Meditation Center**
c.1891
401 Baker St.
This former residence is an unusually large Queen Anne with two towers and a notable profusion of plaster ornament.

15. Brahma Kumaris Meditation Center

16. **House**
c.1895
1588 Fell St.

Thomas Clunie house
1897, William Curlett
301 Lyon St.
These two houses in the Queen Anne style are typical of the scale of residences in this prime location on the panhandle to Golden Gate Park. The Panhandle, as it was officially called, was landscaped in the 1870s under the park administration of William Hammond Hall; it was originally private and fenced. The eucalyp-

16. Thomas Clunie house

18. 411-15, 426 Shrader St.

20. Alonzo McFarland house

21.Phelps house

tus trees are the park's oldest; they shaded a curving drive that was crowded with the carriages of the wealthy on Sundays. The pretentious houses that line the one-by-eight-block park testify to the streets' former status.

Former Southern Pacific Hospital
1907, Daniel Patterson; rehabilitated, 1982, Lanier Sherrill Morrison
Baker and Fell Sts.
A fine Classic Revival style building converted to 185 units of housing for the city's elderly.

17. **Ohloff house**
1891, Charles I. Havens
601 Steiner St.
Another fine Queen Anne house owned by the Episcopal Diocese of San Francisco.

18. **Houses**
c.1890
411-15, 426 Shrader St.
The first house dates from 1890 and was built by Cornelius Murphy; the second is a particularly fine work by Samuel and Joseph C. Newsom. It shows the influence of C.F.A. Voysey and other architects of the the so-called English Domestic Revival Movement, which drew on medieval vernacular buildings and used such quaint detail as the rough-cast plasterwork in the gable ends that incorporates pouchlike swallows' nests.

19. **Apartments**
c.1895
1899, 1907 Oak St.
A matching pair of outstanding apartment buildings.

20. **Alonzo McFarland house**
1895, Coxhead & Coxhead
400 Clayton St.
Ernest Coxhead's manipulation of Classical ornament was so personal that it defies classification. He delighted in overscaling and intertwining traditional motifs and imposing them on plain, boxlike forms.

21. **Phelps house**
1850s; restored 1976, The Preservation Group
1111 Oak St.

Mish house
1885, McDougall & Son
1153 Oak St.
The Abner Phelps house was long thought to have been prefabricated and shipped from New Orleans, but in the course of restoration it was found to be of local construction. Originally a farmhouse and proba-

bly built from a carpenter's plan book, it was moved more than once, ending up in the middle of this block where for years it was invisible from the street. Now turned to face Oak Street and given a front yard, the house can be appreciated for its early Gothic Revival style, unique in the city. The Mish house next door is a grand Stick Style town house, also nicely restored in 1976 as part of this small office park called Phelps Place.

24. 1550 Page St.

22. 1901 Page St.

22. House
1896, Edward J. Vogel
1901 Page St.
A transitional style, called Queen Anne because of its finely scaled plaster decorative detail, and Colonial Revival for its Georgian form. Novelist Kathleen Norris once lived here.

23. House
c.1890, Cranston & Keenan
1777 Page St.
These designers spiced up their Queen Anne houses with unusual plaster ornament such as the owls used here.

24. Houses
1890s
1542-48, 1550 Page St.
The first houses (1891) are by Cranston & Keenan; the house at No. 1550 is either by them or by the Newsoms and is handsome in either case.

25. Houses
1899, Newsom & Myer
1478-80 Page St.

25. 1478-80 Page St.

The Queen Anne style tamed as it merged with Colonial Revival at the century's end.

26. Haight Ashbury Children's Center
1906
1101 Masonic Ave.
A substantial Classic Revival house, typical of the time period and architectural type.

27. 1390-92 Page St.

27. Apartments
c.1900
1390-92 Page St.
Craftsman style apartment houses that look like the work of Edgar Mathews, but have not been identified as such.

28. Former telephone exchange
1890
865 Page St.

28. Former telephone exchange

An exotic Moorish style applied inexplicaby to an early telephone exchange building.

29. 500-06, 508-16 Cole St.

29. Houses
c.1890, Cranston & Keenan
500-06, 508-16 Cole St.
The first house is an interesting switch in scale of the usual components of the Queen Anne house: a small tower is squeezed between two large gables. Typical of most, they were clearly trying to get their money's worth out of this large corner lot.

30. Flats
c.1910, James F. Dunn
1677-81 Haight St.
Parisian style flats.

Commercial building
1907
1660 Haight St.
A rare Art Nouveau storefront. Another example stands at 225 Frederick Street. Designed by August Nordin in 1912, it is less dramatic than the one on Haight Street.

30. Commercial building

31. All Saints Episcopal Church
c. 1915, Willis Polk
1350 Waller St.
A small church with residential scale in the Tudorish half-timber style not typical of Polk's work.

33. 142-60 Central Ave.

32. House row
1896-97, Cranston & Keenan
1214-56 Masonic Ave.
Another wonderful row of Queen Anne houses–especially No. 1226–by these builders, who were particularly active in the area at this time.

33. House row
1899, Daniel Einstein
142-60 Central Ave.
The towers have been fused with the bays so that the houses look as though they were wearing helmets.

34. 91 Central Ave.

34. Apartments
1904, James F. Dunn
91 Central Ave.
An extraordinary Classic Revival facade embellished with wonderful plaster heads.

35. House
1896, Fred P. Rabin
1080 Haight St.

House
1894, John J. Clark
1081 Haight St.
The Haight is introduced appropriately at this edge of the park by towered Queen Anne houses, perhaps the most typical-and certainly the most spectacular-building type in the area. In the next block is the Third Church of Christ, Scientist, 1918, by Edgar Mathews, very like the one at California and Franklin Streets.

36. Apartments
c.1907, Charles J. Rousseau
135-39 Pierce St.
Combination Mission Revival and Art Nouveau.

38. 806, 821-25, 857-61, 880 Ashbury St.

39. Casa Madrona Apartments

37. Haight Street Lofts

37. Haight Street Lofts

1996, Leddy Maytum Stacy

625 Haight St.

Twenty condominium units built on top of an existing garage building. Seventeen are lofts with 15-foot high ceilings, open mezzanines, large windows with industrial sash, and skylights at each end. All units face an interior court. Decorative panels on the sidewalk level are by Michelle Irwin and students in the LEAP program.

38. Houses

1908-12

806, 821-25, 857-61, 880 Ashbury St.

A wonderful potpourri of early 20th-century styles: No. 806 is a squeezed Classic Revival villa; Nos. 821-25 show French influence; No. 833 (1908), by Beasley & Beasley, is planned around a pleasant inner court; No. 857-61 is Elizabethan Revival enriched with plaster male faces; No. 880 (1908), by A. A. Cantin, is vintage Mission Revival. Mixed in are Colonial Revivals and other styles that defy description or easy categorization.

39. Casa Madrona Apartments

c.1920

110-16 Frederick St.

An unexpected oasis of Spanish Colonial Revival-style apartments with a pleasant courtyard. Just down the block at 130 Frederick is an apartment block of 1919 by A.H. Larsen, who did the much larger Clay-Jones Apartments on Nob Hill. And at No. 191 Frederick is the Crossways, a vaguely Mediterranean apartment block.

40. Houses

c.1900

1430, 1450, 1482 Masonic Ave.

Three remarkable houses in the same block. No. 1450 (1891) is by A. J. Barnett; No. 1482 is an unusual shingled Queen Anne with a corner dome.

41. **House**
1910, Bernard Maybeck
1526 Masonic Ave.
A subtle composition in staggered roof planes and voids where the balcony and entrance stair occur. Maybeck's deft touch in a modest shingled house.

42. **Richard Spreckels Mansion**
1897-98, Edward J. Vogel
737 Buena Vista Ave. West

43. 555 Buena Vista Ave. West

41. 1526 Masonic Ave.

A more imposing Queen Anne-Colonial Revival house than Vogel's other work in the neighborhood, but also with literary associations: both Ambrose Bierce and Jack London stayed here. Up the hill at No. 595-97 Buena Vista West is a pair of flats (c.1950) by Henry Hill, one of the post-World War II generation of Modern architects.

43. **Apartments**
c.1925, H. C. Baumann
555 Buena Vista Ave. West
One of Baumann's many neo-Churrigueresque apartment blocks located around the city.

44. **Norma Talmadge house**
1910
439 Roosevelt Way
Anchored to the shelf of the hill by a grand porch with Corinthian columns, this house, built for a famous silent screen star, is larger than it appears because it steps down the hill behind.

In December of 1845, Pio Pico, the last Hispanic governor of California granted the Rancho San Miguel to Jose de Jesus Noe, the last alcalde of Yerba Buena, the precursor of San Francisco under Mexican rule. The Rancho San Miguel comprised the land west of the Mission Dolores that continued west of Twin Peaks.

In 1854, Noe sold 600 acres to John M. Horner,who laid out the 180-block tract called Horner's Addition that stretched from Castro Street to Valencia Street. That same year a financial panic ruined Horner and delayed the development of his tract. When real estate activity resumed in the last quarter of the century, the area's most prominentdeveloper was Fernando Nelson who was born in 1860 in New York and came to San Francisco in the 1880s. Nelson begam work as a carpenter, mainly for other builders, and constructed his first home at 30th and Church Streets at the age of 22. In the 1890s, he acquired several adjacent lots around 20th and Castro Streets and in 1897 built a combination office and home for his family at that intersection. This house now stands at 701 Castro Street, the former site of Nelson's lumber yard. It was set atop a raised brick basement full of garages. Over the next four years Nelson built numerous residences in the Stick and Queen Anne styles in the area. Thirty-one documented flats and single-family houses survive on Castro, 20th, Eureka, Noe, 18th, and Hartford Streets. They may be recognized by a favorite Nelson decorative motif: rows of flat-sawn redwood circles called doughnuts that were joined together and set in a frieze above the front porches. Nelson's career lasted for 60 years during which he embraced new styles as they became popular.

Today the district is densely settled and has two main shopping streets, 18th and 24th, on either side of the hill that rises up between them. Not only is it the heart of the city's internationally known gay/lesbian community, but it is home to a mixed professional and working-class population that also contributes to the neighborhood's identity.

Castro / Noe Valley Diamond Heights

1. Shop and flats *4200 17th St.*
2. House *437-451 Noe St.*
3. Castro Theater *429 Castro St.*
4. Castro Condominiums *2426 Market St.*
5. Apartments *4600 18th St.*
6. Nobby Clarke's Folly *250 Douglas St.*
7. House *4015 21st St.*
8. Houses *700 block of Castro St.*
   House *3755 20th St.*
9. Apartments *741 Noe St.*
10. Casa Ciele *3615 21St.*
11. Former Fire House *3816 22nd St.*
12. Houses *2-6 and 22-24 Vicksburg St.*
13. James Lick Middle School *1220 Noe St.*
14. Commercial/Residential Buildlings *1500 and 1509 Church St.*
15. St. Paul's Church *Church and Valley Sts.*
16. Laidley Street Houses
    102 Laidley St.
    123 Laidley St.
    134 Laidley St.
    135 Laidley St.
    140 Laidley St.
17. Poole-Bell house *196-198 Laidley St.*
18. St. Aidan's Episcopal Church *101 Gold Mine Way*
19. Village Square *Diamond Heights Blvd. at Duncan St.*
20. St. Nicholas Syrian Orthodox Church *Diamond Heights Blvd. at Duncan St.*
21. Diamond Heights Village *Red Rock Way*
22. Twin Peaks Viewpoint

12

Previous page: View down Market Street from upper Market view point.

Parnassus Ave.
Grattan St.
Alma St.
Rivoli St.
17th. St.
Buena Vista Ave.
Hill Ave.
Roosevelt Park
States St.
Clifford Terr.
Roosevelt Way
Castro St.
Market St.
14th.
Henry St.
15th. St.
16th. St.
17th. St.
18th. St.
19th St.
20th. St.
Liberty St.
21st. St.
Hill St.
22nd St.
Alvarado St.
23nd.St.
Elizabeth St.
24th St.
Jersey St.
25th St.
Clipper St.
26th St.
27th St.
Duncan St.
28th St.
Valley St.
29th St.
Day St.
30th St.
Douglass St.
Eureaka St.
Diamond St.
Collingwood St.
Noe St.
Sanchaz St.
Church St.
Dolores St.
Corbett Ave.
Market St.
Grand View Ave.
Castro St.
Army / Cesar Chavez St.
Portola Dr.
Red Rock Way
Diamond Heights Blvd.
Laidley St.
Peaks Blvd.
1
2
3
4
5
6
7
8
9
10
11
12
13
14
15
16
17
18
19
20
21
22
N

12

1. Shop and Flats

1. **Shop and Flats**
   c.1890
   4200 17th St.
   A fine example of a popular 19th century vernacular building type: living quarters over commercial space. Here the corner bay of the flats soars off the hillside at an angle above an almost transparent base.
2. **Houses**
   c, 1890
   437 and 451 Noe St.
   Two Stick-style houses with towers mark the street corners. Across the street, nos. 460-476 Noe St. were built by Fernando Nelson, then a neighborhood resident and a prolific builder in the area.

3. Castro Theatre

3. **Castro Theatre**
   1923, Timothy Pflueger
   429 Castro St.
   Now a major venue for the San Francisco Film Festival and other major cinematic events, this theater was the flagship of the extensive operations of the Nasser Family, a pioneer motion picture family, who built their first theaters in Noe Valley. For their young architect, Timothy Pflueger, this was the first of the seven movie palances that his firm was to design. With seating for 1800 the Castro was still not the largest neighborhood theater of its day, but it was one of the most ornate. The Spanish Baroque style of its facade carries through to the interior where the auditorium itself is an extravaganza with the ceiling cast in plaster in to resemble a tent with swags, ropes, and tassels.

4. Castro Condominiums

4. **Castro Condominiums**
   1982, Dan Solomon & Assocs.
   2426 Market St.
   A skeletal entrance marks this cluster of stepped, white boxes nicely arranged on an awkward site.
5. **Apartment house**
   c. 1900
   4600 18th St.
   An elegant late Queen Anne house converted to apartments.

6. Nobby Clarke's Folly

6. **Nobby Clarke's Folly**
   1892
   Alfred Clarke was an assistant to the chief of police for some 30 years and somehow managed to save enough to build this Queen Anne mansion, which originally stood in a 17-acre park. It appears that

Clarke never lived in the house, and in 1904 it became a hospital. Following other uses and the sale of the grounds, the building was converted to apartments.

7. **House**
   1952, Wurster Bernardi & Emmons
   4015 21 St.
   A fine example of the kind of informal, yet clearly defined, house designed in many variations by this firm from the 1940s through the 1950s.

8. 740-46 Castro St.

8. **Houses**
   1897, Fernando Nelson
   701 Castro St.
   c. 1890
   712 Castro St.
   1894, Charles Hinkel
   740-46 Castro St.
   Two of the city's prominent late 19th century builders lived on this block. Nelson's own house at 701 Castro Steet. was originally on an adjacent lot; it was moved over the brick garages at a later date. By that time Nelson himself had moved to his fashionable new development, Presidio Terrace. Builder Hinkel, the builder, lived at 740 Castro St.

9. Moderne apartments

9. **Moderne apartments**
   c. 1940
   741 Noe St.
   White stuccoed boxes stepping down the hillside.

10. Casa Ciele

10. **Casa Ciele**
   1930
   3698 21st St.
   Built by James Rolph, son of one of San Francisco's colorful mayors, "Sunny Jim Rolph", this period-revival English cottage, hidden away in the pines, has a commanding view of downtown San Francisco.

11. **Former Fire House No. 44**
   c. 1910; remodeled 1962, Lanier & Sherrill
   3816 22nd St.
   A Mission Revival firehouse converted to artists' studios and residence.

11. Former Fire House No. 44

12. **Houses**
   1875
   2-6 Vicksburg St.
   c. 1910
   22-24 Vicksburg St.
   A lofty Italianate and a California Craftsman double house.

13. James Lick Middle School

13. James Lick Middle School
1932, Crim Resing & McGinniss; rehabilitated.
1973, City Architect
1220 Noe St.
Stylish Moderne ornamental detail distinguish this school building in contrast to the Spanish Colonial style of other school buildings in the Mission district.

14. Commercial-residential buildings
c.1890
1500, 1544 Church St.
Two unusually fine examples of this once common building type.

15. St. Paul's Roman Catholic Church and School

15. St. Paul's Roman Catholic Church and School
c. 1900, Frank Shea
Church and Valley Sts.
A rare local example of a Gothic Revival style, more common east of the Mississippi, that combined a monumental towered stone facade with an interior dimly lit by stained glass and punctuated by attenuated columns supporting plaster vaults. The interior is worth seeing.

16. Laidley Street houses
1981-1991

102 Laidley St.
Kotas/Pantaleoni

123, 135 Laidley St..
Jeremy Kotas

134 Laidley St.
Shaffer and Kotas

140 Laidley St.
Kotas and Shaffer

Rarely do architects have a chance to transform an entire street, one house at a time, and thus try out new ideas. In their work on this block of Laidley Street, Jeremy Kotas and Skip Shaffer have produced a series of sometimes funky and always adventurous houses.

16. 134 Laidley St.

17. Poole-Bell house
1872
196-198 Laidley St.
Built by an attorney, Cecil Poole, the house was sold in 1900 to Theresa Bell, ward of a notorious madam, Mammy Pleasant, who had considerable political power in late 19th century San Francisco politics.

18. St. Aidan's Episcopal Church
1963, Skidmore Owings & Merrill; 1979, school building, George Homsey, EHDD
101 Gold Mine Dr.

17. Poole-Bell house

An irregular hexagon with an interior lit by a hidden clerestory and windows in the manner of southwest missions. The repainted mural on the exterior is by Mark Adams, who also executed murals on the interior, which retain their original colors. The flame was St. Aidan's symbol.

18. St. Aidan's Episcopal Church

19. **Village Square**
    1972, Morris & Lohrbach
    East side of Diamond HeightsBlvd. between Duncan and Valley Sts.
    Good site planning and landscaping make this one of the more attractive developments on the Heights.

19. Village Square

20. **St. Nicholas Syrian Orthodox Church**
    1963, William F. Hempel
    Diamond Heights Blvd. and Duncan St.
    A contemporary version of the traditional domed plan of the Eastern Orthodox church.

20. St. Nicholas Syrian Orthodox Church

21. **Diamond Heights Village**
    1972, Gensler Assocs./Joseph Esherick & Assocs.
    Red Rock Way
    A well-sited group of shingled buildings that replaced the high-rise buildings of the original plan for Diamond Heights.
22. **Twin Peaks Viewpoint**
    On clear days you can see the city spread out like a carpet densely woven with a pattern of buildings that ripples over the hills and ends in the garden of form created by the downtown towers.

22. Twin Peaks Viewpoint

CESAR CHAVEZ STUDENT CENTER

In 1911, the A.S. Baldwin Residential Development Company purchased 725 acres of Adolph Sutro's vast oceanside estate. Ultimately, this land became Forest Hill,St. Francis Wood, Westwood Park, Balboa Terrace, and Monterey Heights. At first, the inaccessibility of these communities to the downtown business district was a problem. Although the United Railroad Company built a line out Ocean Avenue, the literal breakthrough was the Twin Peaks Tunnel, which made rapid transit available to downtown starting in 1918. Thereafter the communities west of Twin Peaks became popular for their remoteness from what many middle-class citizens regarded as urban chaos. City Engineer Michael O'Shaughnessy, who sponsored the tunnel, also blessed the area with another important link to downtown. This was Portola Drive, a scenic route that connected St. Francis Circle to the Twin Peaks extension of Market Street. From the Circle, Sloat Boulevard, also sponsored by O'Shaughnessy, completed the scenic tour to the ocean. The major north-south arterial, 19th Avenue, was paved in 1924; its intersection with Sloat deflned the borders of Sigmund Stern Memorial Grove.

While the following destinations do not cover all that is worth seeing in western San Francisco, they present a range of posibilities available to sightseers who are curious about what used to be called the "outer lands" and is still not readily identified with the city east of Twin Peaks.

13

West of Twin Peaks

1. Ingleside Terrace
   Houses:
   a. 282 Urbano Dr.
   b. 855 Urbano Dr.
   c. 77 Cedro Ave.
   d. 90 Cedro Ave.
   e. 140 Cedro Ave.
2. Westwood Park
   Houses
   598, 600, and 701 Miramar Ave.
3. San Francisco State University
   19th and Holloway Sts.
   Student Center
4. San Francisco Zoological Gardens *Sloat Blvd. and Zoo Rd.*
   The Mothers Building
5. Sigmund Stern Grove and The Trocadero Inn
   19th and Sloat Blvd.
6. St. Francis Wood
   Houses:
   a. 98 St. Francis Blvd.
   b. 30 St. Francis Blvd.
   c. 67 San Leandro Way
   d. 195 San Leandro Way
   e. 44 San Benito Way
   f. 61 San Andreas Way
   g. 85 Santa Monica Way
7. Forest Hill:
   a. Erlanger house
   270 Castenada Ave. at Lopez Ave.
   b. House *35 Lopez Ave.*
   c. E. C. Young house *51 Sotelo Ave.*

Previous page: Cesar Chavez Student Center on the San Francisco State University campus

ida Blvd.
c
b
a
Sotel Ave.
Lopez Ave.
Castenada Ave.
19th.
Woodside Ave.
7
Dewey Blvd.
Taraval St.
Vicente St.
Santa Monica
Portola Dr.
5
d
e
Santa Clara Ave.
4
Sloat Blvd.
6
St. Francis Blvd.
a
b
c
f
Monterey Ave.
Miramar Dr.
19th.
Junipero Serra Blvd.
e
d
Cedro Ave.
c
2
a
Ocean Ave.
Francisco State University
1
3
b
N
Holloway Ave.

13

1\. 140 Cedro

1\. 90 Cedro

1. **Ingleside Terrace**
   Urbano Drive traces the loop of the former Ingleside Race Track, opened in 1885. When the track shut down in 1909, Joseph Leonard and his Urban Realty Company purchased 148 acres of the track property and planned a parklike subdivision with the help of engineer J. M. Morser. The company managed the track until 1924 when it was largely built up with houses of various styles and sizes on lots 50 by l20 feet, twice the standard width. A special feature was a large sundial, located at the apex of the angled Entrada Court, that once had a reflecting pool and flower beds. Examples of the early houses designed by Leonard are 77 and 90 Cedro Avenue, 1911, in a shingled Craftsman style; 282 and 855 Urbano Drive, 1915, are also by Leonard. No.140 Cedro Avenue,1913, by William Curlett is an accomplished design in a mixed Mediterranean mode sometimes called "California." Other stripped down versions of the Mediterranean revival styles are common, and even the Californian International Modern style is represented.
2. **Westwood Park**
   1917-27, John M. Punnett, engineer
   Main entrance off Ocean Ave. at miramar Dr.
   The success of Ingleside Terrace may have influenced the plan of streets tracing concentric loops around a green in this subdivision of single-family houses uniformly set back from the streets. Representative examples of the houses are by Charles Strothoff at 598 Miramar Avenue and Ida F. McGain at 600 and 701 Miramar Avenue.

3. San Francisco State University, Student Center

3. **San Francisco State University**
   19th and Holloway Aves.
   Following the state's acquisition of land from the Spring Valley Water Company in 1937, the State Architect's office prepared a master plan for the university campus. Construction did not begin until

the late 1940s. The OSA was responsible for the design of the buildings until 1970, when the office ceased to be the official planners. The most architecturally interesting building on the campus is the 1980 neo-Corbusian Student Union designed by Paffard Keatinge Clay. The building is dominated by two pyramidal elements, one of which serves as an outdoor amphitheater. The lobby is a diagonal street entered through a pivoting slab door of enameled steel inspired by Le Corbusier's Chapel at Ronchamp in France.

5. Sigmund Stern Grove and the Trocadero Inn

4. **San Francisco Zoological Gardens**
   Sloat Blvd. and Zoo Rd.
   c. 1925, Lewis Hobart

   The Mothers Building
   1925, George W. Kelham
   A number of architects and landscape architects have worked at the zoo over the years refurbishing and remodeling its components. Fortunately, their contributions blend in with their surroundings. The whole site and its ensemble of structures is well worth a visit.

Entrance to St Francis Wood

5. **Sigmund Stern Grove and the Trocadero Inn**
   c.1890
   19th and Sloat Blvd.
   The site of one of the "outer lands" race tracks that was planted by George M. Greene with eucalyptus trees to shelter the crowds from sand-laden winds. Greene also built and named the picturesque Trocadero Inn, a remnant of the race track, that is now the park headquarters. In 1932, Mrs. Sigmund Stern purchased the site and gave it to the city. In 1938, the grove's free summer music festival was established–it continues to attract huge crowds.

St. Francis Wood

St. Francis Wood, the most prestigious residential tract west of Twin Peaks, featured 50-by-100-foot lots, underground utilities, a boulevard with a landscaped median strip, and tree-lined streets separated from sidewalks by planting. Because many of the trees came from the 1915 Panama Pacific Exposition's closing sale they were mature enough to give this suburb a proper garden setting. In 1912, the Olmsted Brothers laid out a central boulevard punctuated midway by a circle with a fountain and terminating in another fountain and terrace at the top of the rise. The entrance gates at Junipero Serra Boulevard and the terraces and fountains were designed by John Galen Howard and Henry Gutterson and installed in 1912-13. The main boundaries are major arterials:

6.b. 30 St. Francis Blvd.

6a. 98 St. Francis Blvd.

6d. 195 San Leandro Way

6f. 61 San Andreas Way

6g. 85 Santa Monica Way

Portola Drive, Santa Clara Aveue, Monterey Boulevard, and Ocean Avenue.

Three model homes designed by Louis C. Mullgardt and Henry Gutterson were built in 1913-15 at 40-44 San Benito Way,. Their simplifled Mediterranean styling struck a nice balance between historicism and modernism. Building proceeded slowly until the 1920s, when prosperous times and the effect of the Twin Peaks Tunnel connection to downtown brought the tract close to completion.

The largely Irish population seems to have come from the Mission district and other neighborhoods of the inner city where accelerating development threatened the suburban ambience of the streetcar neighborhoods. Those who moved to the Wood were not urbanites. They enjoyed the remote, near-wilderness quality of this outer fringe area where hunting small game was still a major diversion. A strong neighborhood association controlled architectural design and enforced the racial convenants, which were not broken until the 1950s. Architecturally, St. Francis Wood is a period piece of revivalism. Despite the fact that a number of notable architects contributed their talents, homogeneity of scale, color, and style–achieved through the controls–is the dominant effect. The outstanding achievement that distinguishes St. Francis Wood from the rest of the city's residential areas is the lushness and continuity of the landscaping, which is integrated with the general plan. Following is a selection of houses that attempts to cover the range of styles and to present designs by major architects. Although the list is not comprehensive, we hope the reader will be led on to make personal discoveries.

6. **St. Francis Wood houses**

a. **98 St. Francis Blvd.**
1917, Henry Gutterson; rem. 1929,

b. **30 St. Francis Blvd.**
1927, Masten & Hurd

c. **67 San Leandro Way**
1921, Julia Morgan

d. **195 San Leandro Way**
1917, Julia Morgan

e. **44 San Benito Way**
1913, Louis C. Mullgardt

f. **61 San Andreas Way**
1925, Henry Gutterson

g. **85 Santa Monica Way**
1925, Henry Gutterson

7. **Forest Hill**
1912-1913, Mark Daniels, plan and landscape design
Main entrance on Pacheco Street off Dewey Boulevard
As in Sea Cliff, Daniels's other subdivision, streets were laid out to follow the contours of the hill. Between the branching streets before Magellan, a triangular plot of lawn with a monumental urn suggests-but fails to create-a formal entrance like that of St. Francis Wood. Forest Hill is blessed with two houses by Bernard Maybeck, in addition to his 1919 Tudorish clubhouse for the Forest Hill Association at 381 Magellan Street. Houses of various sizes and styles line the curving streets. Do explore and enjoy the view from the vest-pocket park at the end of Mendosa Ave.

7a. Erlanger house

7c. E. C. Young house

a. **Erlanger house**
1916, Bernard Maybeck
270 Castenada Ave. at Lopez Ave.
The clients wanted a medieval English manor house, but the product resists classiflcation. The design reveals Maybeck's compositional skills and his ability to manipulate eclectic elements with originality.

7b. 35 Lopez Ave.

b. **House**
1915, Glenn Allen
35 Lopez Ave.
A Prairie style house with Sullivanesque ornament by an architect whose best known work is in Stockton. Another good Prairie style house is at 343 Montalvo Ave.

c. **E. C. Young house**
1913, Bernard Maybeck
51 Sotelo Ave.
An intriguing play on the Tudorish half-timber style, with some features (the pulpitlike corner balcony with quatrefoils and the half-timber supergraphics) that are architectural puns.

Most of today's visitors to Golden Gate Park are probably unaware that it was once miles of shifting sand dunes well west of the city's edge. The concept of a park in this sparsely settled area arose in the 1860s when members of the Outside Lands Commission invited Frederick Law Olmsted, creator of New York's Central Park, to consider the idea. He pronounced the prospective site hopeless, but, happily, his advice was ignored. In 1870, William Hammond Hall, an ex-Army engineer, was appointed the park's first superintendent. In five years, despite inadequate support, he had designed the park, figured out how to anchor the sand dunes by planting imported sand grass and how to make trees grow. He had also started to landscape the barren waste at the park's east end. But he was no politician, and after struggling vainly against budget cuts and political intrigue he resigned in disgust. In 1887, he was wooed back, but assumed his former position only long enough to hire his successor, the famous "Uncle John" McLaren, who is now widely and erroneously assumed to have designed Golden Gate Park.

McLaren's tenure as superintendent lasted from 1886 to 1943, when he died in office at the age of 96. A wise tyrant, skilled gardener, and adroit politician, he completed the park, landscaped the Panama-Pacific International Exposition, planted Dolores Street's parks, and generally dominated the city's landscape planning for 60-odd years. The park that Hall designed and McLaren built is one of the country's great examples of romantic landscape design. About three miles long and only one-half mile wide, The park provides maximum green frontage to the city on either side and, thanks to careful grading and planting, a great variety of sheltered and secluded areas. The fog insures the survival of the lawns despite intensive use. Since much of the vegetation is not deciduous, the park is perennially green. Major museums occupy the park along with monuments and notable works of architecture. But above all it is, as all great urban parks are, a piece of the country in the city.

The history of the Outside Lands was tied to the development of transportation. Before they were tamed by rail and car lines, horse racing, dairy farming, and gunpowder production occupied these sandy lands. The Sunset was so named by its first developer, Aurelius E. Buckingham, in 1887. His residential tract extended a few blocks south of the park on 5th Avenue and along Lincoln Way. At that time there were hardly 20 houses between Stanyan and the ocean. Development lagged until the 1894 Mid-Winter Exposition in Golden Gate Park and gained momentum in the decades after the completion of the Twin Peaks Tunnel in 1918. As the streets and car lines multiplied, prospective buyers began to settle the western areas, often to escape the density of the older inner city neighborhoods. The Sunset's many builders borrowed and stole designs from each other, keeping a weather eye out for what was selling.Thus, despite the studied variation in facade treatment, the area's architectural homogeneity is its most memorable trait.

Golden Gate Park & Vicinity

1. **St. Ignatius Church** *Fulton and Parker Sts.*
2. **Neptune Society Columbarium** *1 Lorraine St.*
3. **Roosevelt Middle School** *460 Arguello St.*
4. **Former clubhouse** *325 Arguello St.*
5. **McLaren Lodge** *Kennedy Dr. near Stanyan St.*
6. **Alford Lake Bridge near the** *Conservatory on Kezar Dr.*
7. **Conservatory of Flowers** *John F. Kennedy Dr. south side*
8. **Children's Playground** *between Kezar and Bowliing Green Dr.*
9. **U. C. S. F. School of Dentistry** *707 Parnassus St.*
10. **Parkview Commons** *Frederick and Willard Sts.*
11. **Music Concourse** *between Tea Garden and Concourse Drs.*
12. **M. H. de Young Memorial Museum** *Tea Garden Dr.*
13. **Japanese Tea Garden** *Tea Garden Dr.*
14. **California Academy of Sciences** *Concourse Dr.*
15. **Strybing Arboretum and Botanical Gardens** *Martin Luther King Jr. Dr.*
16. **Christ the Savious Greek Orthodox Church** *490 12th Ave.*
17. **Alice Fong Yu Alternative Middle School** *1541 12th Ave.*
18. **Former San Francisco Conservatory of Music** *1201 Ortega St.*
19. **Former Shriners Hospital** *1701 19th Ave.*
20. **The Dutch and the Murphy Windmills** *park west end near the Great Highway*
21. **The Beach Chalet** *1000 Great Highway*
22. **Doelger City** *27th-39th Ave, Kirkham-Ortega St.*

14

Previous page: Japanese Tea Garden pavilion in Golden Gate Park

14

1. St. Ignatius Church

1. **St. Ignatius Church**
   1914, Charles J. Devlin; chapels restored in 1995 by Brayton & Hughes
   Fulton & Parker Sts.
   Although its hilltop location guaranteed that this monumental church would be seen from many parts of the city, its scale and accomplished Neo-Baroque style make it a major city landmark. Built to replace the St. Ignatius Church at Van Ness Avenue and Hayes Street that burned in 1906, the church is part of the Jesuit University of San Francisco. The interior is well worth seeing; its excellent accoustics make the church a popular concert venue.

   Geschke Learning Center
   1997, Esherick Homsey Dodge & Davis
   Main campus, east of St. Ignatius Church and in front of the Gleeson Library
   A 36,000 sq. ft. addition to the University libraries to expand services, its most prominent feature is the 5,000 sq.ft. Monihan Atrium that anchors the east end of the center.

2. Neptune Society Columbarium

2. **Neptune Society Columbarium**
   1898; B.J. S. Cahill
   1 Loraine Court off Anza St.
   This columbarium was originally associated with the Lone Mountain cemeteries, which were removed to Colma beginning in 1917 because of public health regulations. Since the columbarium was technically not a burial site, it survived the removal, but was closed for many years. Recently acquired by the Neptune Society, the building has been restored and is once again in use and open to the public. The Neo-Baroque rotunda has a 75-foot high dome crowned with a stained glass cap; the richly decorated interior is a wonderful surprise.

2. Neptune Society Columbarium

3. **Roosevelt Middle School**
   1934, Miller & Pflueger
   460 Arguello Blvd.
   Fine constructivist brickwork reminiscent of European Expressionist buildings of the late 1910s and 1920s make this building one of the city's most distinguished works of public school architecture.

3. Roosevelt Middle School

4. **Former clubhouse, now a private residence**
   1929, Henry Gutterson
   325 Arguello Blvd.
   A residentially scaled complex with an inviting forecourt and a rich combination of Arts and Crafts materials.

5. McLaren Lodge

5. **McLaren Lodge**
(park museum and information center)
1897, E. R. Swain
North of John F. Kennedy Dr. near the east entrance
Built as the superintendent's residence, this Romanesque Revival style building in rusticated sandstone with a tile roof is reminiscent of H. H. Richardson's work and that of his successor firm, Shepley Rutan and Coolidge, at Stanford University.

6. **Alford Lake Bridge**
1889, Ernest Ransome
Pedestrian underpass
Kezar Dr. opp. Haight St.
Although the design does its best to deny its material

7. Conservatory

by using concrete to imitate stones dripping with mossy stalactites, this is the country's first reinforced concrete bridge.

7. **Conservatory**
1878, Hammersmith Works, Dublin, Ireland; 2003, rehabilitation by Architectural Resources Group/ Jeffrey Miller, landscape architect
John F. Kennedy Dr. opp. 4th Ave.
James Lick died before the magical greenhouse he had ordered for his San Jose estate could be erected. Later, Leland Stanford and others purchased it for the park. In 1995, a winter storm severely damaged the structure–the park's oldest–but it has been beautiful restored and restocked with a veritable jungle. The building, its setting, and its contents marvelously recapture the 19th-century obsession with collecting exotic vegetation.

8. Sharon Children's House

10. Parkview Commons

11. The Music Concourse

12. M. H. de Young Memorial Museum, under construction

8. **Children's Playground**
   Sharon Children's House
   1886, Percy & Hamilton; 1978, Michael Painter & Associates, landscape architects
   Kezar Dr. near 1st Ave.
   The playground occupies the site of a lake filled by leveling a nearby hill. The precedent for a children's playground came from New York's Central Park. The concept was typical of the social planning of the time and had great popular support. The Children's House, which holds all manner of child-oriented delights, is the city's purest surviving example of Richardsonian Romanesque. Heavily damaged in the 1906 earthquake, as were other masonry structures in the park, it was rebuilt within the year. The carousel dates from c.1892. In 1978 Michael Painter redesigned the playground.

9. **U. C. S. F. School of Dentistry**
   1980, John Funk & Assocs.
   707 Parnassus St.
   A well-detailed building that steps down the slope in terraced forms that diminish the effect of its size.

10. **Parkview Commons**
    1990, David Baker & Assoc.
    Frederick and Willard Sts.
    An exemplary development designed to integrate 114 units of affordable housing into the older fabric of the Haight-Ashbury using three-story buildings containing both flats and two-story houses.

11. **The Music Concourse**
    The sculptural rhythm of the pollarded plane trees makes this great formal space a perfect contrast to the surrounding lush, romantic landscape. The focus is the Music Pavilion, given by Claus Spreckels and designed by the Reid Brothers in 1899.

12. **M. H. de Young Memorial Museum**
    2005, Herzog & de Meuron/Fong & Chan; Walter Hood, landscape architect
    Tea Garden Dr.
    The new de Young museum, scheduled to open in the fall of 2005, replaces a remodeled 1915 building by Louis Christian Mullgardt demolished in 2003. The new building's exterior is clad with 7,200 perforated copper panels with patterns modeled after images of light filtering through tree foliage that give the interior a transparency and a linkage to the park outside. The copper will turn blue-green over time as the salt air reacts with the metal. The building is internally divided into three long interwoven fingers punctuated by Interior garden courts that contribute

to a varied sequence of spaces designed to match the wide range of exhibits. The museum's three levels have 293,000 sq. ft. with more than 84,000 square feet of exhibition space. A large central court inside the main entrance provides access to the galleries. A spiraling 9-story tower, 144 feet tall, houses the museum's education programs; the observation deck on the top floor offers panoramic views in all directions.

13 . Japanese Tea Garden

13 . Japanese Tea Garden

1894, George Turner Marsh/Makoto Hagiwara

Conceived by Marsh, an Australian, who was the country's first Oriental art dealer, and designed and built by a Japanese landscape gardener, this garden attracts a major share of the park's visitors with good reason. Originally built for the 1894 Mid-Winter Exposition, the park's first major public event, the garden proved so popular that it was preserved. From 1907 to 1942 the Hagiwara family ran the concession and along the way invented fortune cookies. In 1942

13 . Japanese Tea Garden

13 . Japanese Tea Garden

13 . Japanese Tea Garden,

they were evacuated to an internment camp in Utah. In 1978 Ruth Asawa, who was also a victim of the World War II Japanese relocation program, designed a bronze plaque honoring the Hagiwaras; it is located near the entrance. The Japanese Tea Garden has many special features that are marked for visitors.

14. California Academy of Sciences

2008, Renzo Piano/Gordon Chong & Partners

S. side of the Music Concourse

The former Academy of Sciences was demolished in 2004; its replacement, designed by Renzo Piano, has an undulating green–yes, planted–roof to reflect the city's hilly terrain.

This roof will shelter a new complex of buildings, the design of which is not set at this writing. If all goes well, the opening is planned for 2008.

17. Alice Fong Yu Alternative Middle School

18. Former San Francisco Conservatory of Music

19. Former Shriners Hospital

20. The Dutch Windmill

15. The Strybing Arboretum and Botanical Gardens
1940
Martin Luther King, Jr. Dr. south of the Japanese Tea Garden
Now occupying some 55 acres of the park, the gardens have over 7,000 plant species that represent different parts of the world.

16. Christ the Saviour Greek Orthodox Church
1966, Esherick Homsey Dodge & Davis
490 12th Ave.
A serenely simple design that effectively communicates its purpose through a small, blue onion dome.

17. Alice Fong Yu Alternative Middle School
2001, Herman & Coliver/Levy Design Partners/ Nancy Severan; Brian Lazco, landscape architect
1541 12th th Ave.
A modernization and expansion of a K-5 elementary school dedicated to immersion in the Chinese language. The design of the new middle school responded to the client's wish to create a different identiry for its campus. The new classrooms, library, science lab, and arts studio step up the hillside site and recall a Chinese rural village with a covered walkway as its street. The Chinese emphasis is also reflected in the buildings' color scheme. The school garden is the product of many years of volunteer work by parents and children that was amplified in the new landscaping created by a professional designer.

18. Former San Francisco Conservatory of Music
1928, Louis C. Mullgardt
1201 Ortega at 19th Ave.
A monumental Mission Revival style building designed by an architect who had considerable talent but few commissions in the city.

19. Former Shriners Hospital
1923; 2002, BAR
1701 19th Ave.
A landmark on this crosstown arterial notable for its terra cotta ornament and human scale. Converted to housing for the elderly, the building is associated with new row housing located behind it on a secondary street off 20th Avenue.

20. The Dutch Windmill and the Murphy Windmill
Golden Gate Park, west end
The so-called Dutch Windmill was designed by Alpheus Bull, Jr., a mechanical engineer employed by the Union Iron Works, and completed in 1903. The base is a five-foot thick, concrete wall, 33 feet in diameter. The wooden tower and sails were restored by 1981, but they produce no power. When completed

in 1905, the Murphy Windmill was said to be the largest one in the world; it stands 95 feet tall with spars measuring 114 feet from tip to tip. The windmills were built to alleviate the park's chronic water shortage by pumping thousands of gallons of water underground. However, they have not pumped water since 1927, when an electric pump installed in the Murphy mill assumed that function.

21. Beach Chalet

21. **Beach Chalet**

1924, Willis Polk; 1936-37, murals and other decorative art by Lucien Labault

This hipped-roof pavilion in a Spanish Colonial Revival style is reputed to be Willis Polk's last design; he did not live to see it built. In the late 1930s, the artist Lucien Labault obtained funds from the Works Progress Adminitration's Federal Art Project to create mural paintings, mosaics, and wooden sculptures for the ground floor and staircase. The subject matter, the recreational activities of San Franciscans of the time, included portraits of prominent people. The building was closed from 1981 until 1996, when it reopened after restoration and installation of a visitor center.

22. Doelger City

22. **Doelger City**

1930s to 1950s

Kirkham to Ortega St., 27th to 39th Ave., approximate boundaries

Kirkham to Ortega St., 27th to 39th Ave., approximate boundaries

The Sunset was mainly developed in the post-World War II decades by the Big Five: the Gellert Brothers, the Stoneson Brothers, the Doelgers, Chris McKeon, and Ray Galli, who began building in the 1920s and 1930s. Miles of bare land were carpeted with homes, some built by Henry and Frank Doelger at the rate of two a day. While not exclusively built by the Doelgers, Doelger City suggests the magnitude of their operations: from 1934 to 1941 they were the country's largest single home builders. The Doelgers were committed to building well for the average family. Creating the floor plan was the first step in the design process; the last step was, as Henry put it, "puting on the architecture." This involved drawing up house fronts with various stylistic themes, English Cottage, French Provincial, Regency, and Colonial, which were then adapted to the plan and built. The contrast between the house fronts and backs reveals this process. In the post-World War II housing boom some of the period-revival styles were replaced with versions of the California ranch house.

The area west of Presidio Avenue and north of California Street is known as Presidio Heights because its northern boundary extends along the ridge above the Presidio grounds; the area's character does not differ from that of Pacific Heights. However, those residents who enjoy the Presidio forest as "borrowed scenery" may be a bit more fortunate.

Arguello Boulevard marks the passage from Presidio Heights to the Richmond district, which grew westward toward the ocean from the 1910s through the post-World War II decades. The availability of cheap land with some transportation encouraged developers who were building in the Mission and other inner neighborhoods at the turn of the 19th century to buy up small parcels in the outer areas and build modest homes. Fernando Nelson, for example, who had built many houses in Noe Valley, created Jordan Park and Presidio Terrace. Lot-by-lot construction of single houses mainly took place in the inner Richmond. More custom-designed homes were designed for the dead-end blocks next to the Presidio, which enjoyed the same parklike scenery as Presidio Heights. The opening of the Municipal Railway line on Geary Boulevard in 1912 was a boon to development because it offered good transit to downtown. In 1917 the area was officially named Park Presidio, partly to avoid confusion with the city of Richmond across the bay but also to signal an end to the past when the area was known as the "Great Sand Waste." The new name did not stick.

The Richmond's varied ethnicity–Russians and East European Jews settled here in significant numbers–has not stamped its architecture in any significant way. But the gastronomic impact of the Asians, particularly the Chinese who overflowed from Chinatown, has been considerable. The commercial strips along Geary Boulevard, Clement, and California Streets from Park Presidio Boulevard to Arguello Boulevard offer enough eateries to assuage the hunger of tourists and residents alike.

Presidio Heights/The Richmond

1. **Houses** *3200 block of Pacific Ave.*
2. **Double house** *21-23 Presidio Ave.*
3. **Houses** *2 Laurel St. and 3300 block of Pacific Ave.*
4. **King house** *50 Laurel St.*
5. **House** *3450 Washington St.*
6. **House** *3340 Washington St.*
7. **House** *3362 Clay St.*
8. **House** *3581 Clay. St.*
9. **Houses** *250 and 301 Locust St.*
10. **House** *3779 Clay St.*
11. **House** *3550 Jackson St.*
12. **Roos house** *3500 Jackson St.*
13. **Houses** *3638 and 3690 Washington St.*
14. **Goldman house** *3700 Washington St.*
15. **Russell house** *3778 Washington St.*
16. **Koshland house** *3800 Washington St.*
17. **Batten house** *116 Cherry St.*
18. **Presidio Terrace**
19. **House** *166 Arguello St.*
20. **Temple Emanu-El** *Arguello Blvd. and Lake St.*
    St. John's Presbyterian Church *Arguello Blvd. and Lake St.*
21. **Jordan Park** *Arguello Blvd. to Commonwealth Ave.; California St. to Geary Blvd.*

The Presidio

22. **New Letterman Digital Arts Complex** *Letterman Dr.*
23. **Thoreau Center for Sustainability** *Torney Ave. and Licoln Blvd.*
24. **Bay School** *35 Keyes Ave.*
25. **Army Museum former Wright General Hospital** *Funston Ave.*
26. **Officers Quarters** *Funston Ave.*
27. **Pershing Hall** *head of Funstron Ave.*
28. **Moore Foundation Building** *Mesa St.*
29. **Barracks** *Montgomery St.*
30. **Crissy Field Center** *Mason St.*
    Crissy Field *Bay shore to Mason St.*
31. **Marine Sanctuary Visitor Center** *on the Bay off Mason St.*
32. **Ft. Point** *on the Bay by Golden Gate Bridge*
33. **Artillery Gun Emplacements** *Lincoln Blvd.*
34. **Fort Winfield Scott** *Ralston Ave.*

Seacliff and Lincoln Park

35. **Houses 9 25 45 Scenic Way**
36. **Palace of the Legion of Honor Art Museum** *34th Ave. and Clement St. or El Camiino del Mar*
37. **Sutro Heights and the Cliff House** *Point Lobos Rd. at the Pacific Ocean*

Previous page: Presidio grounds

3rd. Ave.
2nd. Ave.
Angello Blvd.
Palm Ave.
Jordan Ave.
Commonwealth Ave.
Parker Ave.
Arguello Blvd.
Cherry St.
Maple St.
Spruce St.
California St.
Locust St.
Laurel St.
Walnut St.
Presidio Ave.
Lyon St.
Sacramento St.
Clay St.
Washington St.
Jackson St.
Pacific Ave.
1
2
3
4
5
6
7
8
9
10
11
12
13
14
15
16
17
18
19
20
21
22
23
24
25
26
27
28
29
30
31
32
33
34
35
36
Golden Gate Bridge
Wedemeyer St.
Washington Blvd.
Kobe Ave.
Park Blvd.
McDowell Ave.
101
Doyle Dr.
Lincoln Blvd.
Presidio Blvd.
Lombard St.
Lake St.
Clement St.
N

15

1. 3200 block Pacific Ave.

1. 3200 block Pacific Ave.

1. 3232 Pacific Ave.

2. 21-23 Presidio Ave.

Presidio Heights/The Richmond

1. **Houses:**

   3200 Pacific Ave.
   1918

   3203 Pacific Ave.
   c. 1890; remodeled c. 1904, Willis Polk

   3232 Pacific Ave.
   1902, Ernest Coxhead; remod. 1959, John Funk

   3233 Pacific Ave.
   1909, Bernard Maybeck

   3234 Pacific Ave.
   1902, Ernest Coxhead

   3235 and 3236-40 Pacific Ave.
   c. 1910, William F. Knowles

   3255 Pacific Ave.
   c. 1910, Ernest Coxhead; remod., Willis Polk

   This steep block is an architectural treasure trove for admirers of what has been called the First Bay Tradition, a west coast Shingle style that mixes elegant details with informality in materials and form. Nowhere else in the city is there such a harmonious stand of such houses. The architect's names are a roster of the turn-of-the-century group of easterners who produced the first flowering of regional design.

2. **Double house**
   c. 1900; remod. 1915, Bruce and Robert Porter
   21-23 Presidio Ave.

   Bruce Porter, a talented amateur, contributed to the First Bay Tradition in architecture, stained glass, and landscape design. His own house, designed for him by his friend, Ernest Coxhead, is around the corner at 3234 Pacific Avenue.

3. **Houses:**

   2 Laurel St.
   c. 1945; remod. Clark & Beuttler

   3377 Pacific Ave.
   1908, Julia Morgan

   3355 Pacific Ave.
   1925, Louis M. Upton

   3343 and 3333 Pacific Ave.
   1903, Albert Farr

   3323 Pacific Ave.
   1963, Joseph Esherick

   Though not a showcase for idiosyncratic design like the next block, the houses in this block quietly affirm the strength of the tradition. No. 2 Laurel and No. 3323 Pacific Ave. are respectful modern additions.

4. **Frank King house**
   1917, Bliss & Faville
   50 Laurel St.
   A huge Georgian Revival house on a small site. Another one is across the street.

5. **House**
   1929, Willis Polk
   3450 Washington St.

5. 3450 Washington St.

6. 3340 Washington St.

7. 3362 Clay St.

9. 250 Locust St.

6. **House**
   1912 Oliver Everett
   3340 Washington St.
   A lavishly decorated town house in a version of the French Second Empire style that seems several decades behind the times.

7. **House**
   1895, Coxhead & Coxhead
   3362 Clay St.
   Compare this house with those by Coxhead in the 3200 block of Pacific Avenue. A garage was added to the front side in 2003.

8. **House**
   1909, Bliss & Faville
   3581 Clay St.

9. **Houses**
   250 Locust St.
   1945, Wurster, Bernardi & Emmons

11.House, 3550 Jackson St.

12. Roos house, balcony

13. 3638 Washington St.

301 Locust St.
1954, Wurster, Bernardi & Emmons
From Modernistic formality to Modern Bay Region informality.

10. **House**
1907, Stone & Smith
3779 Clay St.
A quirky design on a corner lot that combines elements of the Craftsman and the Mission Revival styles. Next door is a house with a facade appliqued with ornament like a costume.

11. **House**
1940 Michael Goodman
3550 Jackson St.
An straightforward expression of the International Modern style that later acquired a more regional character.

12. Roos house

12. **Roos house**
1909, 1925, Bernard Maybeck
3500 Jackson St.
Maybeck's most imposing residence in the city for which he designed the interior appointments and some furniture. The half-timbered English Tudor mode is enlivened by Maybeck's personalized Gothic ornamental details in the roof brackets and balcony railing.

13. **Houses**
c. 1900, Bliss & Faville
3638 Washington St.
1928, Arthur Brown, Jr.
3690 Washington St.
Two houses that draw on the Classical vocabulary

of form and ornament in different ways. Note the variety of stair windows on the side elevation of the first house.

14. Goldman house

14. **Goldman house**
1951, Joseph Esherick
3700 Washington St.
A straightforward wooden box that balances the barnlike informality of vertical siding and double-hung windows with delicate railings and concrete columns that used sonotubes as forms. The L-plan creates an elegant garden court and a processional entranceway sheltered from the street.

16. Koshland house

15. **Russell house**
1952, Eric Mendelsohn
3778 Washington St.
Except for the trace of early Mendelsohn streamlining in the rounded corner bay and porthole windows, this house, well sited in its parklike setting, is a fine example of the second wave of Bay Area regionalism.

16. **Koshland house**
1902, Frank Van Trees
3800 Washington St.
The facade of Marie Antoinett's Petit Trianon copied and incorporated into a grand house where guests were invited to musical evenings held in an interior court with a glazed dome. A comparison with the Russell residence across the street reveals how the image of a mansion changed in 50 years.

17. **Batten house**
1892, Willis Polk
116 Cherry St.
An early house by Polk that is a study in the manipulation of facade elements to create balanced asymmetry.

18. **Presidio Terrace**
1905, Fernando Nelson, developer
This exclusive development with house by prominent architects was the crowning achievement of Nelson's prolific building career. His own house of 1930, designed by W. R. Yelland, occupies the most prominent site on the left just past the entrance at No. 30.

9 Presidio Ter.
c.1910, Albert Farr

10 Presidio Ter.
c.1910, Charles Whittlesey

16 Presidio Ter.
1905, Bakewell & Brown

18. 30 Presidio Ter.

20. Temple Emanu-El

20. St. John's Presbyterian Church

19 Presidio Ter.
c.1910, Charles Whittlesey

20 Presidio Ter.
1910, Lewis P. Hobart

23 Presidio Ter.
c.1910, Julius E. Krafft & Sons

28 Presidio Ter.
1908-09, A. F. Whittlesey

30 Presidio Ter.
1930, W. R. Yelland

32 Presidio Ter.
c.1910, Charles Whittlesey

34 Presidio Ter.
c.1910, George Applegarth

36 Presidio Ter.
1911, Julia Morgan

19. House
c. 1903, Sidney B. Newsom & Noble Newsom
166 Arguello Blvd.
The second generation of Newsoms designed this high and narrow, vaguely Elizabethan house.

20. Temple Emanu-El
1924-26, Arthur Brown, Jr., John Bakewell, Jr., Sylvan Schaittacher; Bruce Porter, int. dec.; Bernard Maybeck, G. Albert Lansburgh, Edgar Walter, consultants
NW corner Arguello Blvd, and Lake St.
A monumental Neo-Byzantine temple with a handsome forecourt. The interior is richly appointed and well worth visiting. The stained glass windows, Fire and Water, installed in 1972-73, are by Mark Adams.

St. John's Presbyterian Church
1905
SW corner Arguello Blvd. and Lake St.
A fine brown-shingled church with a country parish look that reflects the Richmond district's state of development in the early 1900s. The building incorporates pews, pulpit furnishings, and the rose window from the original church of c. 1870. Other fine stained glass windows come from a second church of 1888.

21. Jordan Park
1900-1920s, Joseph Leonard, Urban Realty Co.
Arguello Blvd. to Commonwealth Ave.; California St. to Geary Blvd.
Detached houses uniformly set back from the street compose a suburban streetscape with landscape amenities such as palm trees on Palm Avenue. The

houses listed here were chosen both for architectural interest and to present the range of styles in Jordan Park. Joseph Leonard also developed Ingleside Terrace.

21. 12 Jordan Ave.

12 Jordan Ave.

55 Jordan Ave.

57 Jordan Ave.

71 Jordan Ave.

85 Jordan Ave.

20 Palm Ave.

104 Palm Ave.

129 Palm Ave.

30 Euclid Ave.

620 Euclid Ave.

The Presido

The history of the Presidio spans over 200 years of development under three nations: Spain, Mexico, and the U.S.A. Established by the Spanish in 1776 as the military counterpart of the Mission Dolores, the Presidio began as a small compound with a few structures of adobe–a sorry excuse for a fort. In 1847 an American Presidio garrison was established, but in 1855 its five buildings were described as "unsightly mud enclosures." In 1862 the Army built twelve wooden cottages for officers along the eastern side of the parade ground. The post hospital was built in 1864 along with some other wooden structures and a stone magazine.

The Main Post continued to expand during the 1880s and 1890s. A forestation plan prepared by Major William A. Jones in 1883 proposed planting the Presidio's three ridges with trees and leaving the valleys treeless so that the ridges would appear higher and the valleys larger than they were. The plan was designed to create a background of forest overlooking extensive grassy stretches. No other military base in the country had such a landscape plan. San Franciscans joined in the subsequent landscaping campaigns such as one that called for planting 60,000 Monterey pines by 1896. The Presidio also benefited from the expertise of an army engineer, Major William W. Harts, who created a master plan for the reservation in 1907. Whether Harts consulted Daniel H. Burnham (who prepared the famous, unimplemented 1904 plan for San Francisco), whom he knew, or simply drew on Burnham's planning ideas, his plan has elements of the City Beautiful Movement's approach to civic design.

Beside the main post, the other architecturally notable campus is Fort Winfield Scott, built on a ridge on the west side of the reservation from about 1910 to 1912. Major Harts was again involved, calling for buildings designed in "the old Spanish style," now known as Mission Revival. Although the style was already popular in California, this was the first use of it for military buildings.

In 1994, the U. S. Army closed the base and turned over the management of the Presidio to the National Park Service. In 1996, Congress created the Presidio Trust, which shares both the management of the site with the NPS and the goal of preserving the Presidio's natural and historic resources. Since that time plans have evolved to rehabilitate the historic buildings and lease them to private owners. The William Penn Mott, Jr. visitors center in the former Officers Club has maps and information about current uses of the buildings and the restoration of the natural landscape. There are 473 historic structures and numerous historic landscape features. The Presidio buildings encompass a range of architectural styles adopted by the military over time. Standard plans issued by the Army were used but adapted when necessary to unusual conditions. Contemporary idioms are used for the interiors of rehabilitated buildings, which must preserve their historic exteriors.

23. Thoreau Center for Sustainability

22. New Letterman Digital Arts Complex
2005, Gensler Architecture Design and Planning; Lawrence Halprin, landscape architect
Letterman Dr.
The overall site has nearly 25 acres with two important view corridors, one of which focuses on the Palace of Fine Arts rotunda. The four new buildings are sited in a L-plan with an 8-acre undulating meadow within the ell and a 170-foot long lagoon. The buildings themselves were designed to complement the utilitarian aesthetic of the Presidio's historic buildings on the Main Post.

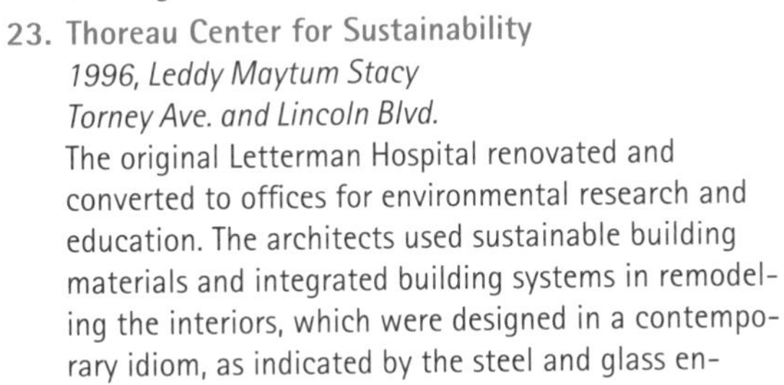
23. Thoreau Center for Sustainability
1996, Leddy Maytum Stacy
Torney Ave. and Lincoln Blvd.
The original Letterman Hospital renovated and converted to offices for environmental research and education. The architects used sustainable building materials and integrated building systems in remodeling the interiors, which were designed in a contemporary idiom, as indicated by the steel and glass entrance canopy.

25. Army Museum

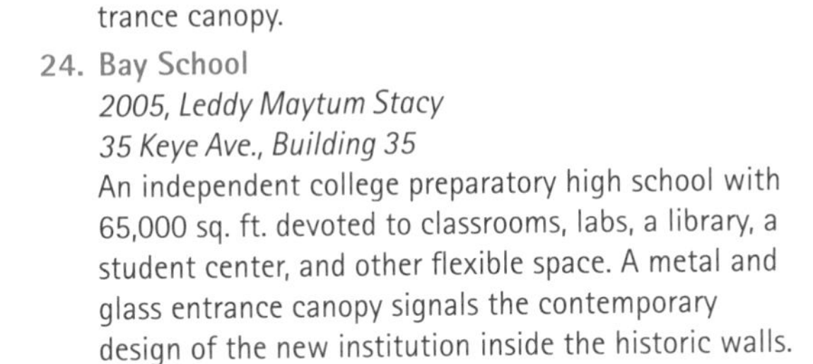
24. Bay School
2005, Leddy Maytum Stacy
35 Keye Ave., Building 35
An independent college preparatory high school with 65,000 sq. ft. devoted to classrooms, labs, a library, a student center, and other flexible space. A metal and glass entrance canopy signals the contemporary design of the new institution inside the historic walls.

25. Army Museum
(former Wright Army Hospital, 1863)
The former post hospital was built in 1864. In 1897 an octagonal tower was added to the building to increase the amount of daylight for the surgery that was the tower's function by providing more windows . The Army Museum has occupied the building since 1973. The simple yet gracious porches–the top one was also originally open–make this is the Presidio's most distinguished early building. Views of its unaltered state are in the museum.

26. Officers' quarters

26. Officers' quarters
1862-64
Funston Ave.
A row of Classic Revival/Italianate style officers' quarters that originally faced the first parade ground.

27. Pershing Hall

27. Pershing Hall
1903
Head of Funston Ave.

28. Moore Foundation Building (Former 6th Army Headquarters)

A well proportioned brick building in the Classical Revival style that was rebuilt after a 1915 fire damaged the General's residence and took the lives of his wife and children.

28. Moore Foundation Building (Former 6th Army Headquarters)
1940; 2001 renovation, Leddy Maytum Stacy with Gensler Assocs., interior design
Building 38, Mesa St.
A multi-tenant building rehabilitated using sustainable design practices, technologies, and materials.

29. Barrack

29. Barracks
1895-97
Montgomery St.
This row of brick barracks facing the parade ground was constructed in response to a large increase in personnel for the Army's infantry, artillery, and cavalry that resulted from the initiation of the coastal defense system of forts in the 1890s. Built of brick the barracks were fireproof and of a higher quality than the wooden buildings that preceeded them. Today they strengthen the character of the former parade ground and indicate the importance of the base in the late 19th century.

30. Crissy Field Center

30. Crissy Field
1996-2001, George Hargreaves Associates, landscape architects
North from Lyon St. along Mason St.
Once a tidal marsh, Crissy Field became a U.S. Army air field in 1921 on the site of the 1915 Panama Pacific International Exposition's Grand Prix race track. The air field remained until 1936. Under the management of the National Park Service since 1994, the site has been rehabilitated as wetlands and dune fields with bayside trails.

Crissy Field Center
2001, Eliot Fisch, architect
Mason St.
Originally an Army commissary, this building has been converted to a multi-use information and education center using using sustainable building materials. The outdoor decks on the upper level offer fine views.

31. Marine Sanctuary Visitor Center

31. Marine Sanctuary Visitor Center (former U.S. Coast Guard Station)
1890
On the bay off Mason St.
Built in the Dutch Colornial Revival style favored by the Coast Guard and planted with palm trees. Neither the style nor the trees are native to the area, but they go well together and signal an oasis.

32. **Barracks and Stables**

The route along Lincoln Boulevard toward the Golden Gate Bridge, includes a white wooden Classic-Revival building of 1902 with a two-story veranda, which was built as barracks for the Cavalry division. Below are five handsome brick stables of 1902, each for 102 horses.

32. Stables

32. Barracks

33. **Fort Point**

1853-61

Now a museum, this polygonal, brick, coastal-defense fort of 1853-61 is one of the finest surviving examples of a group of such forts that includes Fort Sumter in Charleston Harbor. Well worth a visit for its history alone, it also offers a wonderful view of the bay from beneath the Golden Gate Bridge.

33. Fort Pointand Golden Gate Bridge

Golden Gate Bridge

1937, Irving Morrow, consulting architect;
Joseph Strauss, chief engineer

The 4,200-foot clear span was, until 1959, the longest in the world. The great achievement of placing tower foundations in the swirling currents of the Golden Gate, the superb setting, and the orange-red color of the bridge make it a landmark of bridge building. The Moderne detailing expresses its time.

34. **Artillery gun emplacements**

Lincoln Blvd.

On Lincoln Boulevard past the bridge, there is a string of well marked abandoned coastal artillery gun emplacements facing the Pacific.

35. **Fort Winfield Scott**

1910-12

Ralston Ave.

A fine stand of Mission-Reviva stylel buildings set around a grassy parade ground. Along Kobbe Avenue is a handsome row of Classic-Revival style officers'

35. Fort Winfield Scott

quarters, built around 1910, that are part of Fort Scott. Further on there is a 1937 "log cabin", built as a non-commissioned officers' community club, in an ecclectic Craftsman style that benefited from the skill of Public Works Administration workmen.

35. Fort Winfield Scott

36. Houses

37. Palace of the Legion of Honor with Marin headlands in the background.

Sea Cliff and Lincoln Park

Sea Cliff was planned as an eclusive residential development in 1912 by Mark Daniels, who went on to plan Forest Hill the following year. Masonry gates signal the entrances into Sea Cliff; streets follow the contours of the sloping site. To reflect the city's chosen identification with the Mediterranean region, the mainly stuccoed houses were to be designed in Mediterranean Revival styles and painted in light colors to counter the fog that lingered along the coast. The houses are easily seen while driving or walking around this special enclave. Perhaps more rewarding are the fine views of the Golden Gate.

36. Houses

1914, Willis Polk & Co.

9 Scenic Way

25 Scenic Way

45 Scenic Way

Polk's late Classical style, which has none of the idiosyncrasies of his early work.

37. Palace of the Legion of Honor

1924, George A. Applegarth; 1995 remodeling Mark Cavagnero Associates/Edward Larabee Barnes

34th Ave. and Clement St. or El Camino Del Mar

Lincoln Park occupies the top of the Point Lobos Headland. Like Lone Mountain, it once had a cemetery –aptly called the Golden Gate–where the golf course is now. Near the first tee an arch from a Chinese tomb commemorates this piece of the past. Matchless views of the Golden Gate Bridge, the Marin Headlands, and the city to the east delight those who walk along the north edge of the park. The California Palace of the Legion of Honor, an art museum devoted largely to 16th- to 18th-century European painting and a Rodin sculpture collection, was given to the city by Adolph and Alma de Brettville Spreckels as a memorial to the WW I dead. The building is a modified copy of the Parisian palace of the same name, here given a country rather than a city setting. From 1992 to 1995, the museum was closed for renovation and expansion of its facilities. In addition to seismic upgrading, 35,000 sq. ft. were added in a two-level, below grade expansion that included six special exhibit galleries organized around a central skylit marked by a glazed pyramid centered in the ground level entrance court.

38. Sutro Heights and the Cliff House

35. Palace of the Legion of Honor

38. Sutro Heights and the Cliff House

38. Sutro Heights and the Cliff House

1890s to 1909, first four Cliff House buildings; 2005, C. David Robinson Architects
Point Lobos Rd. at the Pacific Ocean

Adolph Sutro began developing his 1,000-acre oceanfront estate in the 1880s. He purchased the burned-out hulk of the second Cliff House, which burned in 1894, and held a competition for the design of the new building that was completed in 1896. This fanciful, chateauesque structure achieved lasting fame in photographs although it too burned in 1907. The fourth Cliff House was built on the stone foundations of the third but had little architectural interest. Now it has been rehabilitated and given a new north wing with a lobby, gift shop, and a 2-story dining area. Terraces have panoramic ocean views. No vestiges of the veritable pleasure palace that was the Sutro Baths with six indoor saltwater pools remain.

Across Point Lobos Road is the site of Sutro's mansion, a rustic lodge that overlooked the Cliff House and the ocean and burned in 1907. The splendid gardens were populated with statues of classical deities, nymphs, fawns, etc., and were open to the public. Now a city park, the site can be explored although it is a pale reminder of its former splendor.

The original plan for the Stanford University campus, commissioned by Leland Stanford from landscape architect Frederick Law Olmsted and the architectural firm of Shepley, Rutan and Coolidge in 1886-1887, was strongly influenced by their client. Stanford had been in charge of building the western part of the transcontinental railroad. Elected governor in the 1860s, he became a U. S. senator in 1885. The university was intended to memorialize his son, Leland Jr., who died in 1884 at age fifteen.

Stanford's goal for the 8,400 acres of land he had acquired by 1882 was an experimental horse farm, which had buildings set around a huge quadrangle. The Red Barn, 1878-1879, is the main surviving structure on the stock farm site; it was restored in 1986 by Esherick Homsey Dodge & Davis.

Stanford dictated the form of a parallelogram for the campus buildings that were to extend in linked quadrangles across the broad plain and symbolize the university's indefinite expansion of intellectual knowledge.Although this vision did not survive Stanford's death in 1893, the original buildings are among the country's most architecturally significant academic complexes. Stanford also took credit for specifying the stylistic evocation of the California Missions. Coolidge described the design as Mission Style with Romanesque details in the tradition of Henry Hobson Richardson, the firm's recently deceassed founder. Certainly the label Richardsonian Romanesque more accurately describes the early campus buildings.

Palm Drive traces the grand approach to the original buildings along a north/south axis that terminates in the Memorial Church. Olmsted's Mediterranean landscape has survived mutations and changes in species of trees and other vegetation. The 1906 earthquake damaged the original structures, some of them beyond repair. Among the most conspicuous losses were the monumental Memorial Arch and the tower of the Memorial Church. The 1989 earthquake also took its toll of the early campus buildings, but a combined program of seismic reinforcing and renovation has remediated much of the damage. Among its achievements are the northeast or History corner and Building 120 just east of the main gate, both by Esherick Homsey Dodge & Davis in 1979 and 1982.

Stanford Univesity

1. Main Quad

   Memorial Court
   Serra St. at end of Palm Dr.
2. Memorial Church *Quadrangle opposite the main gate*
3. Thomas Welton Stanford Art Gallery *off Lasuen Mall*
4. Hoover Tower *Serra Mall*
5. Cecil H. Green Library *Lasuen Mall*
6. Encina Hall *Serra St. W. of the Quadrangle*
7. Schwab Residential Learning Center *Serra St. at Campus Dr. E.*
8. Escondido Village *Escondido Rd. at Campus Dr. East*
9. Alvarado Row and Salvatierra Walk *Lasuen Street and Mayfield Ave.*
10. Hoover House *Cabrillo and Santa Inez St.*
11. The Knoll *Lomita Dr.*
12. Paul and Jean Hanna House *737 Frenchman's Rd.*

    Mazour house *781 Frenchman's Rd.*
13. Haas Public Services Center *Campus Dr. E.*
14. Center for Educational Research at Stanford, CERAS *Galvez Mall*

    Law School *Abbot Way near Galvez Mall*
15. Post Office and Bookstore *E. side of White Memorial Plaza*

    White Memorial Plaza

    Donald Tresidder Memorial Union *SW. corner of the plaza*

    White Memorial Plaza

    Formaer Student Union *West side of White Memorial Plaza*
16. Thornton Center for Engineering Management *Santa Teresa St.*
17. Roble Gymnasium *Santa Teresa St.*
18. Lagunitas Court *Santa Teresa St.*
19. Lyman Residential Center *Campus Dr. W. near Governor's Ave.*
20. The Red Barn *Stockfarm Rd.*
21. Science and Engineering Complex *Stone Pine Plaza Sequoia Plaza*
22. Co-Generation Facility *Campus Dr. W. near Via Ortega*

    Charles H. Gilbert Biology Building *Serra Mall opp. Via Cresqi*
23. Paul Allen Center for Integrated Systems *Via Palou Mall*
24. William Gates Computer Sciences Building *Serra Mall*
25. James Clark Center *Campus Dr. W.*
26. Center for Clinical Sciences Research *off Campus Dr. W.*
27. Stanford Medical Center *Quarry Rd. and Medical Lane*
28. Cantor Center for Visual Art *Lomita Dr. at Museum Way*
29. Stanford Shopping Center *Sand Hill Rd., Arboretum Rd., Quarry Rd., and Vineyard Rd.*

Palo Alto

30. Palo Alto train station *El Camino Real and University Ave.*
31. Ramona St. Historic District *500 block of Ramona St.*
32. Main Post Office *380 Hamilton St.*
33. Downing house *706 Cowper St.*
34. St. Thomas Aquinas Roman Catholic Church *NE corner of Homer and Waverly Sts.*
35. Kellogg house *1061 Bryant St.*
36. Pettigrew house *1336 Cowper St.*
37. Mendenhall house *1570 Emerson St.*
38. Haehl house *1680 Bryant St.*
39. The Misses Stern houses *1950 and 1990 Cowper St.*
40. House *2101 Waverly St.*
41. Raas House *2240 Cowper St.*
42. Lucie Stern Community Center *Middlefield Rd. at Melville Ave.*
43. Rinconada Park *Embarcadero and Middlefield Rds.*
44. Main Public Library *1213 Newell Ave.*
45. Palo Alto Art Center *Embarcadero Rd. at Newell Ave.*
46. Fairmeadows residential tract *E. Meadow Dr. and Alma St.*

    Greenmeadows residential tract *Greenmeadow Way off Alma St.*

Previous page: Hoover Tower, Stanford University campus

Greer Rd.
Newell Rd.
Louis Rd.
Channing Ave.
California Ave.
Middlefield Rd.
Middlefield Rd.
Oregon Expwy
Webster St.
Cowper St.
Waverly St.
Bryant St.
Ramona St.
Emerson St.
Alma St.
University Ave.
Embarcadero Rd.
Hamilton St.
Forest Ave.
Komer Ave.
Channing Ave.
Addison Ave.
Lincoln Ave.
Kellogg Ave.
Churchill Ave.
Colleridge
Lowell Ave.
Tennyson Ave.
California Ave.
El Camino Real
82
Stanford University
Arboretum Rd.
Palm Dr.
Quarry Rd.
Campus Dr. East
Galvez St.
Stanford Ave.
California Ave.
Page Mill Expressway
Serra St.
Hanover St.
Escondido Rd.
Bowdoin St.
Welch Rd
Alvarado Row
Mayfield Ave
Santa Teresa St.
Stock Farm Rd.
West Campus Dr.
Campus Dr. East
Gerona Rd.
Junipero Sera Blvd
N
280
1
2
3
4
5
6
7
8
9
10
11
12
13
14
15
16
17
18
19
20
21
22
23
24
25
26
27
30
31
32
33
34
35
36
37
38
39
40
40
41
42
43
44
45

1. The Oval

1. Main Quad

1. View into Main Quad

1. Entrance to Memorial Court

Stanford University

1. **The Inner and Outer Quadrangles and Memorial Court**
   1887-1891 and 1898-1906, Shepley, Rutan and Coolidge; original master plan, Frederick Law Olmsted, landscape architect
   Serra St. at end of Palm Dr.
   Although the first master plan, which called for continuing the march of quadrangles linked by arcaded buildings across the plain, did not prevail, what was built still dominates and gives focus to today's sprawling campus. Rising above a terrace along Serra Mall, the south elevation of the outer quad of two-story buildings presents an heroic face to the Oval at the end of Palm Drive. The Memorial Court, originally introduced by the Memorial Arch, is now open-ended; Auguste Rodin's bronze Burghers of Calais stand on its southeast side. The buildings of the

1. Memorial Court with Rodin Sculpture

outer quad, constructed by Jane Stanford after Leland's death in 1893, have two stories; the inner quad, completed in 1891, is made up of 12 single-story buildings devoted to academic departments. The whole complex rewards careful study; note particularly how the arcade and roof systems tie together a considerable variety of building sizes and shapes and how the outdoor spaces range in scale from intimate to grand. The sandstone masonry and its exemplary ornamental detail, unequaled in the state, was executed by Italian stone masons imported for the work. Another benchmark of the outer quad's construction was the use of Ernest Ransome's patented reinforced concrete system in the library and assembly hall, designed by Percy and Hamilton for the east side.

2. **Memorial Church**
1887, Charles Coolidge; revisions and additions, 1899-1902, Clinton Day; rebuilt 1913, C. E. Hodges; seismic upgrading, 1989-1991
Main Quadrangle opposite the main gate
Coolidge designed the church with H. H. Richardson's Trinity Church in Boston in mind; the loss of the tower in 1906 diminished the allusion to the famous prototype. Jane Stanford dedicated the church as a memorial to her husband and enriched the design with a lavish use of carved ornament, stained glass, and mosaic on the exterior and interior.

2. Memorial Church

3. **Thomas Welton Stanford Art Gallery**
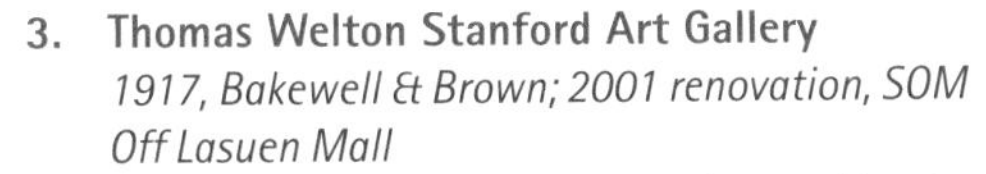
1917, Bakewell & Brown; 2001 renovation, SOM
Off Lasuen Mall
Although designed at the same time and by the same architects as the Green Library, #5, the gallery's style is a more elaborate version of the Richardsonian Romanesque of the quadrangles. The entrance portal is particularly noteworthy for its carved ornament. The structure is concrete faced with a sandstone veneer; a steel truss supports the terra cotta tile roof. The remodeled interior displays changing exhibitions of contemporary art.

3. Thomas Welton Stanford Art Gallery

4. **Hoover Tower**
1938-1941, Arthur Brown Jr. with Bakewell and Weihe
Serra Mall
A 285-foot tower that recalls Bertram Goodhue's Nebraska State Capital of 1919-1932 in its Moderne styling. Don't miss the interior lobby with its outsized eclectic columns.

4. Hoover Tower

5. **Cecil H. Green Library (former University Library)**
1919, Bakewell & Brown; restored 1995-1999, The Architects Collaborative/Fields & Devereux; East Wing, 1980, Helmuth Obata & Kassabaum
Lasuen Mall
The library's site directly east of the arcade that defines the eastern side of Inner Quad terminated the east-west axis through the quads. The building was to be the focus of a large new quad, never completed, which apparently inspired its monumental central section. The sandstone exterior covers a steel frame that facilitated the large arched openings of the tripartite central block. Heavy buttresses projecting beyond the openings and the attic section of small windows heightens the play of light and shadow on the facade. A ground-floor arcade that continues on the wings provides a human scale. The Beauxartsian mix of styles defies labeling but contributes to the design's success in both blending in and standing out

5. Cecil H. Green Library (former University Library)

6. Encina Commons

8. Escondido Village

8. Escondido Village

from the original buildings. The interior features a grand ceremonial stair rising to the former reading room and an upper level lobby with a domed rotunda.

6. **Encina Hall**
1891, Shepley, Rutan & Coolidge; major renovations, 1996-1998, Hardy Holzman Pfeiffer

Encina Commons
1923, Bakewell & Brown
Serar St. west of the quadrangle
The hotel-like dormitory for the original campus, now offices. The Commons behind is another of Bakewell & Brown's well-scaled and detailed variants on the original theme.

7. **Schwab Residential Learning Center**
1997, Legorreta Architectos/The Steinberg Group; Peter Walker & Partners, landscape architects
Serra St. at Campus Dr. East
The traditional hacienda is the model for this 280-unit apartment complex with related facilities, which serves students in the Graduate School of Business and visiting executives. The plan is organized around four courtyards with a forecourt planted with palms. Building heights vary from one to four stories. The earthen tones on the exterior contrast with bold colors–yellow, purple, blue–of the inner courtyards.

8. **Escondido Village**
1959, Wurster Bernardi & Emmons/Thomas Church, landscape architect; 1964-1971, Campbell & Wong/ Royston Hanamoto & Mays, landscape architects; 1971, Ned H. Abrams/Anthony Guzzardo, landscape architect; 2000-2001, Solomon, Inc./ The SWA Group
Escondido Rd. at Campus Dr. East
Originally built as married students housing on 175 acres. A ring road serves as an access route. The first phase designed by Wurster Bernardi & Emmons with landscaping by Thomas Church is notable as an example of Bay Region Modernism, which referenced the California ranch houses with low-pitched shingled roofs and wide overhanging eaves. The 250 two-story units were clad in cement board and redwood board-and-batten with end walls of concrete block. The seven types of one, two, and three-bedroom apartments were grouped in twos or threes with shared courtyards; they were fenced to create safe playgrounds for children. Subsequent developments departed from the early work in scale and style.

9. **Alvarado Row, Salvatierra Walk**
1890s-1910s
Lasuen Street, and Mayfield Ave.
In response to the founders' wish for faculty and student housing to be located on the campus, Olmsted's plan called for residential tracts on curved streets southeast of the main part of the campus. The residential lots were leased, not sold, and requirements for size and quality made the houses relatively expensive. Still, neighborhoods formed as a number of houses were built in the 1890s along the streets listed above. Shepley Rutan & Coolidge built ten houses on Alvarado Row. One of their employees, Charles Hodges, who later became the unofficial campus architect, and Arthur B. Clark designed a number of faculty houses as did other architects outside the university community. These houses exemplify the fashionable revival styles of the time, Colonial Shingle, Spanish Colonial, and Classical. Some examples of noteworthy houses are listed below; the visitor will discover many others by walking the area.

Griffen-Drell house
1892, Charles Hodges
570 Alvarado Row

Dunn Bacon house
1899, Charles Hodges
565 Mayfield Ave.

Grove-Lasuen house
1896, Charles Hodges
572 Mayfield Ave.

9. Alvarado Row, Salvatierra Wal

10. **Hoover House**
1919, Arthur B. and Birge Clark
Cabrillo and Santa Inez
This cubistic house, strongly reminiscent of the work of southern California architect Irving Gill, is often labeled Pueblo Revival. It was designed for Herbert Hoover with much advice from his wife, Lou Henry. It now serves as the Stanford president's house.

10. Hoover House

11. **The Knoll (former president's house)**
1918, Louis Christian Mullgardt
Lomita Dr.
An imposing structure of reinforced concrete coated with pink stucco that was designed as the president's house. The size of the house answered the university's need for a reception center. While the importance of the commission may have inspired the ornate style it was not typical of Mullgardt's other work.

11. The Knoll

12. Paul and Jean Hanna house

13. Haas Public Services Center

14. Center for Educational Research at Stanford, CERAS

15. Post Office and Bookstore

12. Paul and Jean Hanna house

1937, Frank Lloyd Wright; restored 1997-1999, Architectural Resources Group

737 Frenchmen's Rd.

One of Wright's greatest houses, planned on a hexagonal grid and sited on a hill in a sequence of terraces along a zigzagging driveway. The dramatic interior features a double-height, skylit vestibule and a massive sunken hearth. Hexagonal forms are everywhere. The house was left to the University by its original owners in 1975 and was damaged in the 1989 earthquake. Now restored and seismically upgraded, it serves as a conference center. Those who wish to visit the house should request information from the university visitor center.

Mazour house

1947, Ernest Born

781 Frenchman's Row

Exemplary Bay Region style by one of its early post-World War II practitioners.

13. Haas Public Services Center

1993, William Turnbull Associates

Campus Dr. East

A residentially scaled wood-frame building organized around a courtyard. The vocabulary of materials, typical of Turnbull's work, includes board-and-batten and horizontal siding and latticed screens, A stair tower rises above the main entrance. The services center fits comfortably into the neighborhood of early faculty homes.

14. Center for Educational Research at Stanford, CERAS

Galvez Mall

1971-72, Skidmore Owings & Merrill

The CERAS center, visible at the north end of Alvarado Row, reverses the original form of the quads by putting the arcade inside to form an open skylit court framed by several floors of balconies. The building's unusual skewed form permitted long elevations toward the east and south sides.

Law School, Crown Quadrangle

1973-1975, Skidmore Owings & Merrill; Thomas Church, landscape architect

Abbot Way near Galvez Mall

The Law School is one of the buildings that borders the Canfield Sculpture Court.

15. Post Office and Bookstore

1960, John Carl Warnecke

East side of White Memorial Plaza

A reinterpretation of the original idiom of the campus buildings using red-tile roofs over colonnades of concrete piers capped by umbrel forms. The bookstore interior has huge concrete bents that support a skylight 100 feet long above a two-level atrium.

White Memorial Plaza
1964, Thomas D. Church; fountain, Aristides Demetrios
A successful piece of place-making that marks the non-academic center of campus activity.

Donald Tresidder Memorial Union
1962, Spencer Lee & Busse
Southwest corner of the plaza
Stylistically related to the bookstore and post office by its red-tile roof, this dun-colored concrete structure with a broad cantilevered balcony houses many functions and offers a variety of in- and outdoor spaces.

Former Student Union
1915, Charles D. Whittlesey
West side of White Memorial Plaza
Superseded by the Tresidder Union, the old union has a forecourt completed by Bakewell and Brown in 1922 that strengthened the Mission Revival character of the whole. The facade has some elegant ornamental details; the ensemble signals a totally different era from that of its successor.

15. Former Student Union

16. Thornton Center For Engineering Management

16. Thornton Center For Engineering Management
1994, Tanner Leddy Maytum Stacy; Peter Walker/ William Johnson & Partners, landscape architects
Santa Teresa St.
The southern edge of a court defined by the much larger L-shaped Terman Engineering Center of 1977

18. Lagunita Court

designed by Harry Weese Associates. A garden with a reflecting pool designed by Peter Walker occupies the open space. The two buildings also mark the south end of the Science and Engineering area's axis, which begins at the Serra Mall. The Thornton Center has the formal clarity and structural elegance typical of this firm's work as revealed by the metal truss introducing the passage through the building. A balcony on the court's south side accents the passageway.

17. **Roble Gymnasium**
    1931, Bakewell & Brown
    Santa Teresa St.
    Designed for use by women the central section of the building has a domed lobby with entrances through trefoil arches set in a larger archway with a quatrefoil window; the richness suggested by the facade does not carry through into the groin-vaulted lobby. Beyond the lobby is a courtyard into which the gyms open.

18. **Lagunita Court**
    1934, Arthur Brown Jr./Bakewell & Weihe; 1937 additions; 1998, renovation and additions to the dining hall, Gordon Chong & Partners
    Santa Teresa St.
    A residence hall for women built in response to the 1933 decision to increase their enrollment beyond the limit of 500 set by Jane Stanford. The Mediterranean

18. Lagunita Court

Revival-style buildings enclose a generous landscaped courtyard. Wings were added in 1937 on either side of the dining hall, which was renovated in 1998. An innovative structure engineered by faculty members used a lightweight steel frame made of open-web studs prefabricated in panels that were brought to the site and set up on a concrete foundation. The Craftsman character of the wood trusses and wall paneling in the diningroom put an historicist mask on the concealed steel frame.

19. **Richard W. Lyman Graduate Resident Center**
1998, Tanner Leddy Maytum Stacy; Hargreaves Assoc., landscape architects
Campus Dr. W. near Governor's Ave.
A central commons building focused on a venerable oak tree is the pivotal element of the 112 apartment units in four-story buildings that snake along a narrow site. The exterior walls are clad with cement panels and stucco. The western and southern elevations have red metal screens offset from the walls to provide protection from the sun and add a subtle layer of space.

19. Richard W. Lyman Graduate Resident Center

20. **Red Barn and Stock Farm**
1876-1879; 1986, restored and modernized by Esherick Homsey Dodge & Davis
Stock Farm Rd. off Campus Drive West
The Red Barn was the centerpiece of Leland Stanford's horse farm. Today the individual horses may be forgotten, but Eadweard Muybridge's motion-study photographs of them, which Stanford funded, are internationally famous. The barn, a massive wooden structure with High Victorian features, is still in use.

20. Red Barn and Stock Farm

21. **Science and Engineering Quad**
1995-1999, Pei Cobb Freed & Partners; Olin Partnership, landscape architects
Serra Mall
Several buildings dedicated to engineering, materials research and related sciences line a landscaped quadrangle divided into four sections framed with Italian stone pines. Freestanding arcades of steel covered with translucent material line the edges of the quad, which extends from the Serra Mall to the Panama Mall. A plaza at the Serra Mall end of the complex is flanked appropriately by two buildings named for major donors David Packard and William Hewlett, Stanford's best known and most successful engineering graduates. The SEC Quad is a successful work of urban design that has brought order to a formerly meaningless part of the campus.

21. Electrical Engineaing Building

21. Science and Engineering Quad

22. **Cogeneration Facility**
1988, Spencer Assoc./Kaiser Engineers
Campus Drive West
This khaki green, prefabricated metal building strikes an alien note, but certainly expresses its mechanical function in an appropriate way. It is joined to a 1978 building by the same firm that also employed high tech imagery.

24. *William Gates Computer Sciences Building*

25. *James Clark Center*

25. *James Clark Center*

Charles H. Gilbert Biology Building
1991, Arthur Erickson/McClellan & Copenhagen
Serra Mall opp. Via Crespi
The walls of sand-colored precast concrete are enlivened with bands of green glass either angled into the walls or bowed out. The ground level toward Serra Mall is below grade and has a faceted and curved glass wall recessed under the central block. The eaves of the red-tile roof are also of green glass and project over the glazed attic. The attempted merger of various styles and materials is not a very comfortable one, but provokes curiosity about the building's function.

23. *Paul Allen Center for Integrated Systems Addition*

23. **Paul Allen Center for Integrated Systems Addition**
1995–1999, Antoine Predock; Scott Sebastian & Assoc., landscape architects
Via Plalou Mall
Indian sandstone exterior cladding and a copper-shingled roof that appears to float above the walls distinguish this quietly elegant design. A landscaped inner atrium provides the interior with natural light.

24. **William Gates Computer Sciences Building**
1996, Robert A. M. Stern & Partners, Sebastian & Assoc., landscape architects
Campus Dr. W. and Serra Mall
One might have expected the client for this building to have wanted something more high-tech in style than this Post-Modern version of the Richardsonian Romanesque style of the original quads. The ell has a pleasantly landscaped court.

25. **James Clark Center**
2003, Norman Foster Architects/MBT-interiors; landscape architect Peter Walker & Partners
Campus Dr. W.
At a distance this complex of three buildings appears

to be one limestone-clad structure. But from the north a courtyard opens up to reveal two long buildings that curve inward toward each other and a shorter curved end building that frames the court on the south side. A red metal canopy supported on four-foot columns appears to float above the rooftops, providing glimpses of the sky. The glazed courtyard walls have outside corridors accessed by metal stairways. The overall elegance of form, materials, and detailing make this one of the most successful of the recent additions to the campus.

26. Center for Clinical Sciences Research

26. Center for Clinical Sciences Research
2000, Norman Foster & Partners/Fong & Chan; Peter Walker & Partners, landscape architects
Campus Drive East

Two structures of cast-in-place concrete clad with a precast concrete and metal-and-glass curtain wall. Natural lighting with solar control where needed is dramatically enhanced by trellises made of aluminum and painted steel at the height of the buildings. Two identical four-story buildings housing labs, offices, and support spaces face each other across a courtyard with a trellis roof. The walls of rounded bays with stairways and elevators frame the lushly landscaped ground floor, which is below grade and traversed by metal walkways.

26. Center for Clinical Sciences Research

27. Stanford University Medical Center
1955-1959, Edward Durrell Stone; Thomas Church, landscape architect
1976, addition, CRS; 1987, renovation, NBBJ
Quarry Road Extension at Medical Lane
A very large three-story building punctuated by landscaped courtyards connected by covered arcades. The walls of the reinforced concrete structure have sunscreens of perforated concrete that recall Frank Lloyd Wright's "textile block" houses. The main courtyard, which can be visited, is particularly exotic. Stone viewed his buildings as continuing the tone and texture of the original quads in a contemporary way.

27. Stanford University Medical Center

28. Cantor Center for Visual Art
1891 and 1898-1899, Percy & Hamilton; 1902-1906, north, south, and west annexes, Charles Hodges and Clinton Day; 1996-1998, restoration and addition, Polshek & Partners
Lomita Dr. and Museum Way
The design of the museum dedicated to Leland Stanford, Jr. was faithful to the Classical Revival style in being bilaterally symmetrical with a central domed block flanked by gable-roofed wings. However,

28. Cantor Center for Visual Art

28. Cantor Center for Visual Art, Andy Goldsworthy sculpture

its reinforced concrete construction was a significant departure from the masonry technology of the time. Ernest Ransome, engineer for the structure, used twisted and fretted iron rods to stop poured concrete from shifting in the portico's 60-foot tall columns and for the longest reinforced concrete beams yet made, which were used in the lobby ceiling to support the skylight. (He later patented this technique.) The walls were unreinforced concrete with the aggregate left exposed. The high and airy grey marble lobby with its grand staircase is a surprise. The addition by Polshek and Partners is an harmonious yet distinctly contemporary design that opens graciously to an inner garden court and an outside terrace and sculpture garden featuring Auguste Rodin's work.

28. Rodin Sculpture Court

29. Stanford Shopping Center

1954-1957, Welton Becket; Lawrence Halprin, landscape architect; 1976, alterations, Bull Field Volkmann, Stockwell

Arboretum Rd. and Sand Hill Rd.

Although it was not common for a university to be associated with a shopping center, Skidmore Owings & Merrill included plans for one in their 1954 master plan for the university. Happily, the complex was not enclosed when that strategy later became fashionable so that the landscaped pedestrian street and passageways linking the anchor stores are still "open air."

28. Cantor Center for Visual Art

Palo Alto

30. Palo Alto Train Station

1941, Southern Pacific Railroad architects

El Camino Real and University Ave.

The Streamline Moderne style of this station would have matched the design of the Southern Pacific trains of that era.

29. Stanford Shopping Center

31. 500 block of Ramona St., Historic District:

Gotham Shop

1925, Pedro de Lemos

520 Ramona St.

Commercial building

1938, Pedro de Lemos

533-539 Ramona St.

De Lemos was a graphic artist, craftsman, teacher, and curator of the Stanford Art Museum; he was also active in civic affairs and apparently purchased the Ramona Street property to save a venerable oak tree. His work draws on California's Spanish Colonial heritage in a fanciful way. Other notable buildings in

31. Commercial building

the district include the former Medico-Dental Building, now the University Art Center, designed by Birge Clark, and the Cardinal Hotel by William Weeks.

32. **Main Post Office**
1932, Birge Clark
380 Hamilton St.
A gracious Spanish Colonial Revival-style building with fine metal work in light fixtures and grills inside the service area.

33. **Downing house**
1894
706 Cowper St.
A large house in the flamboyant Queen Anne style with abundant decorative detail and shingle work. When built the house must have commanded more land than the present corner lot.

34. St. Thomas Aquinas Roman Catholic Church

34. **St. Thomas Aquinas Roman Catholic Church**
1902, Shea & Shea
NE corner of Homer and Waverly Sts.
A late well-executed example of the Gothic Revival style in a wooden church by a firm that designed many Bay Area churches.

35. Kellogg house

35. **Kellogg house**
1899, Bernard Maybeck
1061 Bryant St.
A rare early work of Maybeck's. The big gambrel roof gave this house its nickname, the "sunbonnet house."

Professorville

The area bounded roughly by Cowper, Addison, Emerson Streets, and Embarcadero is known as "Professorville" because many Standford faculty members built homes there around the turn of the 19th century. These houses are typically comfortable, inostentious and often designed in then popular "brown shingle style." A drive or walk around the area will reward the viewer with a range of stylistic examples.

37. Mendenhall house

36. **Pettigrew House**
1925, George Washington Smith
1336 Cowper St. N. of Kellog Ave.
A fine example of the Spanish Colonial Revival style by a famous practitioner whose work is mainly in Santa Barbara.

37. **Mendenhall house**
1937, William W. Wurster
1570 Emerson St.
An unusual early Wurster in the Moderne style, even more Moderne now because of the addition of a rounded glass block stair tower.

38. Haehl house

38. Haehl house
c.1910, John Hudson Thomas
1680 Bryant St.
One of Thomas's Viennese Secession houses, larger than most of his Berkeley works, which were on smaller, hillier lots.

39. The Misses Stern houses

39. The Misses Stern houses
1930, Birge Clarke
1950 & 1990 Cowper St.
A charming matched pair of Spanish Mediterranean Revival houses designed for two of Palo Alto's great benefactresses. See the Lucie Stern Community Center, #42.

40. 2101 Waverly

40. House
1934, Carr Jones
2101 Waverly at Santa Rita
A half-timbered Norman farmhouse with a slate rood in the middle of old Palo Alto, beautifully executed in the favorite craftsmanly mode of this exemplary Bay Area "carpetect."

40. 2101 Waverly

41. Raas house
1939, William W. Wurster
2240 Cowper St
Wurster's early modern style used in a proto-ranch house.

41. Raas house

42. Lucie Stern Community Center

42. Lucie Stern Community Center
1935, Birge Clarke
Middlefield Rd. at Melville Ave.
A gracious building with a forecourt and other features that recall the patios of the Spanish Colonial haciendas.

43. Rinconada Park
1953, Eckbo, Royston & Williams
Embarcadero & Middlefield Rds.

This style of free-form landscape design has been so well assimilated into the California scene that one forgets how pioneering it was in the '50s.

44. Main Public Library

1959, Edward Durrell Stone

1213 Newell Ave.

Designed by Stone's then local representative, Lloyd Flood, the use of openwork tiles in screen walls combined with a long low-pitched shingled roof has made this library one of the most successful of the firm's Bay Area works.

46. Eichler House

45. Palo Alto Art Center

1953, Leslie Nichols

Embarcadero at Newell Ave.

Originally built as the City Hall, this woodsy civic building with a ranch-house image was replaced in 1970 by a mannered white cube designed by Eward Durrell Stone on Hamilton Avenue downtown. The older building suits its role as a cultural center very well.

46. Eichler House

Eichler Houses

Joseph Eichler, the now famous developer of post-World War II innovative middle-income tract housing, built two of his best known tracts, Fairmeadows and Greenmeadows in this south Palo Alto area, which was well away from other residential neighborhoods in the 1950s. The siting of the houses around concentric circular roads that makes the Fairmeadows tract stand out on the map was not copied elsewhere. But the architects who designed the houses, Anshen & Allen and Jones & Emmons, designed other tracts and individual houses for Eichler in his numerous Bay Area developments. As tasteful adaptations of various bay regional styles of the times, the houses have weathered the decades very well; their owners have cared for them and seen their moderate original prices multiply many times. Today the houses in these tracts are shrouded in lush vegetation, but for afficionadas glimpses of them from the streets are worthwhile.

46. Eichler House

46. Eichler House

46. Fairmeadows

1952, Anshen & Allen; Jones & Emmons

E. Meadow Dr. and Alma St.

Greenmeadows

1953, Anshen & Allen; Jones & Emmons; Claude Oakland

Greenmeadow Way off Alma St. between E. Charleston and San Antonio Rds.

Founded in 1777, San Jose is California's oldest civic settlement and was briefly the state capital after the adoption of the first state constitution in Monterey on November 13, 1849. The first legislature convened in San Jose a month later in a two-story adobe and wood-frame building near the Plaza. Despite some hard work on the part of its members, it has passed into history's dustbin as the lesiglature "of a thousand drinks." The second legislature voted to remove the capital to Vallejo. For nearly two hundred years the seat of San Jose's government was around the second site of the Mexican pueblo (the first site was subject to flooding from the Guadalupe River) between San Fernando and San Carlos Streets in the loop of Market Street. But beginning in 1959 with the completion of a new City Hall, a new civic center was built north of downtown. In the same period much of the central downtown was declared a redevelopment area, and a swath was cut across town to 4th Street that remained more or less barren until the 1980s. However, as of 1991 an impressive stand of new buildings now occupies the old wasteland with only a few holes waiting to be filled. A new light rail system runs along 1st Street with a transit mall designed by CHNMB that starts at San Carlos and runs north to St. James Street. An addition to the art museum, a convention center and the Children's Museum have also been completed in the central downtown area, creating a new civic center closer to the old heart of the pueblo. The Plaza has been re-landscaped and has a very successful fountain by George Hargreaves, who has also designed a new linear park for the Guadalupe River, now under construction west of downtown. When completed it will mitigate the damage to downtown wrought by the freeway, which runs north-south close by. In sum, a new downtown for San Jose is bursting out all over with old buildings being renovated as new ones are built.

Near downtown are 19th- and early 20th-century residential neighborhoods with blocks of fine buildings. North of Julian Street between 1st and 11th Streets are more blocks of vintage houses and bungalows, and the blocks east and south of downtown on both sides of I-280 are rewarding to those interested in late 19th-century architectural styles. Southeast of I-280 is Kelly Park, location of the Historical Society Museum and a collection of old buildings moved there to save them from bulldozers.

San Jose State University occupies several blocks east of central downtown and although not covered in detail in this tour, it is certainly worth a visit. At this point in time, San Jose seems to be at last reaping the cultural benefits of being the major South Bay city and to be getting its share of the wealth produced by Silicon Valley. Having surpassed San Francisco in population, San Jose is now distinguishing itself in the fields of culture and architecture.

1. Hensley Historic District Houses *E. Julian St. to Empire St., 1st-6th Sts.*
2. St. James Park *E. St. James St., E. St. John St., N. 2nd St., N. 3rd St.*
   - a. Former First Church of Christ Scientist *E. St. James St. at N. 2nd St.*
   - b. Former St. Claire Club *65 E. St. James St.*
   - c. St. James Place *E. St. James St. and N. 3rd St.*
   - d. Former Scottish Rite Temple *N. 3rd St. and E. St. James St.*
   - e. First Unitarian Church *160 N. 3rd St.*
   - f. Trinity Episcopal Church *N. 2nd and E. St. John St.*
   - g. St. James Branch U. S. Post Office *E. 1st St. at E. St. John St.*
   - h. Santa Clara County Courthouse *N. 1st at E. St. James St.*
3. Peralta Adobe and Fallon House historic site *184 W. St. John St. at N. San Pedro St.*
4. De Anza Hotel *W. Santa Clara St. between N. Almaden Blvd. and Notre Dame St.*
5. Guadalupe River Park headquarters *River St. and W. Santa Clara St.*

   San Jose Arena *The Alameda and Autumn St.*
6. Former Bank of America Building *S. 1st at E. Santa Clara St.*
7. New Century Block *52-78 E. Santa Clara St.*
8. San Jose City Hall and Civic Center *E. Santa Clara St. between 4th and 6th Sts.*
9. Howard Gates house *62 S. 13th St.*
10. Housing *101 E. San Fernando St.*
11. Dr. Martin Luther King Jr. Library *S. 4th St. and San Fernando St.*

    Tower Hall, San Jose State *University campus; S. 4th St. to S. 10th St.; E. San Fernando St. to E. San Salvador St.*
12. Paseo Plaza housing *E. San Fernando between 3rd and 4th Sts.*
13. Letitia Building *66-72 S. 1st St.*
14. St. Joseph's Roman Catholic Church *Market St. at W. San Fernando St.*
15. San Jose Museum of Art *Market St. at W. San Fernando St.*
16. Plaza de Cesar Chavez *Market St. loop*
17. San Jose Repertory Theater *Paseo de San Antonio between 2nd and 3rd Sts.*
18. California State Office Building *E. San Carlos St. between 2nd and 3rd Sts.*
19. U. S. Courthouse and Federal Building *S. 1st St. at E. San Carlos St.*
20. Tech Museum of Innovation *201 S. Market St.*
21. Former Civic Auditorium *145 W. San Carlos St.*
22. San Jose San Center for the Performing Arts *255 Almaden Blvd.*
23. Children's Discovery Museum *W. San Carlos St. and Woz Way*
24. Former Main Public Library *180 San Carlos St.*
25. McEnery Convention Center *W. San Carlos St. at Market St.*
26. Former St. Claire Hotel *302 S. Market St.*

    Montgomery Hotel *201 S. 1st St. at E. San Carlos St.*
27. Former California Fox Theatre *S. 1st St. near E. San Salvador St.*
28. Rucker House *418 S. 3rd St.*
29. Plaza Maria housing *115 E. Reed St. at S. 3rd St.*
30. Col House *1163 Martin St.*
31. Kelly Park: Japanese Friendship Garden and the History Park *Senter and Story Rds.*
32. Rosicrucian Egyptian Museum *Park and Naglee Aves.*
33. Winchester Mystery House *525 S. Winchester Blvd.*
34. Hanchett Residential Park *The Alameda, Hester Park and Race Sts.*
35. Villa Montalvo *Montalvo Rd. off the Saratoga-Los Gatos Rd.*

Previous page: Plaza de Cesar Chavez fountain

Empire St.
E. Washington St.
E. Julian St.
E. St. James St.
E. St. John St.
E. San Fernando
E. San Carlos Ave
W. Santa Clara St.
San Jose State University
E. San Salvador St.
E. Williams St.
E. Reed St.
Park Ave.
W. San Carlos Ave.
Paseo De San Antonio
Auzerais Ave.
Keyes St.
N 1st St.
N. 2nd St.
N. 3rd St.
N. 4th St.
N. 5th St.
N. 6th
N. 7th
N. 8th
N. 9th St.
N. 10th
N. 11th
N. 12th
N. 13th
N. 14th
N. 15th
N. 16th
N. 17 th
Market St.
Almaden Blvd.
S. 1st St.
S. 2nd. St.
S. 3rd St.
S. 4th St.
Woz Way
Vine St.
87
280
N
1
2
3
4
5
6
7
8
9
10
11
12
13
14
15
16
17
18
19
20
21
22
23
24
25
26
27
28
29
30
31
32
33
34
a
b
c
d
e
f
g
h

2b. Former St. Claire Club

2c. St. James Place

2d. Former Scottish Rite Temple

1. **Hensley Historic District Houses**
   1870s to 1910s
   1st St. to 6th St., E. Julian to Century St.
   Many fine examples of 19th houses from the 1870s to the 1890s are in this district. The larger and more elaborate houses along N. 3rd. Street include the home of Major Hensley, a gold rush baron, at 456 N. 3rd. Street. Built in 1884, the house shows the transition from the so-called Stick-Eastlake style to the Queen Anne style of the 1890s.

2. **St. James Park**
   1848 survey by Chester Lyman
   E. St. James, E. St. John, N. 2nd, N. 3rd Sts.
   Part of Chester Lyman's 1848 plat of the city, this park became the focus of its civic aspirations in the latter part of the century. It was landscaped in 1868 when the first courthouse was built in an attempt to attract the state capital back to San Jose. N. 2nd Street was allowed to bisect the park in 1955, but today it is closed to automobile traffic and has been re-landscaped by Michael Painter. Having been spared major redevelopment in the post-war period, the scale of the park and its buildings is unusually harmonious.

a. **Former First Church of Christ, Scientist**
   1905, Willis Polk
   E. St. James and N. 2nd St.
   A Classic Revival design by an important San Francisco architect. The building also contributes, even in its currently abandoned state, to the civic dignity of St. James Park.

b. **Former St. Claire Club**
   1893, A. Page Brown
   65 E. St. James St.
   A subtle design in the Craftsman mode with brickwork as decoration.

c. **St. James Place**
   1986, Daniel Solomon Assoc.
   E. St. James and N. 3rd St.
   A commendable attempt to design a much larger building to be compatible with the older St. Claire Club.

d. **Former Scottish Rite Temple**
   1924-25, Carl Werner
   N. 3rd and E. St. James St.
   An imposing Classic Revival temple by an architect based in Oakland. In 1981 the building was rehabilitated for the San Jose Athletic Club.

e. **First Unitarian Church**
1891, George M. Page
160 N. 3rd St.
This Romanesque Revival church interrupts the march of the Classic Revival mode down this side of the park. Next door is the Doric portico of the former Masonic Temple, now fronting for a recent high-rise behind it.

2f. Trinity Episcopal Cathedral

f. **Trinity Episcopal Cathedral**
1863, John W. Hammond
N. 2nd and E. St. John Sts.
The oldest church in San Jose; built in the Gothic Revival style by a sea captain, John W. Hammond, who was a member of the parish. Originally constructed of redwood logged in Santa Cruz, the church was doubled in size and cut in half in 1876; the front half was moved to face N. 2nd Street. In 1887 the church was enlarged again, and the steeple added.

2h. Santa Clara County Courthouse

g. **St. James Branch Post Office, former Main Post Office**
1933, Ralph Wyckoff
N. 1st at E. St. John St.
A showpiece of the 1930s Depression-era WPA work with fine terra-cotta detail inside and out.

h. **Santa Clara County Courthouse**
1866-67, Levi Goodrich
N. 1st bet. E. St. John and S. St. James Sts.
A grand Classic Revival building that was even grander before it lost its upper story and dome in a 1932 fire; the present top is post-fire. The building was restored in 1973 and again after the 1989 earthquake in 1994.

3. Peralta Adobe and Thomas Fallon House

3. **Peralta Adobe and Thomas Fallon House**
c.1805; rest. 1976
184 W. St. John St.
The city's oldest remaining Spanish colonial structure from the original pueblo. The 1797 house belonged to Luis Maria Peralta, Comisionado of the pueblo after 1807. It may be the oldest Bay Area adobe. The restored Thomas Fallon House, also part of this historic park, dates from 1855 and contains a museum devoted to the history of the area.

4. De Anza Hotel

4. **De Anza Hotel**
1931, William Weeks
W. Santa Clara between N. Almaden Blvd. and Notre Dame St.
A representative example of Art Deco styling, the historic De Anza Hotel was completely renovated in 1990. The lobby is lavish.

5. San Jose Arena Pavilion

6. Former Bank of America Building

5. **Guadalupe River Park**
   1980's, Hargreaves Associates, landscape architect
   Autumn St., W. St. John St., River St., extending down the river to Woz Way and Almaden Blvd.
   The transformation of a grading plan for a flood control channel into a linear park that extends for about three miles south of Confluence Park at the intersection of Los Gatos Creek and the Guadalupe River to beyond the bridge over the river at Woz Way. The park incorporates several gardens including the four-acre Courtyard Garden, part of a 200-acre network of public gardens adjacent to downtown. Hargreaves has used a variety of undulating terraces and land forms to enhance the river's edge as well 245as bikeways and walks.

5. Guadalupe River Park

   San Jose Arena/HP Pavilion
   The Alameda and Autumn St.

6. **Former Bank of America Building**
   1925-26, H. A. Minton
   S. 1st at E. Santa Clara St.
   The major landmark of downtown for many years. A. P. Giannini, founder of the Bank of America, was a native son.

7. **New Century block/de Saisset Building**
   1880 and 1900
   52-78 E. Santa Clara St.
   The city's finest commercial palace of its time had two later additions; it was renovated in 1984-85.

   I.O.O.F. Building
   c.1883, T. Lenzen
   82-96 E. Santa Clara St.
   A stylistically complementary building to the New Century block.

8. **San Jose Civic Center**
2005, Richard Meier/The Steinberg Group
E. Santa Clara St. between 4th and 6th Sts.
A commanding complex of buildings that includes an 18-story tower on the east side of the site and a three-story council chambers building with a central domed rotunda on the west side. A large plaza framed by a curved wall and the ground level of the parking garage opens to East Santa Clara Street, the main pedestrian entrance.

9. Howard Gates house

9. **Howard Gates house**
1904, Bernard Maybeck
62 S. 13th St.
A showpiece of Maybeck's inventiveness with stylistic idioms. Neo-Baroque elements such as moldings and arches are vigorously modeled to give the asymmetrical facade a depth and boldness difficult for a lesser talent to achieve.

10. 101 E. San Fernando Street housing and commercial

10. **101 E. San Fernando Street housing and commercial uses**
2003, Solomon E T C
Built around landscaped courtyards with fountains, this five-story block-size building also has shops and offices on the streets. Despite a density of more than 100 units per acre, over half of the 322 apartments have street-level entrances. The continuous row of balconies on the upper floor doubles as a cornice of ornamental wrought iron; the stair towers function as piers to give depth to the walls. The net result is a gracious and sophisticated building that stands out from the mainstream examples of mixed-use design.

Mixed-use building
2003, Berger Detmer Ennis, Inc.;
landscape architect, Michael Dillon
33 S. Third St.
Another example of the downtown boom in mixed-use development, which has 89 rental units and 3 commercial spaces

11. Dr. Martin Luther King Jr. Library

11. Dr. Martin Luther King Jr. Library

11. **Dr. Martin Luther King Jr. Library**
2003, Gunnar Birkerts-Design Associates/
Carrier Johnson
S. 4th and W. San Fernando Sts.
A somewhat lacklustre exterior introduces this eight-story library building, the result of a unique collaboration between the city of San Jose and the San Jose State University. As the city's main library and the university's only library, the building required equally important entrances from the campus and the city street. Inside, the central atrium features warm beech

14. St. Joseph's Roman Catholic Church

15. San Jose Museum of Art

15. San Jose Museum of Art

wood and glass used to good effect to define the rising floors. The bookcases themselves contribute importantly to the visual impact of the space.

11. Morris Daley (Tower) Hall

Morris Daley (Tower) Hall
1909, Walter Parker, State Architect
The campus' oldest building, which draws on the Richardson Romanesque style, and is memorable for standing out rather than fitting in with its later neighbors.

12. Paseo Plaza Housing
c. 2000
E. San Fernando St. bet/3rd and 4th Sts.

13. Letitia Building
1890, Jacob Lenzen
66-72 S. 1st St.
A business block in the Romanesque Revival style that was once more common in 19th-century downtowns. Since such buildings were usually built in stone, they were particularly subject to earthquake damage, and have become quite rare.

14. St. Joseph's Roman Catholic Church
1877, Hoffman & Clinch; restored in the 1990s
Market at W. San Fernando St.
The first pueblo church of adobe was built on this site; two other structures followed before this grand edifice was built. Architect Brian Clinch was chosen for his erudition and his talent–he read the New Testament in Greek every day. The interior is equally grand.

15. San Jose Museum of Art
1892, Wiloughby Edbrooke; addition, 1991, Skidmore Owings & Merrill
Market at W. San Fernando St.
Another Romanesque Revival stone building that suffered earthquake damage in 1906–the upper part of the tower was lost–and 1989, as well as two

changes of use. The recent addition by SOM is a handsome design in its own right that, happily, does not try to ape the style of the older building.

16. Plaza de Cezar Chavez
1989, George Hargreaves, landscape architect
Market St. loop
A popular fountain composed of water jets that form a cluster of columns suitable for walking through on hot days, of which there are many.

16. Plaza de Cezar Chavez

17. San Jose Repertory Theater
1993, Holt Hinshaw
N. 2nd and Paseo de San Antonio
A forthright example of contemporary industrial design clad in mostly blue metal sheeting that is a highly visible downtown landmark.

17. San Jose Repertory Theater

18. California State Office Building
1983, ELS Assoc.
E. San Carlos bet. 2nd and 3rd Sts.
One of a series of state buildings designed to conserve energy and provide a humane working environment with landscaped interior couryards

18. California State Office Building

19. United States Courthouse and Federal Building
1984, Hellmuth, Obata & Kassabaum
S. 1st at E. San Carlos St.
Another building that advertises energy conservation in a giant sunshade over the court. Outside the eastern entrance is a bronze memorial with reliefs by sculptor Ruth Asawa depicting the internment of Japanese-American citizens during World War II.

19. United States Courthouse and Federal Building

20. Tech Museum of Innovation

20. Tech Museum of Innovation
1998, Ricardo Legorreta
201 S. Market St.
Bright orange and blue tilework signal the importance of this multi-story building filled with hundreds of interactive and other kinds of informative exhibitions on technological achievements.

21. Former Civic Auditorium

22. San Jose Center for the Performing Arts

23. Children's Discovery Museum

21. Former Civic Auditorium
1934, William Binder & E. N. Curtis
145 W. San Carlos St.
A Spanish Colonial Revival building with a pleasantly scaled colonnade on the street.

22. San Jose Center for the Performing Arts
1972, William Wesley Peters
255 Almaden Blvd.
Late Wrightian design by the architect who headed Taliesin West after the master died.

23. Children's Discovery Museum
1991, Ricardo Legorreta
W. San Carlos St. and Woz Way
A sculptural composition in geometric forms and subtle colors that are the hallmarks of this noted Mexican architect, who once worked with Luis Barragan.

24. Former Main Public Library
1971, Norton S. Curtis
180 San Carlos St.
A period piece that used to look lonely and pretentious but has now been assimilated into a new cultural context.

25. McEnery Convention Center

25. McEnery Convention Center
1990, Mitchell/Giurgola
W. San Carlos at Market St.
A well-scaled civic design that attracts attention with a sprightly mural. Not the least of the convention center's contributions is that it has involved the main library next door and the old civic auditorium across the street in an urbanistic streetscape accentuated by the light rail station by Wallace Roberts Todd.

26. St. Claire/Hyatt Hotel
1926, Weeks & Day
302 S. Market St.
A dignified and urbane building designed by the

architects of other notable hotels such as the Mark Hopkins and the Huntington on Nob Hill in San Francisco. The hotel was financed by T. S. Montgomery, the premier developer of downtown San Jose.

Montgomery Hotel
1911, William Binder; restored 2004, Architectural Resources Group
201 S. 1st St. at E. San Carlos St.
A grand hotel in the Classical Revival style built by T. S. Montgomery, and since its 2004 restoration grander than ever. The building was moved here in 2000 from its original site at 1st. Street and San Antonio following damage by the 1989 earthquake.

27. Former California Fox Theater

27. Former California Fox Theater
1927, Weeks & Day; restoration in progress, ELS
S. 1st St. near E. San Salvador St.
The ornate exterior of this Neo-Churriguerresque movie palace is being restored and the interior rehabilitated to be a performing arts center and to house the San Jose Opera.

28. Rucker house

28. Rucker house
c.1883
418 S. 3rd St.
This great Queen Anne villa offers a taste of San Jose's 19th-century residential neighborhoods. The blocks nearby on S. 5th and S. 6th are also worth exploring to see more fine houses. Try the 500 block of S. 6th Street.

29. Plaza Maria housing

29. Plaza Maria housing
1995, David Baker & Partners
115 E. Reed St.
A richly colored 53-unit housing complex announced by a corner tower that bristles with wood beams suggesting a trellis. The facades of the four-story building on 3rd. Street are also enlivened with trellis-shaded balconies on the upper floors. The two-story side of the complex on 4th. Street is compatible with the neighboring houses.

31. Kelly Park, History Park

30. Col House
c. 1910, Wolfe & Wolfe
1163 Martin St.
A bungalow version of the larger Prairie-school houses in the midwest rendered with great care. At 1208 Martin Street, 1151 Sierra Street, and 1299 Yosemite Street are other less lavish examples of the style by the same firm.

31. Kelly Park
Senter and Story Rds.

32. *Rosicrucian Park and Egyptian Museum*

a. **Japanese Friendship Garden**
1300 Senter Rd.
A gift to the City of San Jose from its sister city of Okayama, Japan. The design of the garden echoes that of Okayama's Korakuen Park and offers the pleasures of plants and water elements typical of a traditional Japanese garden.

b. **History Park**
1600 Senter Rd.
A successful theme park, featuring a collection of 19th-century structures moved here over several decades and restored. At this writing they include the Pacific Hotel, various houses, a firehouse, and the Lick Tanning factory as well as trolleycars that take visitors around the park.

32. *Rosicrucian Park and Egyptian Museum*

32. Rosicrucian Park and Egyptian Museum
1927-c.1972, mostly by Earle Lewis
1342 Naglee Ave. at Park Ave.
This fanciful complex was built as a romantic evocation of ancient Egyptian architecture for the World Headquarters of the Ancient, Mystical Order of the Rosae Crucis. The main museum's collection of Egyptian mummies, art objects, and other artifacts is the largest on the west coast and well worth seeing. A planetarium is associated with the museum. The grounds are restful.

33. *The Winchester Mystery House*

33. The Winchester Mystery House
1884-1922
525 S. Winchester Blvd.
Sara Pardee Winchester's fortune came from the sales of Winchester Repeating Rifles, first used during the Civil War. After the death of her husband, rifle manufacturer William Wirt Winchester, Sara moved from the east to San Jose. In 1884, she bought a 43-acre parcel in the countryside with an eight-room farmhouse. She then embarked upon a compulsive building campaign that lasted the rest of her life and kept a small army of workmen employed. No systematic plan for the house is discernible; the 160 rooms, which cover six acres, are in various stages of completion and appear to have been used or unused according to whim rather than need. No architect has been identified, but Sara subscribed to builders' plan books, and one might surmise that she was a "closet architect."

Directly to the east is Santana Row, an exaggerated version of Main Street dedicated to consumption that was developed by Federal Realty of Maryland. Various historical shards scavenged from faraway places are used to suggest a place with layers of time. We leave it to visitors to judge the result.

34. Hanchett Residence Park

c. 1910-1920, Wolfe & McKenzie and Wolfe & Wolfe, architects, T. S. Montgomery, developer; John McClaren, landscape designer

The Alameda, Hester, Park, and Race Sts.

Although Frank Delos Wolfe designed hundreds of houses in a range of styles from Queen Anne to Craftsman to Mediterranean Revival during his long career from the late 1890s to 1926, his firms' work in this subdivision was mainly in the Prairie style associated with Frank Lloyd Wright. The predominant house type in Hanchett Park is the bungalow, which appears in several variations. Wolfe's best known house here is the 1913 Col house at 1163 Martin Avenue. At 1208 Martin, 1151 Sierra, and Yosemite Avenues are other Prairie-style bungalows by Wolfe. Other fine bungalows not by Wolfe are clustered along Martin Avenue at 1225, 1233, 1241, 1249, and 1257.

35. Villa Montalvo

35. Villa Montalvo

35. Villa Montalvo

35. Villa Montalvo, Folly

35. Villa Montalvo

1912, William Curlett/Alexander Curlett and E. C. Gottschalk; John McClaren, landscape architect

From 280 take 17 to 9, the Saratoga-Los Gatos Rd., and turn left on Montalvo Rd.

James D. Phelan, a three-term mayor of San Francisco and later a state senator, acquired 160 acres of land in the Saratoga foothills in 1911. He commissioned this 19-room mansion in the Mediterranean Revival style, which opened in 1914. For the remainder of Phelan's life his estate was a major northern California center for politics and art. Following his death in 1930, the San Francisco Art Association assumed the trusteeship of the buildings and grounds and instituted an artists residency program, the third such in the country. In 1953 the Montalvo Association was established to administer the programs in art, music, and architecture. Several performing arts facilities are located in the complex of buildings; the spacious grounds are open free to the public.

PARAMOUNT
PARAMOUNT
PARAMOUNT MOVIE AUG 27
20,000 LEAGUES UNDER SEA
PARAMOUNT
MOVIE CLASSIC
20

Oakland's central downtown retains a rich diversity of architecture from its major periods of growth. The successive downtown centers lie along Broadway beginning at the waterfront with the heart of the 1850s settlement, now called Jack London Square. Over the next hundred years the city grew to the northeast away from the water. At the turn of the 20th century the heart of downtown remains more or less where it was in the post-1906 boom period around the five-points intersection at 14th Street, Broadway, Telegraph and San Pablo Avenues.

The vast Rancho de San Antonio, which was granted to Luis Peralta who lived out his life in a humble adobe in San Jose, encompassed the area that became Oakland. A sharp and acquisitive-minded Yankee, Horace Carpentier, managed to lease land from the Peraltas on the waterfront. He joined with two other Yankees to hire Julius Kellsberger in 1850 to map a townsite in a grid plan with streets 80 feet wide-except for Broadway, which was 110 feet wide-running through blocks 200 by 300 feet square. Seven blocks were allocated for public open space. In 1852 Carpentier got the state legislature to pass an act incorporating the settlement as Oakland, a fitting name at the time because the land was largely covered with oak groves. This "walking city" lasted until the railway era that followed the arrival of the transcontinental railroad at the Oakland Mole in 1868. In the 1870s when railroad lines began to run along the lower east-west streets, business and commercial interests moved up Broadway to the area around 9th to 11th Streets, now called Old Oakland. Civic enterprises blossomed. Mayor Samuel Merritt presided over the creation of public libraries and a new city hall at 14th Street and San Pablo Avenue. He also got the state legislature to create the first-ever wildlife refuge in North America on Lake Merritt in 1870. During this decade the city's wealthy and powerful citizens began to settle around the lake that bore the mayor's name while the central business district consolidated in the east-west blocks around Broadway from 10th to 14th Street.

The 1906 earthquake did less damage to Oakland than San Francisco and sparked another boom, which witnessed the transformation of the low business buildings into skyscrapers in the pre-World War I period. Even the new City Hall of 1912 was built as a skyscraper. When Oakland became the focus of retail shopping for the surrounding East Bay towns the central retail district reached 17th Street. With the completion of the Civic Auditorium in 1914, a civic center began to develop on Lake Merritt.

The impact of the automobile in the 1920s brought the creation of new suburbs in the areas north and west of downtown and produced a new retail and entertainment district uptown around Broadway and 20th Street. By contrast the post-World War II suburban expansion had a minimal, even depressing, effect on downtown and brought declining real estate values, neglect and, ultimately, redevelopment areas.

Today downtown has a new, or renewed, look while retaining its historic diversity. Since most of it is quite walkable, it can be explored on foot.

1. Jack London Square, *Foot of Broadway*
2. Amtrack Station *245 2nd St.*
   The Leviathan *330 2nd St.*
3. Former Western Pacific Depot *3rd and Washington Sts.*
4. Old Oakland Historic District *Broadway to Clay St. 8th to 10th St.*
5. Swann's Marketplace *9th and Clay Sts.*
6. Landmark Place *Martin Luther King Jr. Way between 11th and 12th Sts.*
7. Preservation Park *Martin Luther King Jr. Way to Castro St. 12th to 14th Sts.*
   Pardee House Museum *672 11th St*
   First Lutheran Church *14th and Castro St.*
   African American Museum and Library at Oakland (former Charles Greene Library) *659 14th St. at Martin Luther King Jr. Way*
8. 1111 Broadway building
   Clorox Building *1345 Broadway*
   City Center Buildings & Mall 11th to 14th St. *Broadway to Martin Luther King Jr. Way*
9. Ronald V. Dellums Federal Building
   Elihu M. Harris State Building *Clay St. to Jefferson St.*
10. 1100 Broadway building
    Bank building *1200 Broadway*
    Oakland Tribune Tower *13th and Franklin Sts.*
11. City Hall *1 City Hall Plaza*
12. YWCA Building *1515 Webster St.*
13. Former Howden Building *17th and Webster Sts.*
14. Cathedral Building *Telegraph Ave. and Broadway*
15. Fox Oakland Theater and office building *1515 Telegraph Ave.*
16. Mary Bowles Building *1721 Broadway*
17. Former Oakland Floral Depot *1900 Telegraph Ave.*
18. Former I. Magnin & Co. *Broadway and 20th St.*
19. Paramount Theater *2025 Broadway*
20. Former Breuner Co. *22nd St. and Broadway*
21. Moss Cottage Mosswood Park *Broadway and MacArthur Blvd.*
22. Kaiser Center Ordway Building *Kaiser Plaza and 21st St.*
    Kaiser Center Building *20th and Harrison Sts.*
23. Former Oakland Hotel *270 13th St.*
24. Oakland Main Public Library *125 14th St.*
25. Scottish Rite Temple *1433 Madison St.*
26. Camron-Stanford House Museum *1426 Lakeside Dr.*
27. Alameda County Courthouse *18th and Fallon Sts.*
28. Oakland Museum *Oak St. between 10th and 12th Sts.*
29. California College of the Arts *5212 Broadway*

Previous page: Paramount Theater

W. Grand Ave.
22nd St.
21st St.
20th St.
19th St.
17th St.
15th St.
14th St.
13th St.
12th St.
11th St.
10th St.
9th St.
8th St.
7th St.
6th St.
5th St.
4th St.
3rd St.
2nd St.
Water St.
Embarcadero
San Pablo Ave.
Telegraph Ave.
Harrison St.
Lakeside Dr.
M. L. King Jr. Way
Jefferson St.
Clay St.
Washington St.
Broadway
Franklin St.
Webster St.
Alice St.
Jackson St.
Madison St.
Oak St.
880
1
2
3
4
5
6
7
8
9
10
11
12
13
14
15
16
17
18
19
20
21
22
23
24
25
26
27
28
29
N

2. Amtrack Station

2. Amtrack Station

3. Former Western Pacific Railroad Depot

1. **Jack London Square**
   Beginning of Broadway
   The square was named after the Last Chance Saloon, a favorite haunt of the famous writer and native son. The original waterfront has evolved into a center for offices, entertainment, and tourism.Nearby along Franklin between 2nd and 3rd Streets is the warehouse and produce market district that developed in the 'teens and '20s. Many buildings have been rehabilitated for other uses, but the market still functions in the mornings and the buildings express their function.
2. **Amtrack Station**
   2000, VBN Architects
   245 2nd St.
   One of the largest U.S. rail stations built in recent years, the Oakland station is the hub of the central west coast passenger rail travel that links the San Joaquin Valley with commuter and transcontinental services. The 15,000 sq. ft. station building houses regional supervisors' offices, engineer and crew facilities, and passenger ticket operations. The metal and glass groin vaults recall grand European rail stations.
   The Leviathan
   1990-91, Ace Architects
   330 2nd St.
   A self-consciously outrageous design by architects known for exploiting the fanciful.

2. The Leviathan

3. **Former Western Pacific Railroad Depot**
   1909
   3rd and Washington Sts.
   A relic of the railroad era that has been converted to offices.

4. Old Oakland Historic District

4. Old Oakland Historic District

4. Old Oakland Historic District

1868-1881; rest. 1970s-1980s, Storek & Storek
Broadway to Clay, 8th to 10th St.

A fine collection of 19th-century commercial buildings meticulously restored. Among them are:

The Lawyers' Block
1880-85, Kenitzer & Raun, Frederick Delger, developer
Broadway and 10th St.

Ratto's Deli and International Market
1876, John S. Tibals
827 Washington St.

5. Swann's Marketplace

5. Swann's Marketplace

1917-1940; 2000 rehabilitation, Pyatok Architects
9th and Clay Sts.

For over 60 years Swann's was a major city market occupying an entire block. Colorfulterra-cotta ornament set around the building's cornice advertised its wares. Now converted to mixed-use the building includes 20 co-housing condominium units and a commons, 18 affordable rental units, offices and commercial spaces, and a Museum of Children's Art. Thedesign, which saved 75% of the existing structure, created linked public and private open spaces by peeling away parts of the roof above the metal trusses.

4. The Lawyers' Block

6. Landmark Place

6. Landmark Place

2002, Pyatok Architects
Martin Luther King Jr. Way between 11th and 12th Sts.

A project on the edge of Preservation Park consisting of 92 flats and lofts designed to reflect thetransition between the city's 19th century residential image and contemporary downtown development.

7. 12th St. entrance to Preservation Park

7. Preservation Park

7. Pardee House Museum

7. First Lutheran Church

7. Preservation Park

1970–1991, Architectural Resources Group, consulting architects for historic preservation

12th to 14th Sts. and Preservation Park Way

Of the 16 structures on this site only five stand on their original sites north of 13th Street. The others were moved in 1970 to sites south of 13th Street because of the freeway construction to the northwest. Rehabilitation of the buildings for various non-profit organizations and offices was completed in 1991. Plaques have information about the buildings, which range in date from 1870 to 1911. The office park successfully recalls the vanished upper-class residential neighborhood it replaced.

Pardee House Museum

1868, Hoaglund & Newsom

672 11th St.

One of the best remaining examples of the bracketed Italianate Villa Style complete with carriage house and water tower.

First Lutheran Church

1891, Walter Matthews; 1998 restoration of the east wing and social hall, William Turnbull & Assoc.

14th and Castro Sts.

African American Museum and Library at Oakland (former Charles S. Greene Library)

1902, Bliss & Faville; 2002 restoration and conversion, Michael Willis Architects

659 14th St. at Martin Luther King Jr. Way

Two buildings that shared the Romanesque Revival style of their time of construction as well as damage from the 1989 earthquake that fortunately led to their restoration and revitalization.

8. **1111 Broadway building**
1991, Gensler Assoc.

Clorox Building
1976, Cesar Pelli
1345 Broadway

City Center Buildings and Mall
1990, Ishimaru Design Group
11th to 14th Sts. & Broadway to Martin Luther King Jr. Way

Downtown's latest commercial and office complex, created on land cleared for redevelopment decades ago. The interior of the City Center Mall is asuccessful work of urban design. A pleasant sculpture garden associated with the Oakland Museum is located behind the 1111 Broadway building.

8. City Center Buildings and Mall

8. City Center Buildings and Mall

9. **Ronald V. Dellums Federal Building**
1992, Kaplan, McLaughlin, Diaz
Jefferson to Martin Luther King, Jr. Way

Elihu Harris State Office Building
1998, DMJM/Keating
1515 Clay St.

Two buildings that speak of big government in Post-Modern ways. The ground floor of the state building has the City of Oakland Craft and Cultural Arts Gallery, which exhibits the work of Bay Area artists.

9. Ronald V. Dellums Federal Building

10. **1100 Broadway building**
1911-12, Frederick H. Meyer
1100 and 1200 Broadway

Bank building
1907, Charles W. Dickey; 1909, 1922-23, Reed & Corlett
1200 Broadway

Oakland Tribune Tower
1923, Edward T. Foulkes
13th and Franklin Sts.

The core of the post-1906 downtown, these were the skyscrapers of their time designed in the image of the Italian Renaissance palace. The Tribune Tower is still a favorite skyline landmark.

10. Oakland Tribune Tower

11. **City Hall**
1911-14, Palmer, Hornbostel & Jones;
1995 reopened after restoration and seismic retrofit

1 Frank H. Ogawa Plaza

A skyscraper with a Classical topknot lavishly decorated in white terra-cotta ornament depicting the state's fruits and flowers. The design was a competition winner and reflected a then new idea of putting city halls in skyscrapers. Damaged by the 1989 earthquake, the building's seismic retrofit was completed in

11. City Hall

11. The Rotunda

11. The Rotunda

11. The Rotunda

11. City Hall

1995. The Frank H. Ogawa Plazawas completed in 1998 by Pyatok Architects, Inc. with Y. H. Lee Associates. The design, which has a raised lawn and amphitheater seating around a tiled court leading to the building entrance is part of a paved pedestrian commons. The sculpture and fountain were created by Bruce Beasley in 2002.

Oakland Administration Building; former Broadway Building
1907, Lewellyn B. Dutton; restored 1998, Muller & Caulfield/Fentress & Bradburn/Carey & Co. historic preservation architect
Broadway and 14th St.

The Rotunda, adjoined to the administrations building
1913, Charles Dickey; 2001 restoration architect James Heilhoner
These two historic buildings were joined with a new structure to create a building for city administration offices. The Rotunda was originally the centerpiece of a department store and has been restored to its original splendor.

12. **YWCA Building**
1915, Julia Morgan
1515 Webster St.

Morgan was the YWCA's architect at one time and designed a number of its buildings in the west and in Honolulu. This one has an attractive interior court.

12.YWCA Building

13. **Former Howden Building**
 1915
 17th and Webster Sts.
 Built to advertise the owner's ornamental tile products; the interior is also richly decorated.

13. Former Howden Building

14. **Cathedral Building**
 1913, Benjamin McDougall
 Telegraph Ave. and Broadway
 A chateauesque skyscraper with spikey ornament.
15. **Fox Oakland Theater and office building**
 1928, M. I. Diggs, Weeks & Day
 1815 Telegraph Ave.
 An exotic Arabian nights movie palace awaiting restoration and new life.

15. Fox Oakland Theater and Office building

16. **Mary Bowles Building**
 1931, Douglas D. Stone
 1721 Broadway
 A small gem of Art Deco styling.
17. **Oakland Floral Depot**
 1931, Albert Evers
 1900 Telegraph Ave.
 Another Art Deco jewel box; it was built to prevent a tall building from blocking the view of the department store next door.

17. Oakland Floral Depot

18. Former I. Magnin & Co.

18. **Former I. Magnin & Co.**
 1931, Weeks & Day
 20th St. & Broadway
 Like the previous entry this is a box wrapped in Art Deco terra-cotta tiling.

24. Oakland Public Library

25. Scottish Rite Temple

26. Camron-Stanford House Museum

27. Alameda County Courthouse

19. **Paramount Theater**
1931, Miller & Pflueger; rest. 1976,
Skidmore Owings & Merrill
2025 Broadway
Arguably the greatest Art Deco theater left on the west coast, the billboard-like exterior served its advertising function superbly. The architects designed every bit of the interior and had talented artists, Ralph Stackpole, Robert Howard and others, create the relief sculpture and other decoration. There are tours. Don't miss the ladies' lounge.

20. **Former Breuner Co.**
1931, Albert F. Roller
22nd St. and Broadway
Built for a furniture company, as the chair in terra-cotta relief over the entrance suggests.

21. **Moss Cottage**
1864, S. H. Williams
Mosswood Park, Broadway and MacArthur Blvd.
The finest and most elaborately detailed Gothic Revival Cottage still standing in California.

22. **Kaiser Center**
Ordway Building
1970, Skidmore Owings & Merrill
Kaiser Plaza and 21st St.

Kaiser Center Building
1959, Welton Beckett & Assoc.; Rooftop garden, Osmundsen/Staley
20th and Harrison Sts.
Kaiser's standing as a major property owner and a powerful local institution is expressed in these two buildings. The rooftop garden is a largely unknown treasure that rewards visitors with a well-maintained green oasis and great views of the city.

23. **Former Oakland Hotel**
1910, Henry Janeway Hardenburgh, Bliss & Faville; rest. 1981 and 1991, The Ratcliff Architects
270 13th St.
The post-1906 boom inspired this luxury hotel, still a landmark, but now converted to housing for senior citizens.

24. **Oakland Public Library**
1949, Miller & Warnecke
125 14th St.
Restrained Modern styling with a human civic scale.

25. **Scottish Rite Temple**
1908, O'Brien & Werner
1433 Madison Ave.

A particularly gutsy version of the Mission Revival style.

26. **Camron-Stanford House Museum**
1875, Samuel Merritt
1426 Lakeside Dr.
The last of the stately mansions that once lined the lake.

27. **Alameda County Courthouse**
1935, W. G. Corlett & James W. Plachek
13th and Fallon Sts.
A fine example of the Depression era Public Works Administration's Monumental Moderne.

28. **The Oakland Museum**
1969, Kevin Roche, John Dinkeloo & Assoc.; landscape architect, Dan Kiley
Oak between 10th and 12th Sts.
A justly famous Bay Area building, this sunken museum houses Natural History, History, and Art and has a landscaped courtyard framed by terraced gardens.

28. The Oakland Museum, garden

29. California College of the A rts, Barclay Simpson Sculpture Studio

28. The Oakland Museum

29. California College of the Arts, dormitory

29. **California College of the Arts**
5212 Broadway
Founded in 1907 as the California College of Arts and Crafts, the first such institution west of the Mississippi River. Treadwell Hall, built around 1880, is the oldest campus building. Two notable recent buildings are the Barclay Simpson Sculpture Studio by Jim Jennings, 1993, and a 64-bedroom dormitory at Broadway and Clifton Street, designed by MarK Horton and opened in 2003. The crisp steel and glass box facing Broadway–provides an architectural introduction to the campus, much of which is invisible on its hillside site. Along Clifton Street the building angles back from the street and frames an eliptical zinc-clad building housing semi-public spaces that faces the main campus.

Two separate and distinct communities grew together to form the City of Berkeley, which was incorporated in 1878 with the waterfront community of Ocean View. The open fields that separated the University community from its industrial counterpart were gradually filled in with buildings, but unlike Oakland, Berkeley has remained a largely residential city with a relatively small downtown.

The University got its start in Oakland in 1859 when the Reverend Henry Durant, founder of the College of California, joined with members of an academic committee to purchase a 160-acre tract for the future location of the college, which they felt should be removed from the evil urban influences of Oakland. To help finance the purchase, an adjacent townsite of one-acre lots was platted, and settlement began. The town was finally named after Bishop George Berkeley of Cloyne, whose line, "Westward the course of empire takes it way," seemed appropriate to the founding fathers. The College became the state university after the passage of the Morrill Land Grant Act of 1862. By the terms of the act each state got 30,000 acres of surveyed public land for each of its senators and representatives in Congress as apportioned by the 1860 census. Proceeds from the sale of the land were to be invested and the returns used to develop the campus buildings and grounds.

The University of California graduated its first class in 1873; the graduation ceremony took place in front of the first two buildings, North and South Halls, designed in 1873 by David Farquharson in the fashionable Second Empire style. (Only South Hall remains.) Between them the central axis of Frederick Law Olmsted's 1866 campus plan, now called Campanile Way, defined the visual path to the Golden Gate. Farquharson himself did a plan for the campus in 1873 that somewhat reflected Olmsted's, but it had hardly any effect on the siting of buildings when the University really began to grow in the 1880s. In the mid-1890s Mrs. Phoebe A. Hearst expressed an interest in funding a building for the College of Mining in memory of her husband, Senator George Hearst. Soon after she financed an international competition for a campus master plan that was coordinated by Bernard Maybeck and judged by a distinguished jury of American and European architects in 1899. The winner, Emile Bénard, was awarded the prize money, but as a result of political machinations was not appointed by the regents to serve as supervising architect. Instead the position was filled in 1901-2 by the fourth-place winner, John Galen Howard. As supervising architect for 22 years, Howard revised Bénard's plan and designed the buildings that comprise the central core of the campus. George Kelham followed Howard and held the position from 1927-1036; Arthur Brown, Jr., succeeded him in 1938 and served until 1948 as the last supervising architect. The post-World War II expansion filled the central campus with buildings, most of which are not up to the original standards set by Howard. Yet the campus remains remarkably parklike.

Although the main entrance to the University of California campus is at the end of University Avenue, the pedestrian entrances at Hearst and Telegraph Avenues are equally important. The central campus is bounded on the west by Oxford Street, on the north by Hearst Avenue, and on the south by Bancroft Way. To the east the campus stretches up into the hills, but the central campus ends more or less at Gayley Road.

University of California

1. Hilgard Hall
   Wellman Hall
   Giannini Hall
2. University House
   Haviland Hall
3. Valley Life Sciences Building
4. Sproul Hall and Plaza/Cezar Chavez Student Center complex
   Former Unitarian Church
5. Sather Gate
   Wheeler Hall
6. Durant Hall
   California Hall
7. Doe Library
   Bancroft Library
8. South Hall
   Sather Tower and Esplanade
9. Hearst Memorial Gym
10. Berkeley Art Museum
11. Jean Gray Hargrove Music Library
12. Wurster Hall/College of Environmental Design
13. Haas Business School
14. Women's Faculty Club
    Senior Men's Hall
    Faculty Club
15. Hearst Memorial Mining Building
16. North Gate Hall
17. Foothill student housing and Stern Hall
    Greek Theater
18. Graduate School of Public Policy (Former Beta Theta Pi House) *2607 Hearst Ave.*

Berkeley

19. Delaware Historic District *800 block of Delaware St. and 1800 Fifth St.*
20. First Presbyterian Church of West Berkeley *926 Hearst Ave.*
    Church of the Good Shepherd *1001 Hearst Ave.*
21. H. J. Heinz Factory *2900 San Pablo Ave.*
22. Captain Boudrow house *1536 Oxford St.*
23. Tipping Building *1906 Shattuck Ave.*
24. Whittier Elementary School *1645 Milvia St.*
25. Berkeley Unified School District Building (former City Hall) *2134 Martin Luther King Jr. Way*
26. Berkeley High School *Allston Way and Martin Luther King Jr. Way*
27. Martin Luther King Jr. Civic Center Building *2180 Milvia St. Civic Center Park*
28. Main Public Library *Shattuck Ave. and Kittredge St.*
29. Tupper & Reed Music Store *2277 Shattuck Ave.*
30. Howard Automobile Company building *2140 Durant Ave.*
31. Manville Apartments *2100 Channing Way*
    Fine Arts apartments *Shattuck Ave. and Haste St.*
32. Former S. H. Kress building *2036 Shattuck Ave.*
    Former Golden Sheaf Building *2071 Addison St.*
33. Berkeley City Club *2315 Durant Ave.*
34. Town and Gown Club *2401 Dwight Way*
35. First Church of Christ Scientist *2619 Dwight Way*
36. Thorsen House *2307 Piedmont Ave.*
37. Julia Morgan Center (former St. John's Presbyterian Church) *2640 College Ave.*
38. Normandy Village *1781-1839 Spruce St.*
39. Oscar Mauer Studio *1772 Le Roy Ave.*
    Allenoke Freeman house *1777 Le Roy Ave.*
    Former Cloyne Court Hotel *2600 Ridge Rd.*
40. Kennedy-Nixon house *1537 Euclid Ave.*
41. Rose Walk *Rose between Euclid and Le Roy Aves.*
    John Galen Howard house *1401 Le Roy Ave.*
42. Greenwood Common *off Greenwood Terrace*
    Francis Gregory house *1476 Greenwood Terrace*
    Warren Gregory house *1486 Greenwood Terrace*
43. La Loma Park/Maybeck land *Buena Vista Way and La Loma Ave.*
    Lawson house *1515 La Loma Ave.*
    Mathewson studio/house *2704 Buena Vista Way*
    Maybeck's "Sack house" *2711 Buena Vista Way*
    Wallen Maybeck house *2751 Buena Vista Way*
    House *2753 Buena Vista Way*
    Gannon house *2780 Buena Vista Way*
44. Hume Cloister/Castle *2900 Buena Vista Way*

Previous page: Sather tower, the Campanile, University of California

Sutter St.
Los Angeles Ave.
Mariposa Ave.
Amador Pl.
Arch St.
Oak St.
Laurel St.
High Ct.
Keith Ave.
Sterling Av.
Shasta Rd.
Campus Dr.
Hill Rd.
Eunice St.
Quail Ave.
North Gate Ave.
Queens Rd.
Fairlawn Dr.
Summer St.
Tamalpais Rd.
Glen Ave.
Codornices Rd.
La Loma Ave.
Glendale Ave.
Avenida Dr.
Bay View Pl.
Rose
Greenwood Ter.
Le Roy Ave.
Buena Vista Way
Parnassus Rd.
Campus Dr.
Olympus Ave.
Scenic Ave.
Hawthorne Ter.
Rose St.
La Loma Ave.
La Vereda Rd.
Vine St.
Bonita Ave.
Milvia St.
Henry St.
Walnut St.
Oxford St.
Spruce St.
Arch St.
Cedar St.
Hilgard Ave.
Euclid Ave.
Cedar St.
Virginia St.
Lincoln St.
Le Conte Ave.
Highland Pl.
Shattuck Ave.
Virginia St.
Ridge Rd.
Francisco St.
Hearst Ave.
Cyclotron Rd.
Delaware St.
Gayley Rd.
Hearst Ave.
University Dr.
Berkeley Way
Stadium Rimway
University Ave.
University Dr.
Shattuck Sq.
Addison St.
University of California
Center St.
Allston Way
Piedmont Ave.
Kittredge St.
Prospect St.
Bancroft Way
Fulton St.
Ellsworth St.
Dana St.
Bowditch St.
College Ave.
M. L. King Wy.
Durant Ave.
Channing Way
Etna St.
Warring St.
Haste St.
Shattuck Ave.
Regent St.
Hillegass Ave.
Benvenue Ave.
Parker St.
Dwight Way
Blake St.
Telegraph Ave.
Derby St.
Parker St.
Forest Ave.
Carleton St.
Garber St.
Derby St.
Stuart St.
Cherry St.
Kelsey St.
Ward St.
Russell St.
Stuart St.
Shatt
N
1 2 3 4 5 6 7 8 9 10 11 12 13 14 15 16 17 18 19 20 21 22 23 24 25 26 30 31 32 33 34 35 36 37 38 39 40 41 42 43 44

19

1. Wellman Hall

University of California

1. **Wellman Hall**
   1912, John Galen Howard
   Hilgard Hall
   1917-18, John Galen Howard
   Giannini Hall
   1930, William C. Hays
   As California's major industry along with mining, agriculture was a high priority for the early university. When built, Agriculture Hall, now Wellman, was the first building visitors saw when they entered the campus. Howard's reliance on the Classical Revival styles for academic buildings inspired him to use the vernacular Tuscan farmhouse with its courtyard garden as a model for the college. The bold form and detail of Wellman gave way to the ornate rendition of neo-Classicism used for post-World-War-I Hilgard Hall, for which reinforced concrete coated with stucco sgraffito work was used instead of the more expensive granite. Replete with symbols of the bounty of the state's agriculture, Hilgard will reward those who scrutinize its walls. Giannini Hall was designed at the dawn of the Modern era by Howard's associate, Will Hayes, whose wife Elah created the low relief panels atop the pilasters on the east side of the building. Giannini's lobby is a fine example of Art Deco styling and one of the few significant interiors on the campus.

1. Hilgard Hall

1. Hilgard Hall

1. Giannini Hall

2. University House

2. **University House (originally the President's House)**
   1900-1902, Albert Pissis; 1910, John Galen Howard
   The first building sited according to Emile Benard's competition-winning campus plan was modeled after the classical Italian Villa. The interior was completed years later for President Benjamin Ide Wheeler by

John Galen Howard, who also designed the landscaping and allegedly brought the seeds for the umbrella pine trees from Tuscany.

Haviland Hall
1923-24, John Galen Howard
Haviland occupies the site that Howard designated in his plan for the Fine Arts Museum, the counterpart of California Hall south of the central axis. Built for the School of Education, the building has a fine interior in the style of the 18th-century architect Robert Adam on the upper floor; it originally housed the school library. The exterior is yet another version of the Classical Revival style with cast concrete ornament in a rich variety of motifs.

2. Haviland Hall

3. **Valley Life Sciences Building**
1930, George Kelham; 1989-1994 remodelling, Ratcliff Assoc.
Kelham's imposing building was a true block-buster in its day. It housed the departments assigned in Howard's plan for five small buildings on the site. Styled in one of the exotic modes–say, Neo-Assyrian–favored by the decorative arts movements of the time, the exterior has fine cast sculptural detail created by Robert Howard, John Galen Howard's son. The structure was gutted in 1989; the building re-opened with new interiors in 1994.

3. Valley Life Sciences Building

4. **Sproul Hall and Plaza/Cezar Chavez Student Center complex**
1941, Arthur Brown, Jr.; 1965, DeMars & Reay
Bancroft at Telegraph Ave.
The renown site of student protests during the Free Speech Movement in the 1960s, this spatially integrated complex has proved to be a very successful work of urban design.

Former Unitarian Church
1898, A.C. Schweinfurth; 1999 renovation, Muller & Caulfield
A notable example of the Bay region Shingle style with redwood tree trunks used as columns. Schweinfurth was a member of the group of architects, which included Bernard Maybeck, the Coxhead brothers, and Willis Polk, that spawned the regional craftsman style around the turn of the 19th century. In 1960 the university purchased the church building; the congregation had moved. The building is currently used for a variety of programs.

5. Sather Gate and bridge

5. **Sather Gate and bridge**
1911, John Galen Howard
Before the construction of Sproul Plaza in the 1960s,

5. Wheeler Hall, detail

5. Wheeler Hall, detail

Telegraph Avenue extended to this important campus entrance. Both the ornate gate and the bridge associated with it were funded by Jane K. Sather, widow of Peder Sather who had been a trustee for the College of California. The bas-relief marble panels with nude figures were sculpted by Melvin Earl Cummings.

Wheeler Hall

1917, John Galen Howard; 1973 auditorium remodeling, DeMars & Wells

Named for Benjamin Ide Wheeler, the university's most important president to date, this was the largest classroom building yet erected on the campus. Oriented toward the southern campus entrance, the building's French Baroque style is effectively used to enrich the main facade with elegant sculptural detail

5. Wheeler Hall

such as heads of Apollo over the arched windows and the row of giant urns atop the cornice. The building's other sides have a simpler, more utilitarian character.

6. **Durant Hall (originally Boalt Hall)**

1911, John Galen Howard

A small cubic building intended as one of a pair connected by an arcade to balance California Hall across Campanile Way. The other building, Philosophy Hall, was never built. Despite its size the building conveys the law's gravity and dignity through bold treatment of the molded cornice with its large metopes and the rather severe composition of the elevations. Whether or not Howard had an architectural pun in mind, the granite blocks are so laid at the building corners between the capitals and the bases that they create the illusion of shafts on the flat walls. The upper floor reading room is worth seeing even though computer monitors now clutter the space. The rooftop skylight illuminates the central part of the room framed with Tuscan columns, and

Howard's bronze "lamps of learning" cast in the shape of Greco-Roman oil lamps light the periphery. The Deparment of East Asian Languages and its library now occupy the building.

6. Durant Hall

California Hall

1903-1905, John Galen Howard; 1968-1970 alterations, Germano Milono/Walter Steilberg

The first building of Howard's revised campus plan to be completed housed offices for the president and other administrative services on the upper floor. The first floor had a large lecture hall and classrooms, which were replaced with offices in the 1960s remodelling. A rectangular block with a strong modular rhythm, the steel-frame structure is obvious behind the Neo-Classical granite walls. The most ornate element of the design is the copper-framed skylight with its elaborate acroteria (rooftop ornament)– wonderful to see from a distance.

6. California Hall

7. **Doe Memorial Library**

1907-1911 and 1914-1918, John Galen Howard; 1927-1928, Morrison Library interior, Walter Ratcliff, Jr.; 1975, Theodore Bernardi, Wurster Bernardi & Emmons, East Reading Room restoration; 1992-1994 Information Center and underground Gardner Stacks, Esherick Homsey Dodge & Davis

When Charles Franklin Doe's posthumous gift to the university decreased in value after the 1906 earthquake, the available funds fell short of paying for the library building. The Regents then decided on two construction phases, which meant that the library was completed eleven years later. The main entrance is centered in the facade of the north-facing wing, which contains secondary reading rooms on the ground floor and the main reading room on the upper floor. Howard eschewed the grand entrance stairway, which devoured space in major libraries such as the New York and Boston Public Libraries, in favor of a non-monumental branching stair on the south side of the entrance lobby that leads to the main floor and the 210-foot reading room that stretches the length of the north wing. Skylights and ceiling-height windows on the north side as well as large arched windows on the east and west ends illuminate the interior– second in size only to that of the New York Public Library. A coffered barrel-vaulted ceiling completed the majestic space, decorated with Classical motifs by the San Francisco interiors design and furnishing firm of Vickery, Atkins & Torrey. The library's south block contained nine floors of stacks, seminar rooms, and a second large reading room on

7. Doe Memorial Library

7. Doe Memorial Library, detail

7. Doe Annex/Bancroft Library

8. Sather Tower/The Campanile

8. Sather Esplanade

the east side. The north wing is a major architectural statement both for the library and for the campus as a whole. If the university was proclaimed the Athens-of-the-West the library was a temple to Athena/Minerva, represented by a bronze sculpture mounted over the entrance portal. The north wing recalls a Greco/Roman temple with giant engaged Corinthian columns. The heads of round-arched windows break the pediments on the east and west ends, and the carved granite ornament is richly detailed and original, particularly that of the column capitals, which feature open books upheld by coiled serpents, more symbols of the goddess of wisdom.

In the 1990s the original stacks were removed for seismic reasons, and the books were transferred to underground stacks beneath the north wing's terraces.

Doe Annex/Bancroft Library

1949, Arthur Brown, Jr.

Built on the site of North Hall, South Hall's counterpart that was finally demolished in 1931, this reinforced concrete structure coated with granite-like stucco was designed in a simplified Beauxartsian classical style to respect but not compete with Doe Library.

8. **Sather Tower/The Campanile**

1914, John Galen Howard

Howard had drawn his ideas for a campanile for nearly a decade before one was funded by Jane K. Sather in 1911. The final design was modeled after the tower of San Marco in Venice; its height of 303 feet is shorter and its girth less than its model, but the resemblance is clear. Although the tower's shaft, strengthened by corner pilasters, is severely plain, Howard intended it to "burst into bloom at the summit, like a great white lilly." The ornamental detail is concentrated at the campanile level and above where a balustrade carved with fleur-de-lis provides the base for the pyramidal spire capped with a bronze lantern symbolizing the enlightenment of learning. Although nearly a century has passed and much development has occurred around the Bay, Sather Tower remains a significant landmark.

Sather Esplanade

1915-1916, John Galen Howard; landscaping, John W. Gregg and MacRorie-McLaren

Howard's vision of the esplanade as a natural meeting place for students was never fulfilled. Instead, the formally landscaped island planted with pollarded London plane trees and crossed with brick pathways has functioned more as a vantage point for campus views and a place for solitary reverie. Various people are commemorated here, including Howard, for whom a large granite tablet with bronze lettering was designed by Stafford Jory and Warren Perry and set in the brick pavement in front of the Campanile. The most noticeable monument is a bronze bust of Abraham Lincoln by Gutzon Borglum of Mount Rushmore fame that was given to the university in 1909 and sited here in 1921. Lincoln signed the 1862 Morrill Land Grant Act, which led to the creation of the University of California.

8. South Hall

South Hall
1873, David Farquharson; 1968-70 alterations, Kolbeck Cardwell & Christopherson; 1986-88 seismic upgrade and restoration, Esherick Homsey Dodge & Davis
Designed in the fashionable French Second Empire Style by the architect who made a plan for the campus in 1869, South Hall was one of the first two buildings erected on the campus. The building served several purposes. To fireproof the physical and natural sciences laboratories the building had double-walled brick construction and a mansard roof of slate with multiple chimnies and flues. The bas-relief panels on the end walls below the cornice are made of cast-iron dusted with sand to mimic stone and depict California grains and fruit. The main entrance with a branching stair was originally on the west side of the building to conform with the general orientation of the campus buildings to the Golden Gate.

9. Phoebe A. Hearst Memorial Gymnasium

9. Phoebe A. Hearst Memorial Gymnasium

9. **Phoebe A. Hearst Memorial Gymnasium**
1925, Bernard Maybeck and Julia Morgan
Morgan collaborated with Maybeck in planning the building–the drawings were made in her office–and Maybeck designed romantic architectural elements such as the urns and the decorative detail as well as the setting for the pool. The gymnasium was intended to be part of a larger complex with an auditorium, art gallery, and museum that was never built.

10. **Berkeley Art Museum**
1970, Mario Ciampi
2630 Bancroft Way
A segmented cubistic composition in concrete with a dramatic interior in which the galleries fan out along a spiral circulation path overlooking a large atrium. The building's site extends from Bancroft Way to Durant Avenue. A theater, gallery, offices, service spaces, and a cafe occupy the lower level entered from Durant Avenue. A partial seismic retrofit in 2001 enabled the museum to stay open, but seismic issues continue to make its future uncertain.

11. Jean Gray Hargrove Music Library

12. Wurster Hallollege of Environmental Design

12. Wurster Hall/College of Environmental Design, Library

13. Haas School of Business

11. Jean Gray Hargrove Music Library
2004, MSME Architects
A small boxy building wrapped with slate shingles that prompts comparison with the wood shingled buildings of the Arts and Crafts era. Set into a hillside, the library has two stories on the east side and three on the lower west side; its 28,755 sq. ft. are divided almost equally among the three floors. Within its gray slate skin a skeletal white steel frame is visible through openings that allow daylighting and take advantage of views and orientations. Metal louvers have been set outside some windows to filter sunlight. The white interior is well appointed with warm cherry wood paneling and casework; the floors are also of cherry. Separation of the slate skin from the brace frame will allow it to move independently during an earthquake and mitigate possible damage. The library's rich collections of books and music manuscripts are now available for use in an hospitable ambiance.

12. Wurster Hall/College of Environmental Design
1964, DeMars, Esherick, and Olsen;
2003, seismic retrofit and restoration,
Esherick Homsey Dodge & Davis
College Ave. at Bancroft Way
When built for the departments of architecture, landscape architecture, planning, and the decorative arts, this was the world's largest prefabricated concrete building; its "Brutalist" style, fashionable in the 1960s, has been accused of making the building overwhelm its surroundings. The seismic retrofit for the building necessitated alterations to the interior to protect the structure against seismic shear forces.

13. Haas School of Business
1992-95 Moore Ruble Yudell/VBN Architects
Named for Walter A. Haas, Sr., long time president of Levi Strauss & Co., the school is housed in a building divided into three sections sited around a courtyard, which is entered through monumental arches from the campus and Gayley Road. A steel sculpture by Fletcher Benton titled "Folded Circle Trio" stands in the garden opposite the western gateway. The design, which echoes the informal early regionalism of the Bay Area's wooden buildings as well as the classicism of the campus buildings, is eclectic in the broadest sense of the term.

14. Women's Faculty Club
1923, John Galen Howard
Senior Men's Hall
1906, John Galen Howard
Faculty Club
1902, Bernard Maybeck; 1903-04, John Galen Howard; 1914, 1925, Warren Perry; 1959, Downs & Lagorio
Along Strawberry Creek

An informal group of social buildings on Strawberry Creek, the first in the eastern Shingle Style and the second a monumental redwood log cabin. The third building stands at the end of Faculty Glade. Designed by Maybeck in a modified Mission Revival style, it has been enlarged several times, but the original main hall is intact and well worth seeing.

14. Women's Faculty Club

14. Men's Faculty Club

15. Hearst Memorial Mining Building
1902-07, John Galen Howard; 1948 remodeling to replace the mining laboratory with offices, Michael Goodman; 1998-2002 restoration, seismic retrofit with base isolation, and addition, NBBJ/Rutherford and Chekene Consulting Engineers

The finest building on the campus and one of California's and the nation's architectural treasures. Phoebe Apperson Hearst provided a generous budget for this dedicatory monument to her late husband, Senator George Hearst. Howard's plan for the building housed public and administrative functions in the south

15. Hearst Memorial Mining Building

section and laboratories, offices, and classrooms in the north section. Although Howard rhetorically linked the design to the state's Hispanic missions, it was a far cry from those rudimentary structures. Mediterranean classicism is most evident in the treatment of the Memorial Vestibule block, which dominates the building's southern section. The use of heavy timbers in the brackets supporting the tiled roof's overhang refers to vernacular colonial struc-

15.Hearst Memorial Mining Building

15. Hearst Memorial Mining Building

tures that Howard knew from his youthful visit to southern California. Critics noted their combination with sculpted granite corbels as a novel departure from traditional classicism. Sculptor Robert Aitken carved the corbel blocks with male torsos symbolizing the "primal elements" on the west side and "the eternal forces" on the east side. In the center female torsos represent the "ideal arts". A high level of craftsmanship is evident in all the decorative detail. If the exterior no longer seems novel, the interior of the Memorial Vestibule never fails to astonish visitors. The three-tiered galleries that provide circulation are framed with slender cast iron columns, which support an arcade capped with three glazed domed skylights that bring daylight into the hall. Their pendentives are clad with thin terra-cotta tiles set in a herringbone pattern. This tilework was the invention of Rafael Guastavino, whose company installed it in many structures in the eastern United States, but very rarely in the west. The hall had to be dimensioned with the tilework in mind, and a company crew installed it. The contrasting colors of the cool metalwork and the warm tile and brickwork enhance the airy effect of the space; its kinship to Labrouste's design for the reading room of the 1868 Bibliotheque Nationale in Paris is notable. After World War II, when mining no longer dominated the state's economy, the laboratory section of the building was gutted and remodeled as office space. However, further changes in the field produced the Department of Materials Science and Mineral Engineering for which, at the turn of the 20th century, the building was rehabilitated. The most dramatic aspect of the rehab work was the use of base-isolation in which the building's many tons of stone were set on hundreds of isolators, which in an earthquake will allow it to move about 29 feet in any direction and thus avoid maximum damage.

16. North Gate Hall/Graduate School of Journalism

16. North Gate Hall/Graduate School of Journalism
1906-12, John Galen Howard; 1935-36 additions, Warren Perry; 1936 library, Walter Steilberg; 1993 restoration, Stoller Knoerr Architects
This building for the first department of architecture west of the Rockies was fondly called the Ark–Howard was Father Noah. Since his ultimate goal for the school was a proper masonry building, he considered this one a temporary structure, hence its simple brown-shingled form and residential scale. The building grew by additions set around a pleasant courtyard that was finally enclosed on the south side with a library in 1936. This innovative structure has a roof and interior arches of concrete. The walls are made of Underdown concrete tiles, a forerunner of the now common concrete block. Uphill to the east is the former Drawing Building, 1914, also by Howard. The east end of this building was demolished in 1929.

16. North Gate Hall/Graduate School of Journalism

16. North Gate Hall/Graduate School of Journalism

17. Foothill Student Housing
1991, William Turnbull Assoc./Ratcliff Assoc.
Stern Hall
1942, 1959, Wurster, Bernardi & Emmons
A well-planned complex sensitively sited on difficult terrain that incorporates an older dormitory.

18. Goldman School of Public Policy (former Beta Theta Pi house)
1893, Coxhead & Coxhead;
1909 east addition, Bakewell & Brown;
1999 east building, Architectural Resources Group
Hearst at LeRoy Ave.
A good example of Ernest Coxhead's regional work, the building was designed in a Tudor revival style and composed of four interconnected sections that suggest a village. The university acquired the fraternity house in 1966. Parts of the interior are relatively unaltered and give a sense of Coxhead's work.

18. Goldman School of Public Policy

Berkeley

19. Delaware Historic District
1854-1910; designated in 1979, William Coburn, historic preservation architect
800 block of Delaware St. and 1800 block of Fifth St.
Berkeley's first settlement, Ocean View, connected a wharf called Jacob's Landing with Bowen's Inn on the Contra Costa Road, which became San Pablo Avenue. Buildings on these blocks from the 19th and early 20th centuries have been restored and rehabilitated for various uses. Notable among them are the 1878 house of Joseph Alphonso, a Portuguese cabinetmaker and carpenter who built other homes in the area–see

19. Delaware Historic District

20. First Presbyterian Chuch of West Berkeley

21. H. J. Heinz Factory

23. Tipping Building

the Silva house at 1824 5th Street–and the Heywood house of 1878, at 1808 Fifth Street, built by a son of Zimri Brewer Heywood, owner of the nearby Heywood and Jacobs Lumberyard and Planing Mill. In 1992 the Babilonia Wilner foundation restored the house with David Smith & Associates, architects. Information plaques exist for many of the buildings.

20. First Presbyterian Chuch of West Berkeley
1879, Charles Geddes
926 Hearst Ave.

Church of the Good Shepherd
1878, Charles Bugbee
1001 Hearst Ave.
Berkeley's two oldest churches. Both were designed in a Gothic Revival style often called Carpenter Gothic because of its typical wooden construction. Although not considered small when built, the two nicely painted churches now seem a bit like charming miniatures of their much larger kin.

21. H. J. Heinz Factory
1927, The Austin Co./Albert Kahn
2900 San Pablo Ave.
A huge factory in an eclectic Mediterranean mode by an architect well known for the design of industrial buildings. As the place where many of Heinz's 57 Varieties were manufactured, it gives a sense of the scale of such operations. Now converted to other uses, it retains its status as one of the city's grandest buildings.

22. Captain Boudrow house
1889, Julius Krafft
1536 Oxford St.
The finest Queen Anne style house in Berkeley, built for a sea captain, Joseph Hart Boudrow, who came to Berkeley from Nova Scotia in the 1880s. In England, the towers of Queen Anne houses symbolized the adage, "a man's home is his castle," but in the Bay Area the tower was mainly an empty symbol; the interior was usually left unfinished with no way to get into it. Captain Boudrow may have specified a house with a high tower because he wanted to view the progress of his ships in the Bay. Details such as fishtail shingles and ornamental friezes and panels are typical of the style.

23. Tipping Building
1995, Fernau & Hartman
1906 Shattuck Ave.
A three-story mixed-use building housing an engineering firm and apartment on the upper floor and a

coffee shop on the street level. The use of different materials and colors as well as separate roofs for the two upper-floor sections break up the building's mass.

24. Whittier Elementary School
1939, Schmidts Hardman Dragon Officer
1645 Milvia St.
An outstanding example of the so-called Streamlined Moderne style, which joined the curvilinear aesthetics of industrial design and the International Style.

25. Berkeley Unified School District Building (former City Hall)
1908, Bakewell & Brown; rest. 1991
2134 Martin Luther King, Jr. Way
Beaux-Arts Classicism used to create an American version of a French provincial city hall, which the city outgrew some years ago, but has carefully restored.

25. Berkeley Unified School District Building

26. Berkeley High School campus

26. Berkeley High School campus
1938-1950, Henry H. Gutterson and William Corlett, Sr.; Jacques Schnier and Robert Boardman Howard, scultors; 2004, Milvia Way buildings, ELS Architects
Allston Way and Martin Luther King Jr. Way
The original buildings on the high school campus were funded by the Depression-era Works Progress Administration. The Shop and Science Buildings were built in 1938-39; the Little Theater followed in 1940. Wartime shortages delayed the completion of the Community Theater until 1950. The buildings' early Modern or Moderne styling, a version of stripped-down classicism, was enriched by sculpted panels in bas-relief of various sizes by two of the Bay Area's best known local artists. Two recent buildings, a student center and gymnasium/natatorium, have contributed a welcome contemporary tone to the campus along its Milvia Way frontage.

28 Main Public Library

30. Howard Automobile Co. building

31. Manville Apartments

27. Martin Luther King Jr. Civic Center Building (former Federal Land Bank)

1938, James W. Plachek

This very large austere building expressive of the Great Depression era became Berkeley's new city hall in 1977. The Martin Luther King Jr. Civic Center Park west of the building, completed in 1942, was the outcome of years of planning that drew on the talents of prominent contributors such as Bernard Maybeck, Julia Morgan, Henry Gutterson, Lewis Hobart, and John Gregg. The square and its fountain completed the City Beautiful movement concept of government buildings grouped around a landscaped open space.

28. Main Public Library

1930; James W. Plachek; 2001 expansion and renovation, Ripley/BOORA Associated Architects

Shattuck and Kittredge Sts.

A building in the Art Deco style, sometimes called Zig-Zag Moderne, that recently received a much-needed and well-designed western addition. The high airy reading room was restored; its exterior sports zig-zag ornament along with sgrafitto panels that depict Egyptianesque figures making books.

29. Tupper & Reed Music Store

1925, W. R. Yelland

2277 Shattuck Ave.

Architecture from Mother Goose, delightfully dressed up.

30. Howard Automobile Co. building

1930, Frederick H. Reimers

2140 Durant Ave.

A garage and automobile showroom in the Art Deco style originally built for Charles Howard, owner of the famous racehouse Seabiscuit.

31. Manville Apartments

1995, David Baker & Assoc./Topher Delaney, landscape architect

2100 Channing Way

To minimize the massing of this 132-unit apartment building for university graduate students, it was designed to appear as three buildings through the use of different colors and exterior features. Ground floor commercial uses contribute to street life. A gated entrance between the two sections on Shattuck Avenue leads to a second-level court designed by Topher Delaney and furnished with lively geometric sculptures by Buddy Rhodes.

Fine Arts Apartments
2004, Solomon ETC
Shattuck Ave. and Haste St.
A lively contemporary rendition of the Moderne mode of the 1920s for a 100-unit apartment building with an interior courtyard. A 200-seat theater designed as the location for the former Fine Arts cinema occupies the ground floor along with a lobby and other uses.

31. Fine Arts Apartments

32. **Former S. H. Kress building**
1932, Edward F. Sibbert
2036 Shattuck Ave.
Originally built for the Kress chain of variety stores and adorned with terra-cotta ornament typical of the Zig-Zag Moderne branch of the post-1925 Art Deco style. The building is now part of the Arts District as is the former Golden Sheaf Bakery building next door at 2071 Addison Street. This 1905 brick building with cast terra-cotta ornament was designed by Clinton Day, the architect of a number of early buildings for the university campus.

32. Former S. H. Kress building

33. **Berkeley City Club (former Berkeley Women's City Club)**
1929, Julia Morgan
2315 Durant Ave.
A reinforced concrete structure with a massive six-story residential tower flanked by wings. The decorative detail has a modified Romanesque character. Public spaces are on the two lower floors, and two interior garden courts help to light the interior. The blue tiled swimming pool is worth seeing as is the upper floor dining hall–the heavy timbers of the ceiling are actually concrete. Those who wish to visit the interior may apply at the office near the entrance.

33. Berkeley City Club

34. **Town and Gown Club**
1899, Bernard Maybeck
2401 Dwight Way

34. Town and Gown Club

35. *First Church of Christ, Scientist*

Composed of shingled boxy sections, the tallest of which has a broadly overhanging roof supported by a framework of outrigger joists and posts that extend into the interior of the assembly room. Although Maybeck relished using structure to give buildings an expressive character, critics wrote that his breaking with convention bordered on the "freakish."

35. *First Church of Christ, Scientist*

35. *First Church of Christ, Scientist*

35. *First Church of Christ, Scientist*

36. *Julia Morgan Center*

35. First Church of Christ, Scientist
1910, Bernard Maybeck
Sunday School add.,
Dwight Way and Bowditch St.
1927, Henry Gutterson
Maybeck's masterwork and one of this country's most remarkable buildings. An amalgam of styles but a copy of none, the design demonstrates his genius for fusing innovative structure with original ornament and for making the most of a restricted site. The auditorium with its cruciform structure of four great boxed trusses set on concrete piers to create a flattened dome must be seen to be believed. The exterior cement-asbestos siding and metal-framed windows were typically used for industrial buildings; the original standing-seam metal roof, which leaked and was replaced with terra-cotta tiles, would have added to the church's industrial palette of materials. The church is open to the public after services on Wednesday night and Sunday morning. The interior is as magical at night as during the day.

36. Julia Morgan Center
(former St. John's Presbyterian Church)
1908-10, Julia Morgan
2640 College Ave.
Designed to fit into this early neighborhood of brown-shingled houses, many of them owned by university faculty and personnel, the building appears smaller

than it actually is. The barnlike character of the interior was deliberate; its frankly expressed structural framework was enriched with Craftsman lighting fixtures. Built at the same time as Maybeck's nearby church, it cost a quarter as much. The building is now used as a theater.

37. Sigma Phi Fraternity house

37. Sigma Phi Fraternity house (former Thorsen house)

1910, Greene & Greene

2307 Piedmont Ave.

A rare and notable example in northern California of the work of this famous Pasadena firm. The well known Blacker house in Pasadena was designed for Mrs. Thorsen's sister; Mr. Thorsen was a retired lumberman and thus an ideal client for whom the Greene brothers created this example of comsummate craftsmanship in wood complemented by clinker brick.

38. Normandy Village

38. Normandy Village

38. Normandy Village

38. Normandy Village

1929, William Raymond Yelland

1781-1839 Spruce St.

Also known as Thornburg Village, this complex of apartment buildings was designed to recall villages in Normandy that Colonel Jack Thornburg had visited during World War I. Although Yelland had not seen Normandy, he doubtless saw picture postcards of it since his design for the buildings is literally picturesque-shadows and signs of age are painted on the walls along with vines and other motifs. No two apartments in the original buildings are exactly alike, and the view from the street conjurs up storybook illustrations.

39 Allenoke, the Freeman house

40. Former Kennedy/Nixon studio/house

39. Oscar Maurer Studio
1907, Bernard Maybeck
1772 LeRoy Ave.
A small but inviting studio building designed for a photographer and sited along a creek. Although the building's general appearance recalls the humble vernacular of colonial times, the recessed wall of the entrance portico has a Maybeckian flourish in the Corinthian column that bisects its wall-size "picture" window.

Allenoke, the Freeman house
1904-06, Coxhead & Coxhead
LeRoy Ave. at Ridge Rd.
A large Colonial Revival house of strong character in a suitable setting by a firm that contributed importantly to early Bay Area regional architecture.

Former Cloyne Court Hotel
1904, John Galen Howard
2600 Ridge Rd.
A shingled structure built around three sides of a generous garden courtyard. The hotel was funded by many investors with university connections and intended for long and short stays–recitals and lectures were offered in addition to room and board. In 1946 the hotel was purchased by the University Student Cooperative Housing Association.

40. Former Kennedy/Nixon studio/house
1914, 1923, Bernard Maybeck
Euclid Ave. and Buena Vista Way
An idiosyncratic design combining Mediterranean and Gothic elements–Maybeck was particularly fond of trefoils and quatrefoils–created for Alma Kennedy, a popular piano teacher. Maybeck designed the furniture and cabinetry in the redwood recital hall, which has fine acoustics. The hall was linked to living quarters; it replaced a building also by Maybeck that burned in 1923.

23. Rose Walk

41. Rose Walk

1913, Bernard Maybeck; 1925-36, Henry Gutterson
Rose bet. Euclid and LeRoy Ave.

A perfectly planned residential development compressed into one block. Maybeck designed the walk and the concrete retaining walls and light standards. After the 1923 fire, owner Frank Gray hired Henry Gutterson, Maybeck's protege, to design houses on the north side. The single and double houses were ingeniously sited to provide privacy and gracious living on a small scale.

41. Howard house

Howard house

1912, John Galen Howard
1401 LeRoy Ave.

Designed in an L-shape to follow the lot frontage, this long and linear shingled house shows how much Howard's eastern formality was modified by western informality. Julia Morgan added a library wing to the north end in 1927.

41. Greenwood Common

Greenwood Common

1950s, Lawrence Halprin, landscape architect
W. side of Greenwood Terr.

William W. Wurster initiated this postwar development on property that belonged to his house, designed by John Galen Howard; it stands east of Greenwood Terrace but is not visible from the street. Like Rose Walk, this is an exemplary residential enclave, but from a different time. The Modern architects of the Second Bay Tradition are well represented in these modest houses, numbered from north to south around the common.

41. Greenwood Common, No 1

No. 1
1955, Donald Olsen

No. 3
1954, Joseph Esherick

No. 4
1954, Harwell Hamilton Harris

No. 7
c.1920, R. M. Schindler and William W. Wurster

No. 8
1953, Howard Moise

No. 9
1954, Henry Hill

No. 10
1952, John Funk

Francis Gregory house
1907, Bernard Maybeck
1476 Greenwood Terr.

41. Gregory house

41. Lawson house

If its age were unknown, one might take this for a contemporary Shingle-style house.

Gregory house
1912, John Galen Howard
1486 Greenwood Terr.
A sensitively sited Craftsmanly chalet.

La Loma Park/Maybeck land
1915-1933, Bernard Maybeck
Buena Vista Way and La Loma Ave.
About 1900 the Maybecks purchased a large tract of land called La Loma Park with two friends and subdivided it in 1902. The Maybecks' portion was built up mainly with family houses although some were designed for friends. Their large family house of 1909 was destroyed in the 1923 fire and replaced with a set of cottages that the family occupied in a somewhat nomadic fashion. Maybeck participated in the construction of most of the houses listed below; they embody innovative ideas and inventive handicraft.

Lawson house
1907, Bernard Maybeck
1515 LaLoma St.
Maybeck designed this innovative, poured-in-place concrete house for Professor Andrew Lawson, the geologist whose studies of the San Andreas and the Hayward faults prompted his desire for an earthquake resistant, fireproof house. Lawson was also one of the buyers of La Loma Park. Inspired by the houses of ancient Pompeii, the walls were incised in a diaper pattern and accented with colored tiles. The concrete was coated with stucco integrally tinted with earthen colors that have faded over time.

Mathewson studio/house
1915, Bernard Maybeck
2704 Buena Vista Way

The "Sack house"
1924, Bernard Maybeck
2711 Buena Vista Way

41. The "Sack house"

Clad with sacks dipped in Bubblecrete, a lightweight concrete, and hung on chicken wire. The original cladding was removed and recreated in the 1980's.

Wallen Maybeck house
1933, Bernard Maybeck
2751 Buena Vista Way
Designed for Maybeck's son and his family.

41. 2753 Buena Vista Way

House
1914, William C. Hays
2753 Buena Vista Way
A Bay Area Shingle-style version of a small Italian palazzo .

Gannon house
1933, Bernard Maybeck
2780 Buena Vista Way
Nearly a twin of Wallen Maybeck's house but adjusted to a different site.

42. Hume Cloister/Castle
1928, John Hudson Thomas
2900 Buena Vista Way
Although difficult to see, this unusual house is worth knowing about. Based on the design of an Augustinian monastery in Toulouse, France, it was revisioned by Samuel and Portia Hume, who furnished their architect with ideas. As director of the Greek Theater and founder of the Berkeley Art Museum, Samuel Hume followed many artistic pursuits. His wife, Portia, a psychiatrist who carried on her practice in the cloister, was an important pioneer in the mental health field. The cloister rambles around an entrance courtyard; sections of the house are visible from below on Buena Vista Way.

Although Marin County has both scenic delights and important architecture, the dense greenery, rugged terrain, and dwellers' insistence on privacy make it difficult to tour. The following circuit begins with two former military bases associated with coastal defense that now house cultural institutions. Sausalito is the next stop, followed by Belvedere and Tiburon, Mill Valley, San Anselmo and Ross. Our tour ends north of San Rafael; it is not comprehensive, but we hope it will encourage further exploration.

Sausalito. William A. Richardson, an English sailor and one of San Francisco's founding fathers, received Rancho Sausalito as the dowry of his Mexican bride. In 1869 1,000 acres were purchased by the Sausalito Land and Ferry Company, which subdivided the property as a speculative development with ferry service to San Francisco. Commuter settlement began in earnest in 1875 when the North Pacific Coast Railroad took control of the ferry. Until the opening of the Golden Gate Bridge, ferries provided the major means of northern entry to San Francisco. The town has evolved from fishing village to bohemian suburb to its present congested but still picturesque state. Precipitous terrain and narrow streets make driving difficult, especially on weekends. On the other side of Route 101 is the portion of the Golden Gate National Seashore that includes the Marin Headlands and the old coast defense installations of Forts Baker, Barry, and Cronkhite.

Next on our circuit are Belvedere and Tiburon, located north off Route 101. The completion of the Northern Pacific Railroad from San Rafael to Tiburon in 1884 brought ferry service from Tiburon to San Francisco–a spectacular commute. The first exurbanites settled along the harbor's edge, mainly in houseboats. Some of these survive as houses along Beach Road. In 1890 the Belvedere Land Company planted pine and eucalyptus on Belvedere "Island" (actually a peninsula), transforming the barren slopes into a Riviera-like paradise. Today most houses are barely visible, but it is worth driving around and climbing a few of the steep lanes to experience the ambience. The Belvedere Lagoon was a real estate development of the 1950s, now so solidly lined with houses that it is difficult to get any sense of either the architecture or its relationship to the water except from a boat.

Mill Valley, east of US 101, got its name from a sawmill built on Cascade Creek to cut the then plentiful redwoods. In 1887 the land was acquired by a group of developers who connected it to the new railroad. By 1890 3,000 lots had been sold, most of them for summer homes. In 1903, when electric rail service came to Mill Valley and linked it to the Sausalito ferry with a commute time as fast as today's, the town's transformation into a bedroom community for San Francisco accelerated. In spite of this, and thanks in part to its setting, it has kept its character as a special place, more rustic than its neighbors. Here, too, houses are difficult to see.

Ross/San Anselmo. Nestled in a glen full of oaks in the heart of the peninsula, Ross was an early summer colony for the very wealthy. The intersection of Sir Francis Drake Boulevard and Bolinas Avenue is a good place to begin a tour of old Ross. Continue up Laqunitas Road past St. Anselm's Church at the corner of Shady Lane to the Theological Seminary loop road and then return to Shady Lane.

North Marin along US 101. A huge amount of development both sightly and unsightly is visible along US 101 north of San Rafael. We have chosen a few outstanding sights that are not too far off the highway. Thecoastal side of Marin County has the scenic wonders of Mt. Tamalpais and Point Reyes and the historic second-home communities of Bolinas and Inverness. All of this is worth exploring, but another book would be necessary to do it justice.

Marin County

1. **Headlands Center for the Arts** former Fort Barry off US 101 *north of the Golden Gate Bridge*
2. **Former Fort Baker off US 101** *south of the Golden Gate Bridge*

Sausalito

3. **Dickinson house** *26 Alexander Ave.*
4. **Sausalito Town Square**
5. **St. John's Presbyterian Church** *100 Bulkley Ave.*
6. **Sausalito Women's Club** *Central Ave. at San Carlos Ave.*
7. **Christ Episcopal Church Santa** *Rosa Ave. at San Carlos Ave.*
8. **Gardner house** *Cazneau St. at Girard Ave.*

Belvedere/Tiburon

9. **Hilarita Reed Lyford house/ Audubon Society** *off Tiburon Rd.*
10. **St. Stephen's Episcopal Church** *Bayview and Golden Gate Ave.*
11. **Golden Gate Ave. houses**
12. **Belvedere Town Square** *Beach Rd. and San Rafael Ave.*
13. **First Church of Christ Scientist** *San Rafael Ave. at Laurel Ave.*

Mill Valley

14. **Marin Outdoor Art Club** *Throckmorton Ave. and Blithedale Ave.*
15. **Depot Plaza and Cafe** *Throckmorton Ave. between Bernard St. and Madrona St.*
16. **Mill Valley Public Library** *Throckmorton Ave. at Elma St.*

Ross/San Anselmo

17. **Ross Town Hall Ross Common** *Lagunitas Rd. and Ross Common*
18. **St. Anselm's Catholic Church** *Shady Lane at Bolinas Ave.*
19. **San Francisco Theological Seminary** *Seminary Rd. off Kensington Rd.*

    Chapel *Bolinas and Richmond Ave.*

North Marin along US 101

20. **Marin County Civic Center** *San Pedro Dr. at Civic Center Dr.*
21. **Lucas Valley Eichler Homes** *Lucas Valley Rd. at Mt. Shasta*
22. **Former St. Vincent's School** *end of St. Vincent Rd.*
23. **Hamilton Field** *Ignacio Blvd. near Novato*

Previous page: Golden Gate Bridge

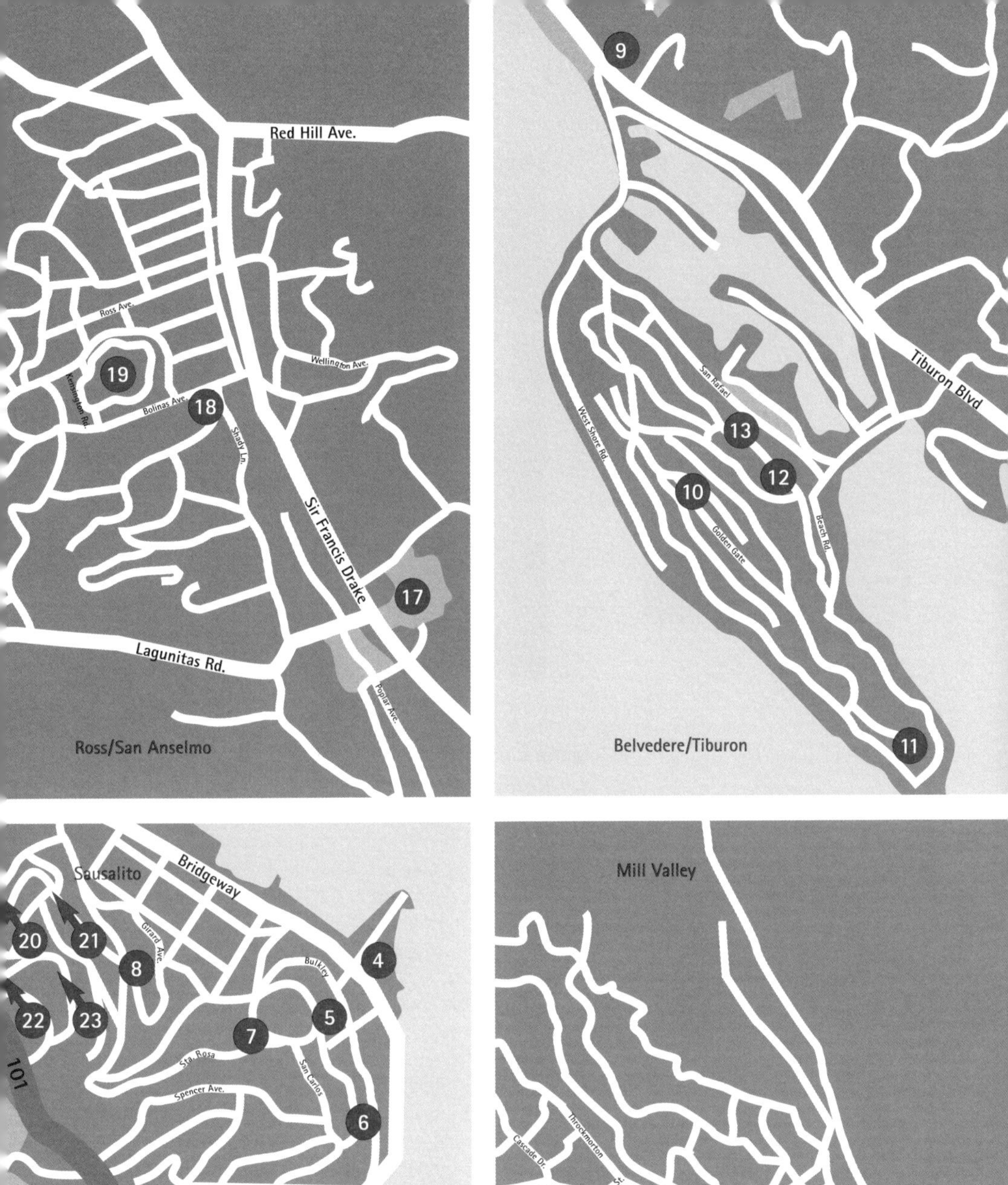
Red Hill Ave.
Ross Ave.
Wellington Ave.
Kensington Rd.
Bolinas Ave.
Shady Ln.
Sir Francis Drake
Lagunitas Rd.
Poplar Ave.
19
18
17
Ross/San Anselmo
9
Tiburon Blvd
San Rafael
West Shore Rd.
Golden Gate
Beach Rd.
13
12
10
11
Belvedere/Tiburon

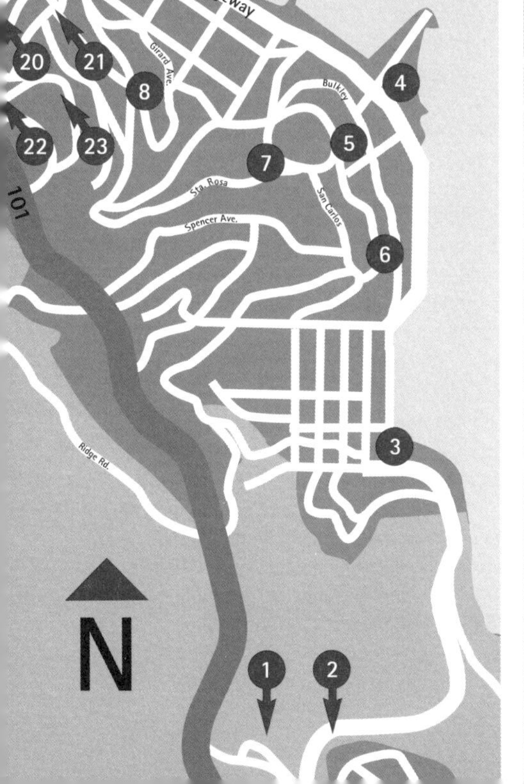
Sausalito
Bridgeway
Girard Ave.
Bulkley
Sta. Rosa
Spencer Ave.
San Carlos
Ridge Rd.
101
20
21
8
4
22
23
7
5
6
3
N
1
2

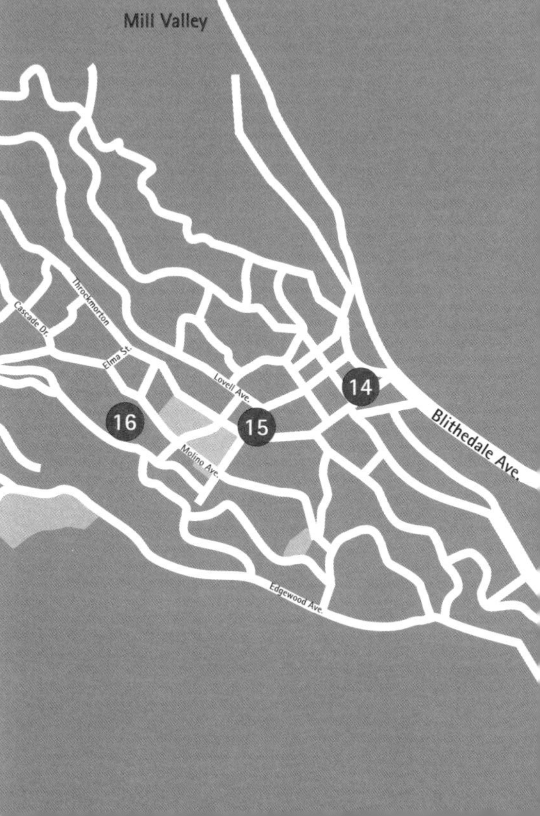
Mill Valley
Cascade Dr.
Throckmorton
Elma St.
Lovell Ave.
Molino Ave.
Blithedale Ave.
Edgewood Ave.
14
15
16

1. Headlands Center for the Arts

2. Fort Baker

1. Headlands Center for the Arts

Marin County

1. **Headlands Center for the Arts**
   1980s
   If traveling north on US 101 after crossing the Golden Gate Bridge, take the Alexander Avenue exit and follow the directions to the Headland Center for the Arts. If going south on US 101, take the last Sausalito exit before crossing the bridge and follow directions to the HCA.
   The HCA is housed in buildings on the former Fort Barry that were converted to a live-in residential program for artists of diverse backgrounds and disciplines. In addition to quarters for some 30 artists, the center provides a variety of public programs. The main building has interiors sensitively re-finished by artist David Ireland, and a remarkable restroom designed by Interim Architecture.
2. **Fort Baker**
   East of the Golden Gate Bridge, Alexander Ave. exit from US 101 north after the bridge
   1898-1910
   A picturesque cluster of simplified Colonial Revival buildings grouped around a 10-acre parade ground that slopes down to the Bay. The Children's Discovery Center is housed in some of the buildings. The site offers hiking trails and fine views of the Golden Gate Bridge and points of interest around the Bay.

Sausalito

3. **Dickinson house**
   1890, Willis Polk
   26 Alexander Ave.
   This dark shingle box is one of the oldest houses in the town. A little beyond it on the left at 215 South Street is a Gothicky cottage that is at even older.
4. **Sausalito Town Square**
   Bridgeway at Excelsior Lane
   Elephant lampposts, palms, and a fountain wonderfully express Sausalito's turn-of-the-19th-century Mediterranean image.
5. **St. John's Presbyterian Church**
   1905, Coxhead & Coxhead
   100 Bulkley Ave.
   Although the interior of Coxhead's last Shingle style church is much starker than his earlier ones, the clerestoried tower provides a wonderful climax.

4. Sausalito Town Square5.

5. St. John's Presbyterian Church

6. Sausalito Women's Club

7. Christ Episcopal Church

6. **Sausalito Women's Club**
   1916-18, Julia Morgan
   Central Ave. at San Carlos Ave.
   One of a series of Women's Clubs that Morgan designed around the Bay Area, this simple shingle building seems as right for its site and purpose today as when it was built.
7. **Christ Episcopal Church**
   1882
   Guild Hall
   1889
   Parish Hall
   1967, Henrik Bull
   Santa Rosa Ave. at San Carlos

7. Christ Episcopal Church, Parish Hall

8. Gardner house

This harmonious group evolves from Carpenter Gothic origins through Shingle Style and finally to a regional version of it in the Parish Hall.

8. **Gardner house**
   1869
   Cazneau St. at Girard Ave.
   A Carpenter Gothic cottage that is Sausalito's oldest largely unaltered house.

Belvedere/Tiburon

9. Hilarita Reed Lyford house/ Audubon Society

9. **Hilarita Reed Lyford house/Audubon Society**
   1874, rest. 1957, John Lord King
   A miniature Italianate villa perched on the edge of Richardson's Bay, this was originally built for the daughter of John Reed, owner of Rancho Corte Madera del Presidio and early settler of Mill Valley, on Strawberry Point.

10. St. Stephen's Episcopal Church

12. Belvedere Town Square

10. **St. Stephen's Episcopal Church**
    1954, 1959, Hansen & Winkler
    Bayview and Golden Gate Ave.
    A stark reinforced-concrete church, unusual in this setting, that looks more European than American. The handsome interior has notable abstract stained glass.

11. **Golden Gate Avenue houses**

    332 Golden Gate Ave.
    1903, Clarence Ward

    334 Golden Gate Ave.
    1904, Albert Farr

    340 Golden Gate Ave.
    1905, Daniel McLean

    428 Golden Gate Ave.
    1893, Willis Polk

    This group is representative of the first wave of settlement on Belvedere. They reflect the fashionable styles of the times.

12. Belvedere Town Square
1905, Albert Farr
Beach and San Rafael Ave.
Architect Albert Farr's design for the Belvedere Land Company Offices derived its long horizontal banding and many gables from the fashionable English architect C. F. A. Voysey's work and clothed them in native shingles. Across the street are cottages and apartments by Farr and the Town Square Apartments of 1955 by Schubart & Friedman.

13. First Church of Christ, Scientist

13. First Church of Christ, Scientist
1952, Charles Warren Callister
San Rafael Ave. at Laurel
Although influenced by Frank Lloyd Wright, this prow-shaped church in redwood and concrete has Callister's personal stamp; it fits neatly into its triangular site. The building is a landmark work of one of the second generation of architects who adapted the Bay Region style to their own time.

Mill Valley

15. Depot Plaza and Cafe

14. Marin Outdoor Art Club
1905, Bernard Maybeck
Throckmorton and Blithedale Aves.
The perfect introduction to Mill Valley and one of Maybeck's masterpieces, this simple hall gets its "architecture" from the inspired, if not altogether logical, projection of the trusses through the roof. A sort of rustic cousin of Mies van der Rohe's Crown Hall in Chicago.

16. Mill Valley Public Library

15. Depot Plaza and Cafe
c.1903; rest. c.1989
Throckmorton bet. Bernard and Madrona Sts.
The heart of town is focused on a former bus depot, probably preceded by electric rail, which was converted to a bookstore-cafe facing a perfectly scaled and very popular plaza.

15. Marin Outdoor Art Club

18. St. Anselm's Catholic Church

19. San Francisco Theological Seminary

16. Mill Valley Public Library

1969, Wurster, Bernardi & Emmons; 1997 addition, William Turnbull Assoc.

Throckmorton at Elma St.

Wurster's simple barnlike library set in the redwoods at the edge of the creek is a fiting companion piece to Maybeck's Outdoor Art Club on the other side of town. A tour down Cascade Drive (left on Laurel off Throckmorton after you pass the Library) behind the Library gives a wonderful sense of Mill Valleyness.

Ross/San Anselmo/North Marin

17. Ross Town Hall and Ross Common

19th and 20th centuries

Lagunitas Rd. and Ross Common

A fitting civic center for one of the Bay Area's early suburban towns.

18. St. Anselm's Catholic Church

1907, Frank Shea

Shady Lane at Bolinas Ave.

A free interpretation of the mix of French-Norman and English half-timbered styles of the times, this is one of the finest of Shea's many churches and perfect for its setting.

19. San Francisco Theological Seminary

1892-97, Wright & Saunders

Seminary Rd. off Kensington Rd.

Chapel

Bolinas and Richmond Ave.

One of the few Bay Area examples of Richardsonian Romanesque, these buildings do credit to the style. The chapel is by far the best of the group, but the setting of the other buildings, Montgomery Hall and Scott Library Hall, on their little knoll is inspired.

20. Marin County Civic Center

30. Hamilton Field/Landing

North Marin along US 101

20. Marin County Civic Center

1957-72, Frank Lloyd Wright/Aaron Green and William Wesley Peters, Taliesin Associated Architects

San Pedro Rd. at Civic Center Dr.

A very late work by Wright that was completed after his death and looks somewhat like a futuristic movie-set. However, the conception is dazzling enough to silence criticism. The first phase was the Administration Building, completed in 1962. Next was the Hall of Justice, completed in 1969. These two buildings bridge three hills; three drive-through entrances under the bridges separate main public access from traffic to the jail. At the foot of the hill is the Post Office, the only U.S. government building ever designed by Wright. The separate Veterans Memorial Auditorium was designed by Taliesin Fellowship and completed in 1972.

21. Lucas Valley Eichler Homes

1963, Claude Oakland; landscape architect, Royston, Hanamoto & Mays

Lucas Valley Rd. at Mt. Shasta Dr.

An outstanding example of subdivision site planning and design by a now renowned "merchant builder" who set a standard for tract housing that has not been surpassed.

22. St. Vincent's School

c.1920

End of St. Vincent Dr. from the US 101 Marinwood exit.

A striking group of school buildings in the Spanish Colonial Revival style that is visible from the freeway and perhaps best seen from that vantage point.

23. Hamilton Field/Landing

1930s, Former Air Force Base

Ignacio Blvd. near Novato, exit off US 101

A fine ensemble of buildings in the Spanish Colonial Revival style–sometimes referred to as "the Hollywood of military bases." The former administration buildings now house the City of Novato Art Center. A map of the site is displayed in front of the main building. The former airplane hangars are being converted to office space. The Marin Community Foundation offices are housed in one hangar remodeled in 2000 by Mark Cavagnero. The 25,000 sq. ft. of space contain conference rooms spaces for public and internal use that are arranged around a central well crossed by an elegant metal bridge hung from the hangar's trusses.

The last and northernmost of the chain of Franciscan missions that extended up the California coast from what is now Mexico, Sonoma is also one of the few California towns that retains any significant imprint of the "Laws of the Indies" codified under Philip II in the late 16th century for the establishment of settlements in the New World. The laws dictated that towns should be laid out on a square grid with the principal public buildings around a central plaza. Commandante General Mariano Guadalupe Vallejo's grand vision for Sonoma resulted in a larger plaza than was specified in the "Laws of the Indies"–the original blocks are also larger–and an unusually wide boulevard leading into it from the south. Even more remarkable is the plaza's enduring influence on town life. People meet there, eat there, celebrate there, hang out there, and behave more like Mexicans than Gringos. It is worth a trip to Sonoma just to spend a few hours in the Plaza, and many people do just that.

The mission was founded in 1823 just after Mexico became independent of Spain. Both the mission and the later town were established to head off the Russians, who were working their way down the coast from Alaska, having established a settlement at Fort Ross in 1812. As it turned out, the Russians were not a threat; in fact, they contributed to the building of the mission, and Sonoma had an amiable trading relationship with Fort Ross until the Russians gave up and went home in 1841.

Born into a military family in Monterey, Mariano Vallejo became Commandante of the San Francisco Presidio in 1833 at the age of 26. In 1834 he was made "Commisionado" in charge of the secularized holdings of the Sonoma Mission. He soon moved his family and most of his troops into the mission buildings and began a long and fruitful involvement in the affairs of the future town and its surrounding countryside. After several unsuccessful attempts to found settlements elsewhere, he laid out his grand plan for the present town in 1835. Although the existing mission buildings doubtless influenced his decisions, the great axis of Broadway, running due north from the Embarcadero at the head of navigation on Sonoma Creek to the Plaza cradled in its backdrop of hills, reveals the sensibility of an urban planner. Of his buildings on the Plaza, only the Barracks and the Mission Chapel are left. Vallejo's Casa Grande with its four-story watchtower on the Broadway axis burned in 1867. Still, reminders of the family around the Plaza remain, including two buildings by his brother Salvador and one by his brother-in-law Jacob Leese. Although buildings gradually framed the Plaza during the 19th century, the town of Sonoma grew slowly in comparison with neighboring Petaluma and Napa. Sonoma's charming small-town ambience, along with its incomparable Plaza, makes it a favorite tourist destination. Happily, it has largely resisted quaintness. Its unique array of architecture from the Mexican and early statehood eras is not as well-known as it should be.

The present city of Napa was first called Nappa City; its original settlement, platted on a grid centered on 3rd Street, followed the river lined with steamboat wharves. To the south was the slightly later Napa Abajo, or Lower Napa, also a grid but set at a different angle. Division Street marks the meeting point of the two grids. Steamboat captains built their stately mansions here. To the west, yet another grid appeared with Brown and Walker's Addition and subsequent additions that developed into the area around Fuller Park, now one of Napa's most attractive residential neighborhoods. Northward from the park, Jefferson Street became the locus of more stately homes and evolved into the town's main north-south artery. Except for the old high school at Jefferson and Lincoln, virtually all of Napa's interesting architecture is in a roughly ten-block area centered on 1st and Seminary Streets.

Sonoma

1. Mission San Francisco Solano *NE cor. Spain St. at 1st St. E.*
2. Blue Wing Inn *125-129 E. Spain St.*
   Vasquez (Hooker) house *129 E. Spain St. inside El Paseo*
3. Ray Adobe *205 E. Spain St.*
4. Cooke house *245 E. Spain St.*
5. McTaggart (Sebastiani) house *400 4th St. E.*
6. Duhring house *532 2nd St. E.*
   Clewe house *531 2nd St. E.*
7. Parmelee (Grinstead) Building *466 1st St. E.*
8. Sebastiani Theater Building *476 1stSt. E.*
9. Duhring General Store Building *492 1st St. E.*
10. First Baptist Church *542 1st St. E.*
11. Green (Nash-Patton) Adobe *579 1st St. E.*
12. Sonoma Valley Visitors Bureau *1st St. E. side of Plaza*
13. Sonoma City Hall *center of the Plaza*
14. Batto Building *457 1st St. W.*
15. Ruggles (Aquilon) Building *447 1st St. W.*
16. Salvador Vallejo Adobe *415-27 1st St. W.*
17. Sonoma (Plaza) Hotel *110 W. Spain St.*
18. Swiss Hotel (Salvador Vallejo house) *18 W. Spain St.*
19. Sonoma State Park *center of N. side of the Plaza*
20. La Casita (Castenada Adobe) *143 W. Spain St.*
21. Lachryma Montis (Mariano Vallejo house) *W. Spain St. at 3rd St. W.*
22. General's Daughter Restaurant (Vallejo-Haraszthy house) *400 W. Spain St.*
23. Andronico Vallejo adobe and barn *700 Curtin Lane*
24. Jack London State Park *London Ranch Rd. Glen Ellen*
25. St. Andrew's Presbyterian Church *16290 Arnold Dr.*
26. Temelec Hall *Temelec Dr. off of Arnold Dr.*
27. MacArthur Place (Burris house) *29 E. MacArthur St.*
28. Buena Vista (Haraszthy) Winery *end of Vineyard Lane*
29. Casa Grande *Adobe Rd. at Casa Grande*

Previous page: View of the Napa Valley

Napa

30. Napa Unified School District *Jefferson St. at Lincoln St.*
31. Apartments *1556 Polk St.*
32. House *2109 1st St.*
    House *1929 1st St.*
    House *1926 1st St.*
    House *1001 Jefferson St.*
    House *1801 1st St.*
33. Noyes Mansion *1750 1st St.*
34. Napa Opera House *Main St. between 1st and Pearl Sts.*
35. Commercial building *942-48 Main St.*
36. Copia 500 *1st St.*
37. Oxbow School *530 3rd St.*
38. Napa County Courthouse *Brown St. 2nd to 3rd Sts.*
39. First Presbyterian Church *3rd and Randolph Sts.*
40. Andrews house *741 Seminary St.*
41. Nichols house *1562 3rd St.*
42. Migliavacca house *1475 4th St.*
43. McClelland houses *569 Randolph St.*
44. First United Methodist Church *625 Randolph St.*
45. E.R. Gifford house *608 Randolph St.*
46. Goodman-Corlett house *1225 Division St.*
    Hayman house *1227-1229 Division St.*
47. Houses *642 705 Seminary St.*
    Houses *1730 1738 Oak St.*
    House *617 Seminary St.*
48. George Goodman Jr. house *492 Randolph St.*
49. Cedar Gables (former E. W. Churchill house) *486 Coombs St.*
50. George Goodman house *1120 Oak St.*
51. Churchill Manor *485Brown St.*
    Manasse Mansion *443 Brown St.*
52. William H. Corlett house *507 Jefferson St.*
53. Turton house *1767 Laurel St.*
54. Martin house *409 Franklin St.*
    Cottages 406 *436 Franklin St.*
55. Yount house *Seminary and Pine Sts.*
56. Sawyer house *39-97 Franklin St.*
    Cottages *355 361 Franklin St.*
    House row *356-86 Franklin St.*
57. Apartments former Holden Mansion *313 Franklin St.*

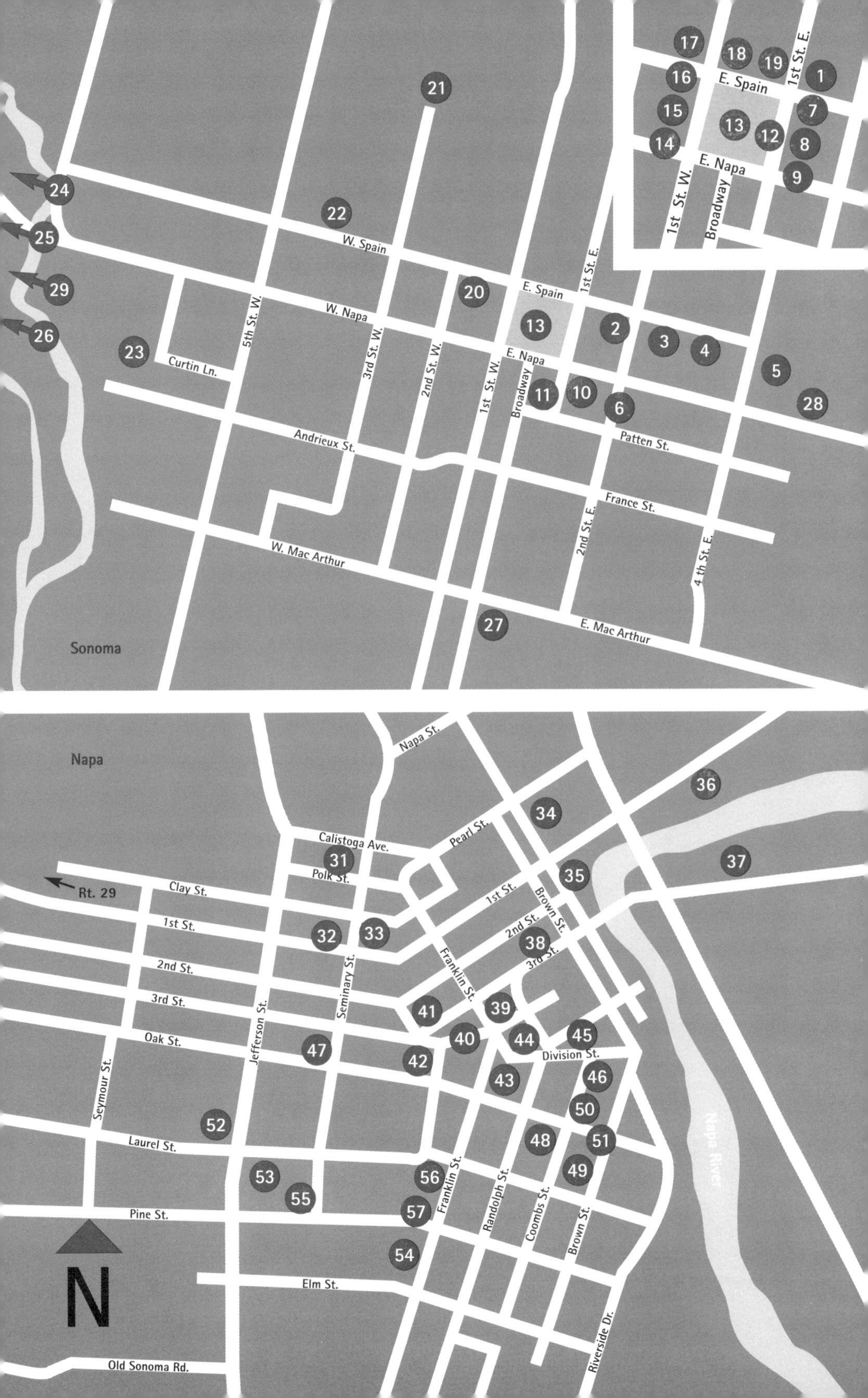

E. Spain
E. Napa
1st St. E.
1st St. W.
Broadway
W. Spain
W. Napa
E. Spain
E. Napa
5th St. W.
3rd St. W.
2nd St. W.
1st St. W.
Broadway
1st St. E.
Curtin Ln.
Andrieux St.
Patten St.
France St.
2nd St. E.
4 th St. E.
W. Mac Arthur
E. Mac Arthur
Sonoma
Napa
Napa St.
Calistoga Ave.
Pearl St.
Polk St.
Rt. 29
Clay St.
1st St.
1st St.
Brown St.
2nd St.
2nd St.
3rd St.
3rd St.
Franklin St.
Oak St.
Division St.
Seminary St.
Jefferson St.
Seymour St.
Laurel St.
Franklin St.
Randolph St.
Coombs St.
Brown St.
Pine St.
Elm St.
Riverside Dr.
Old Sonoma Rd.
Napa River
N

1. Mission San Francisco Solano

2. Vasquez (Hooker) house

3. Ray Adobe

4. Cooke house

5. McTaggart (Sebastiani) house

1. **Mission San Francisco Solano**
   1824-40
   N.E. cor. Spain & 1st St. East
   The entrance is through the remaining fragment of the original convento, or friars' quarters, on East Spain Street. The mission church, now gone, stood to the east; the present church is a later parish church built by Mariano Vallejo about 1840 and heavily restored. Tickets are sold here for the barracks across the street, the Vallejo home, and the Petaluma adobe, the Casa Grande.

2. **Blue Wing Inn**
   1840, James Cooper and Thomas Spriggs
   125-129 East Spain
   The basis for this structure was a modest two-room cottage built by the man sent by Vallejo to look after the newly secularized mission. When two British seamen offered to buy the site Vallejo evicted his majordomo and the new owners built the present two-story adobe, which functioned as a hotel, saloon, and gambling hall. Guests included William Tecumseh Sherman, Joseph Hooker, Henry Halleck, and Sidney Longstreet, all of whom later won military fame in the Civil War.

   Vasquez (Hooker) house
   c.1850
   129 East Spain (in court of El Paseo)
   A prefabricated house from Sweden, bought by then Lt. Joe Hooker on the docks of San Francisco and erected originally on the southwest corner of the Plaza. It is now the headquarters of the Somoma League for Historic Preservation and is open to the public.

3. **Ray Adobe**
   1849-50, John Ray
   205 East Spain St.
   One of the landmarks of early California architecture, the wooden section on 2nd Street East was built first; the adobe portion with its unusual two-story verandah was added after the Virginian John Ray struck gold.

4. **Cooke house**
   1852-57
   245 East Spain St.
   A wood-framed house built like an adobe with rooms opening off a continuous front porch.

5. **McTaggart (Sebastiani) house**
   1923, Samuele Sebastiani
   400 4th St. East

A very grand Craftsman bungalow; humbler versions are further south along 4th Street.

6. **Duhring house**
1859; rem. 1928, Bliss & Faville; Thomas Church, landscape arch.
532 2nd St. East
An imposing Colonial Revival house that began as a simple frontier dwelling. Bliss and Faville were prominent San Francisco architects; Thomas Church later became California's most famous modern landscape architect. Not much remains of this early garden.

6. Duhring house

Clewe house
1876
531 2nd St. East
This handsome Italianate was built by a cousin and sometime partner of the Duhrings across the street.

7. **Parmelee (Grinstead) Building**
1911
466 1st St. East
This is a charming example of early 20th-century commercial building on a very small scale.

8. Sebastiani Theater Building

8. **Sebastiani Theater Building**
1933
476 1st St. East
While somewhat grandiose in scale, this Mission Revival edifice is a local landmark and houses a movie theater.

9. Duhring General Store Building

9. **Duhring General Store Building**
1891
492 1st St. East
A one-story brick building with an octagonal corner cupola built by a German immigrant who was one of the town's pioneer merchants and subsequently

11. Green (Nash-Patton) Adobe

13. Sonoma City Hall

14. Batto Building

16. Salvador Vallejo Adobe

became one of its most prosperous residents. The family still owns the building, which was restored after a fire in 1990.

10. **First Baptist Church**
1870's
542 1st St. East
A simple Gothic Revival church that recalls the New England origen of many of California's post-colonial settlers.

11. **Green (Nash-Patton) Adobe**
1847, Henry Green
579 1st St. East
A typical adobe plan with two ground-floor rooms on either side of a center hall, a large sleeping loft upstairs, and a kitchen in the lean-to at the rear.

Sonoma Valley Visitors Bureau
1913; rehabilitation and seismic upgrade, 1997, Architectural Resources Group, historic preservation architect
1st St. E., east side of the Plaza
A few years after the completion of the City Hall a classical small-town Carnegie Library joined it in breaking the Laws of the Indies by erecting buildings on the Plaza.

13. **Sonoma City Hall**
1906, H. C. Lutgens; rest. 1987, Gerald Tierney
Center of the Plaza
By the end of the 19th century, Sonoma had become north-Americanized enough to warrant emulating mid-western courthouse squares and violating the Laws of the Indies by erecting the City Hall in the center of the Plaza. The vaguely Mission-Revival style building, a dim echo of the Hispanic past, is a perfect termination for Broadway.

14. **Batto Building**
1912
457 1st St. West
A fine early 20th-century commercial building in brick.

15. **Ruggles (Aquilon) Building**
1860's
447 1st St. West
A simple frame building which housed Sonoma's first Chinese laundry.

16. **Salvador Vallejo Adobe**
1836
415-27 1st St. West

Built by General Vallejo's brother, who later extended it north on the site of what is now the El Dorado Hotel.

17. **Sonoma (Plaza) Hotel**
1872, Henry Weil, builder
110 West Spain St.
In atmosphere and furnishings, very much the country hotel of a century ago.

18. **Swiss Hotel (Salvador Vallejo house)**
1840, Salvador Vallejo
18 West Spain St.
Salvador's second building on the Plaza is a smaller version of the barracks down the street with a projecting second-story gallery.

19. **Sonoma State Park**
Center of north side of the Plaza:

20. **Park Headquarters (former boarding house)**
1870
West Spain St.
Originally located where the Cheese Factory now stands.

Indians' quarters and kitchen
1835
to the left of Headquarters
The surviving outbuilding of General Vallejo's residence, which had a four-story flanking tower and stood on Spain Street astride the Broadway axis.

Toscano Hotel
1857-59
Spain St.
Furnished with period furniture by the Sonoma League for Historic Preservation, which provides guided tours.

Barracks
1840
1st St. East at Spain St.
Built by Mariano Vallejo to house his garrison, the building was the headquarters of the 1846 Bear Flag Rebellion and the capitol of the short-lived Republic of California.

20. **La Casita (Castenada Adobe)**
1842-49, Salvador Vallejo
143 West Spain St.
One of several small adobes built by Salvador around the perimeter of his property and first occupied by Juan Castenada, Mariano Vallejo's secretary.

21. **Lachryma Montis (Mariano Vallejo house)**
1852
North of West Spain St. at 3rd St. West
This beautifully restored and maintained complex

20.Toscano Hotel

21. Lachryma Montis (Mariano Vallejo house)

23. Andronico Vallejo adobe and barn

24. Wolf house, Jack London State Park

testifies to the transformation of General Vallejo from a Mexican ranchero to a North American squire and the Americanization of Hispanic California. Vallejo had a commodious house on the Plaza, but in 1852 he bought one of three "frames," as prefabricated houses were called, that had been shipped from Massachusetts around the horn to the San Francisco docks. He then brought the kit-of-parts to Sonoma at vast expense. Using adobe to insulate the walls, he erected the house on this lovely site along with a Gothic Revival carriage house, now gone, and a summer house, as if to show that he was now a Yankee. The surviving "chalet" barn is also a prefab of sorts; its timber frame came from England. Only a little of the original garden remains.

22. General's Daughter Restaurant (Vallejo-Haraszthy house)
1878
400 West Spain St.
The intermarriage of two of Sonoma's first families resulted in this Italianate house, which duplicates the plan of Lachryma Montis.

23. Andronico Vallejo adobe and barn
1852, John Ray
700 Curtin Lane
John Ray sold this large adobe to General Vallejo's

22. General's Daughter Restaurant (Vallejo-Haraszthy house)

wife, who gave it to her son, Andronico. The dormers on the roof, an unusual feature, provided light to the upper floor sleeping rooms.

24. Wolf house, Jack London State Park
1913, Albert Farr
London Ranch Rd., Glen Ellen
When Jack London got rich from his writing, he bought this ranch and built his dream house, an enormous stone and timber structure he named Wolf house–it burned before he and his wife, Charmian,

could move in. After London's death Charmian built the "House of Happy Walls," where she lived until her death In 1959. Now a museum, It houses memorabilia of London. The ruins of Wolf house are some of the most romantic of their kind.

25. St. Andrew's Presbyterian Church

25. St. Andrew's Presbyterian Church
1992, William Turnbull Assoc.
16290 Arnold Drive south of Sobre Vista Rd.
A school, and meeting hall set on a patio defined by a covered walkway. The simple barnlike form of these buildings contrasts with the airy lightness of the interiors.

26. Temelec Hall

26. Temelec Hall
1858, Granville P. Swift
Temelec Drive off Arnold
Now the clubhouse for a retirement community that surrounds it and bears its name, this large stone Italianate mansion with carriage house, barn, and Gothic Revival garden pavilions is a remarkable feat at such an early date. Swift, a member of Sonoma's Bear Flag rebellion who later struck gold, built it with forced Indian labor.

27. McArthur Park Hotel and Spa (Burris house)
c.1840-1860, Nicholas Burris
29 East MacArthur St.
The centerpiece of this complex is a wooden house with a second-story gallery typical of adobe buildings of the period; its wood frame was unusual because of the lack of sawmills at this early date. The recent buildings on the site are imitations.

28. Buena Vista (Haraszthy) Winery

28. Buena Vista (Haraszthy) Winery
1857, Agoston Haraszthy
End of Vineyard Lane
Haraszthy, a Hungarian Count, is usually credited with starting California's wine industry. Recognizing that the climate and soil of the North Bay region were right for making fine wine, Haraszthy returned to Europe to collect root stocks and planted these vineyards. He and his descendants built the two stone wineries with limestone caves excavated in the hillside. Raise a glass to his memory in the tasting room of the older building!

29. Casa Grande

29. Casa Grande
1834, General Mariano Vallejo
Adobe Rd. at Casa Grande
This huge two-story adobe ifs the surviving section of a bulding complex and surrounded a court; it was a combination fort and ranch headquarters for Vallejo's

30. Napa Unified School District Headquarters

31. Apartments

32. 1929 1st St.

extensive land holdings. Manufacturing and storage facilities as well as accomodations for soldiers, ranch hands, and Indians were located here.

29. Casa Grande

Napa

30. Napa Unified School District Headquarters
1922, W. H. Weeks
Jefferson at Lincoln St.
A splendid monument to the days when the local high school was a major cultural landmark, in a free and elegant combination of Beaux-Arts Classicism and Mediterranean Revival.

31. Apartments
c.1885
1556 Polk St.
This neighborhood was apparently originally developed in the 1880s with a variety of housing at different scales.

32. House
c.1890
2109 1st St.
The verandahed bungalow done in the Stick-Eastlake style.

House
c.1875
1929 1st St.
With its Mansard roof and double-bayed front, this house packs a lot of Victorian grandeur into a small box.

House
c.1900
1926 1st St.
The steep gable roof perpendicular to the street was popular around the turn of the century. Here the detailing combines elements of Colonial Revival, Queen Anne, and even Craftsman in the projecting beam ends on the porch.

House
c.1895
1001 Jefferson St.
Queen Anne houses gradually dropped the elaborate bracketing and strapwork of Stick-Eastlake for the simpler surfaces of the Colonial Revival, but kept the complicated massing. How they loved to turn a corner like this!

32. 1926 1st

House
c.1900
1801 1st St.
The strong horizontal banding of the windows and eave lines indicates that something new is happening amidst the Queen Anne jumble of forms.

33. Noyes Mansion
c.1905, attrib. to Luther M. Turton; 19??, rehabilitation, Architectural Resources Group, historic preservation architects
1750 1st St.
Almost certainly by Napa's leading architect of the turn-of-the-century, this house shows the full flowering of the first Colonial Revival style, although the steep-gabled dormers and round central bay hark back to Queen Anne.

32. 1001 Jefferson St.

34. Napa Opera House
1879, Samuel & Joseph Cather Newsom/Ira Gilchrist; 2003, rehabilitation, Architectural Resources Group
Main St. bet. 1st and Pearl Sts.
The long-awaited restoration of this cultural landmark is now complete.

32. 1801 Jefferson St.

35. Commercial building
c.1910
942-48 Main St.
This handsomely restored block anchors the key corner of the old downtown, largely gutted by urban renewal west of here. South of it on Main at 902-12 is a charming little group of Art Deco shops.

34. Napa Opera House

35 Commercial building

Napa Riverfront

The Napa riverfront is undergoing a welcome rehabilitation. The Napa River Flood Protection Project, which mandated channel widening, new bridges, and trails is reconfiguring the river's course and its relationahip to adjacent properties. Planning efforts have focused on two riverfront areas north and south of downtown. The first area extends from Trancas Street south to Randean Way; the second extends from Division/ Seventh Street south to Imola Avenue. A major focus of development is the so-called Tannery Bend on South Coombs Street, location of the historic Sawyer Tannery. The historic A. Hatt Building, 500 Main Street, has been rehabilitated as a hotel, restaurnats, and shops. Design guidelines for a range of building types from residential to commercial have been established, and the riverfront's future is beginning to unfold.

36. Copia

Polshek Partnership Architects

500 1st St.

A cultural center and museum of wine, food, and the arts housed in a large boxy building that looks very corporate. The surrounding gardens are open to the public and overlook the Napa River.

36. Copia

37. Oxbow School

2003, Stanley Saitowitz, Natoma Architects

530 3rd St.

A one-semester fine arts program for high school juniors housed in 15 existing and new buildings on the Napa riverbank near downtown. The well designed new studio buildings have flexible spaces with high ceilings, generous glazed openings, and roll-up glass doors on the river side. The harmonious campus is well worth visiting.

38. Napa County Courthouse

1878, Samuel & Joseph Cather Newsom/Ira Gilchrist
Brown St. bet. 2nd and 3rd Sts.

The Newsoms, later famous for their Carson House in Eureka, are here shown in their reserved civic mode. Gilchrist, the local architect, did a number of houses around town and collaborated on the Opera House. He probably got the job by saying he would bring in the eminent San Franciscans. Across the street at 812-16 Brown is the rusticated stone Napa Law Center of around 1910.

37. Napa County Courthouse

37. Oxbow School

39 First Presbyterian Church

39. First Presbyterian Church

1874, Daley & Eisen
3rd and Randolph Sts.

This spire is the major landmark of downtown. The church's sculptural ornament is a rich addition to this Gothic-Revival confection.

40. Andrews house

1892, Luther M. Turton
741 Seminary St.

Although Turton could do the Eastlake style with the best of them, he shifted to the Prairie style a quarter of a century later in his own house at 1767 Laurel.

41. Nichols house

1879, Ira Gilchrist
1562 3rd St.

A Stick Style house that looks like it might have been a reworking of an earlier Italianate.

42. Migliavacca house

1895, Luther M. Turton
1475 4th St.

This splendid Queen Anne house was moved here from where the new Library now stands on Division St.

42. Migliavacca house

44. First United Methodist Church

45. E. R. Gifford house

46. Hayman house

43. McClelland houses
1879
569 Randolph St.
An Second-Empire style house that turns the corner in an elegant way with a rounded porch.

590 Randolph St.
c.1900, Luther M.Turton
A series of rounded bays pop out from the simpler main mass of this house.

44. First United Methodist Church
1916, Luther M. Turton
625 Randolph St.
Turton's masterwork, this reinforced concrete English Gothic church occupies a pivotal position in Napa both literally and culturally. The exterior is unremarkable, but the interior has a wood-paneled sanctuary, a quarter of a circle in plan, that is a fine example of the auditorium plan typical of American Protestant churches in the late 1800s. The congregation founded the Napa Collegiate Institute, active from 1870 to 1896, which then merged with what is now the University of the Pacific. As its extensive buildings indicate, it is still a major educational presence.

45. E. R. Gifford house
c.1890
608 Randolph St.
A lavishly bracketed Queen Anne house set in a garden that must be as old as the house.

46. Goodman-Corlett house
1882
1225 Division St.

Hayman house
c.1900
1227-29 Division St.
These well-maintained neighbors illustrate the evolution of taste at the end of the last century. The Italianate at 1225 Division was built by George Goodman, who founded Napa's first private bank and donated its first library, and was given to his son Harvey. It was updated with a round Queen Anne tower in the 1890s. The Hayman house has the complex massing and curved eaves of the Queen Anne style combined with fanlights and porch columns of the Colonial Revival style.

47. 617 Seminary St.

47. Houses:

642 Seminary St.
c.1890

1730, 1738 Oak, 705 Seminary St.
c.1865
A group of three Stick-Eastlake houses and an earlier Carpenter Gothic cottage facing Fuller Park.

House
c.1905
617 Seminary St.
A gem of a Colonial Revival cottage with a swoop of Queen Anne in the porch.

48 George Goodman, Jr., house
c.1890
492 Randolph St.
George senior built this Queen Anne house with all the trimmings for his obviously favorite son.

49. Cedar Gables

49. Cedar Gables (former Edward Wilder Churchill house)
1892, Ernest Coxhead
486 Coombs St.
Nearly identical to a house that Coxhead designed at the same time for David Greenleaf in Alameda, this Queen Anne house is one of Napa's great treasures; it displays the architect's skillful handling of shingled surfaces.

51. Churchill Manor

50. George Goodman house
1872-73, MacDougall & Marquis
1120 Oak St.
The senior Goodman's mansion, now unfortunately crowded by modern apartments, is in the Second Empire style with a Mansard roof. Napa's "millionaire's corner" was at Oak and Brown Streets.

51. Churchill Manor (former Edward S. Churchill house)
1889
485 Brown St.
Originally Second Empire style, Napa's grandest mansion was updated to Colonial Revival in 1906. Its interiors are largely intact and are sometimes open to the public.

51. Manasse Mansion

Manasse Mansion
1886, William H. Corlett
443 Brown St.
Another ingenious updating was performed on this Stick-Eastlake around 1900, when it was given a colonial portico. Combined with the two angled corner gables, it gives the look of a house charging off in all directions.

52. William H. Corlett house

54. Martin house

54. 406, 436 Franklin St.

55. Yount house

56. Sawyer house

52. William H. Corlett house
c.1916, William H. Corlett
507 Jefferson St.
The house of this architect/builder, charming as it is, shows how much more conservative Corlett was than his builder colleague Luther Turton.

53. Turton house
1915, Luther M. Turton
1767 Laurel St.
Only a few years before this Turton was designing houses in the Queen Anne and Eastlake styles; for his own house he chose the newly fashionsble Prairie style.

54. Martin house
c.1890
409 Franklin St.

Cottages
c.1870
406, 436 Franklin St.
The Martin house is a two-story double-bayed Italianate that has had a Colonial Revival porch added. Across the street are two charming Gothic Revival cottages.

55. Yount house
1884
Seminary and Pine Sts.
A large Stick-Eastlake house built by the daughter of the founder of Yountville.

56. Sawyer house
c.1875
389-97 Franklin St.

Cottages
c.1880
355, 361 Franklin St.
This block of Franklin is one of the few that uses redwoods as street trees; it also has a fine collection of houses.The Sawyers, founders of one of Napa's principal industries, owned the Sawyer Tannery at 68 Coombs Street. Next door to their double house is a charming pair of Eastlake cottages with curving porches facing each other.

House row
c.1885
356-86 Franklin St.
Five Stick-Eastlake houses obviously built as a speculative development. Some remodeling has taken place, notably at 376, which was transformed into the Shingle Style in the early 1900s.

57. Apartments (Holden Mansion)
c.1886
313 Franklin St.
A fine Italianate mansion that faces a pair of California Bungalows from the early 1900s across the street.

58a. Trefethen Vineyards

Napa Wineries
St. Helena Highway, Route 29
Although sources of information about the hundreds of wineries in the Sonoma and Napa Valleys are too numerous to mention here, they are easily found online and at the chambers of commerce in both cities. The wineries listed here are among the oldest and the newest; they are located either on near Route 29 extending north of Napa to Calistoga.

58a.Trefethen Vineyards
1886, Hamden McIntyre
1160 Oak Knoll Ave., Napa
One of the few remaining three-story wooden wineries that housed the grape crusher on the third floor and allowed gravity to direct the grape juice to fermentation tanks on the second floor and then into barrels on the ground floor.

The fermentation room is a wooden wonder. The architect was also a sea captain.

58a. Trefethen Vineyards, barrel romm

b. Domaine Chandon Winery
1973, ROMA
1 California Dr., Yountville
Dramatic oak-paneled barrel vaults are a prominent feature of this winery; the site plan and landscaping are exceptional.

58b. Domaine Chandon Winery

58c. Napa Valley Museum

c Napa Valley Museum
1985, Fernau & Hartman
55 Presidents Circle, Yountville
The first phase of a museum complex that resulted

58c. Turnbull Wine Cellars

58g. Niebaum Coppola

58fg. Niebaum Coppola

58h. Tra Vigne

from a competition, the main building is a dramatic vaulted structure that alludes to the valley's rural-industrial past and exhibits its varied history.

d. **Dominus Estate Winery**
1997, Herzog abd de Meuron
2570 Napanook Rd., Yountville
Walls of gabions, steel baskets filled with loose basalt rocks, give this winery building the appearance of merging with its site. Air and light permeate the walls and help regulate the temperature inside.

e. **Opus One**
1991, Scott Johnson
1144 Oakville Cross Rd.
Although open and welcoming on its entrance side, much of this dramatically composed winery is hidden from view beneath a grassy mound of earth.

Opus One

f. **Turnbull Wine Cellars**
1962, William Turnbull & Assoc.
8210 St. Helena Highway, Route 29, Oakville
Originally the Johnson-Turnbull winery. The old cottage was remodeled as a part time residence for the owners, one of whom was the winery's architect and a master of contemporary buildings that respected their rural settings.

g. **Niebaum Coppola**
1879, William Mooser/Hamden McIntyre
1991 St. Helena Highway, Route 29, Rutherford
Partly built into the rocky hillside, this winery was known for years as Inglenook. It is now owned by famed film director, Francis Ford Coppola.

h. **Tra Vigne**
1880
1050 Charter Oak Ave., St. Helena
A former winery converted to a restaurant in the 1970s with a fine diningroom interior.

58i. Beringer Vineyards

58j. St Clement

58k. Culinary Institute of America

58l. Close Pegase

58l. Close Pegase

i. **Beringer Vineyards**
1884, William Mooser
2000 Main St.. St. Helena
A San Francisco architect's version of a Rhineland villa; the interior conveys the Victorian image of grandeur in the valley. The Architectural Resources Group were responsible for the rehabilitation of the winery, the main house, and support buildings.

j. **St. Clement**
1878
2867 N. St. Helena Highway, St. Helena
Built as the residence of Fritz H. Rosenbaum, a stained glass maker, who incorporated a stone wine celler in the basement of his high-style mansion. It was restored in 1962 and has since been remodeled under various owners.

k. **Culinary Institute of America**
1889, Percy & Hamilton/Hamden McIntyre
2555 Main St., St. Helena
The former Greystone Winery owned for years by the Christian Brothers, who were able to produce wine during the Prohibition years because they supplied churches with wine for sacramental use.

l. **Close Pegase**
1985, Michael Graves
1060 Dunaweal Lane, Calistoga
A colorful bow to the Classical past by a famous post-modern architect. The owner's art collection is displayed in some of the interiors and on the grounds.

Interest in a rapid transit system for the San Francisco Bay Area gained momentum in the post-World War II period. The Bay Area Rapid Transportation Commission, established by the state legislature in 1951, produced a transportation plan in 1956. The BART District, drawn up in 1957, comprised the five inner-bay counties: San Francisco, Alameda, Contra Costa, Marin, and San Mateo, that would be affected by the system. In 1962 Marin and San Mateo withdrew, and the other three counties authorized construction of a 75-mile system. Voters passed a $792 million bond issue to which was added $180 million in surplus Bay Bridge tolls, $71 million in revenue bonds, and $8 million in federal grants. The first construction contract was let in 1965; the Oakland-Fremont line began operations in 1972. The BART was the first entirely new rapid transit system undertaken in the U.S. in over 50 years. It was also the largest single urban design project then underway in the country and the first land-use plan ever developed for the Bay Area.

A joint venture of three engineering firms, Parsons Brinkerhoff/Tudor/Bechtel, designed the system. Consulting Architect Donn Emmons of Wurster, Bernardi and Emmons, developed the general architectural standards for the system and the stations and designed the award-winning structure for all the elevated sections of track. Emmons also created a list of 14 architectural firms and seven landscape architects for the selection process of the stations' designers. Ernest Born designed the overall signage for the stations, and Lawrence Halprin served as consulting landscape architect.However, in 1965 both Emmons and Halprin resigned to protest their lack of authority in matters relating to architecture and landscape design. In 1966 Tallie Maule succeeded Donn Emmons as consulting architect and coordinated design efforts for the stations constructed during the initial campaign. This phase ended in 1973 with the completion of the sixteen East Bay and ten San Francisco/Daly City stations.

In 1996 the Concord line was extended to Pittsburgh/Bay Point, and the Dublin/Pleasanton line opened.The most recent stations on the list below completed the BART line to the San Francisco Airport (SFO) and Millbrae in 2000.

As of this writing 104 of the 385 miles of rail rapid transit called for in the BART's first plan have been completed along with 43 stations in four counties. (Marin County is still not in the district.) The extension of the Fremont line to San Jose is in progress but is not expected to open before 2008.

While the format of the stations was prescribed from the beginning in respect to the length of platforms and their canopies as well as the plan for interior spaces such as the concourse level, variations in the use of forms and materials were within the purview of the station architects. Although most of the stations are not architecturally notable, the following examples exhibit the range of architectural ideas–very little of the proposed landscaping was implemented–employed in the two major buildings campaigns: 1965-72 and 1992-2000.

Public Art is incorporated in some of the stations, notably in the Embarcadero station where a monumental fiber-art work about 60 feet tall by Barbara Showcroft is hung on the wall in front of the entrance to the tunnels under the bay. The sculpture succeeds admirably in conveying the image of an underworld deity. The South San Francisco station has hologram-like images–a windsurfer riding the waves or an antique streetcar moving by the platform–that appear to move for observers walking by them or riding by on trains. For the Millbrae station Donna Billick created 46 benches with mosaic images in terrazzo that depict Millbrae's physical, cultural, and geographical history. Scott Donahue' six bronze sculptures of people representative of Millbrae's history from 1550 to the present have concrete and ceramic reliefs on side panels and are set in variousareas throughout the station.

Recently, the BART administration has embraced the concept of transit-oriented-development (TOD) and has fostered the creation of so-called "transit villages", which feature mixed-use development near the stations linked when possible to other transportation modes. A Downtown Plan for Hayward produced by Solomon E T C in 2000 has created a TOD area near the Hayward station. At the Fruitvale Station a mixed-use development completed in 2004 and designed by McLarand Vasquez & Partners offers a more compact example of a transit village.

22

Stations Completed in 1972

Embarcadero, SF
Tallie B. Malle/Hertzka & Knowles

Montgomery St., SF
Skidmore Owings & Merrill

Powell St., SF
Skidmore Owings & Merrill

Civic Center, SF
Reid & Tarics

Glen Park, SF
Corlett & Spackman/Ernest Born
Douglas Bayliss, landscape architects

19th St., Oakland
Gerald M. McCue & Assoc.

12th St., Oakland
Gerald M. McCue & Assoc.

Lake Merritt, Oakland
Yuill-Thornton, Warner & Levikov
Douglas Bayliss, landscape architects

Fruitvale, Oakland
Reynolds & Chamberlain/Neill Smith
Anthonay Guzzardo, landscape architects

Hayward
Wurster Bernardi & Emmons
Ralph Jones, landscape architects

Stations Completed in 1996

Pittsburg/Bay Point
Finger & Moy
Merrill Morris Partners, landscape architects

Castro Valley
Group 4
Haygood & Assoc., landscape architects

Dublin/Pleasanton

Dublin/Pleasanton
SMP Architects
Haygood & Assoc., landscape architects

BART / San Francisco International Airport

Stations Completed in 2000

South San Francisco
Stevens+Assoc.

San Bruno
Greg Roja & Assoc.

San Francisco International Airport
MBT and ED2

Millbrae
VBN
Merrill Morris Partners, landscape architects

Stations slated for 2008

Warm Springs
Robin Chiang & Co.
Haygood & Assoc., landscape architects

San Francisco International Airport (SFO)
1995-2000, SOM/Del Campo & Maru/
Michael Willis Architects
Bayshore Freeway, US 101, opposite Millbrae

The new International Terminal is SFO main reception lobby, receiving not only those passengers boarding internatonal flights, but also those who come to the airport via BART or the air train to the parking lots. At this writing the terminal is also the world's largest base-isolated structure. The ultra modern metal and glass building is supported on two sets of cantilevered trusses to enable it to span the main access road that passes underneath. The roof of the dramatic ticketing hall–800 feet long and 80 feet high–features a series of 180-foot-long football-shaped trusses that diffuse light coming from above. Appropriately, the roof appears to hover above the building as though participating in the act of flight.

T